AMERICAN G

Gothic Literary Studies is dedicated to publishing groundbreaking scholarship on Gothic in literature and film. The Gothic, which has been subjected to a variety of critical and theoretical approaches, is a form which plays an important role in our understanding of literary, intellectual and cultural histories. The series seeks to promote challenging and innovative approaches to Gothic which question any aspect of the Gothic tradition or perceived critical orthodoxy.

Volumes in the series explore how issues such as gender, religion, nation and sexuality have shaped our view of the Gothic tradition. Both academically rigorous and informed by the latest developments in critical theory, the series provides an important focus for scholastic developments in Gothic studies, literary studies, cultural studies and critical theory. The series will be of interest to students of all levels and to scholars and teachers of the Gothic and literary and cultural histories.

American Gothic

Charles L. Crow

UNIVERSITY OF WALES PRESS
CARDIFF
2009

www.uwp.co.uk

British Library Cataloguing-in-Publication Data
A catalogue record for this book is available from the British Library.

ISBN 978-0-7083-2008-2 (hardback)
ISBN 978-0-7083-2044-0 (paperback)
e-ISBN 978-0-7083-2248-2

The right of Charles L. Crow to be identified as author of this work has been asserted by him in accordance with sections 77, 78 and 79 of the Copyright, Designs and Patents Act 1988.

Printed in Malta by Gutenberg Press Ltd.

For Fiona and Jacob

CONTENTS

Series Editors' Foreword

The Histories of the Gothic series consists of four volumes: *Gothic Literature 1764–1824*, *Gothic Literature 1825–1914*, *Twentieth Century Gothic* and *American Gothic*. The series provides a comprehensive introduction to the history of Gothic Literature and to a variety of critical and theoretical approaches. Volumes in the series also raise questions about how the Gothic canon has been received and seek to critically challenge, rather than simply reaffirm, commonplace perceptions of the Gothic tradition. Whilst intended as an introduction to the history of the Gothic, they thus also provide a rigorous analysis of how that history has been developed and suggest ways in which it can be critically renegotiated.

The series will be of interest to students of all levels who are new to the Gothic and to scholars and teachers of the history of Gothic Literature. The series will also be of interest to students and scholars working more broadly within the areas of literary studies, cultural studies and critical theory.

Andrew Smith, University of Glamorgan
Benjamin F. Fisher, University of Mississippi

Acknowledgements

Sherry Truffin and Jeffrey Andrew Weinstock generously allowed me to read their forthcoming books in manuscript. Conversations with Lawrence I. Berkove sharpened my understanding of Ambrose Bierce's ironies. My Japanese-speaking son, Jonathan Crow, offered help with references to Japanese fiction and film. An anonymous reader for the University of Wales Press made invaluable suggestions for revision.

My thanks to series editors Andrew Smith and Benjamin Fisher for their encouragement and patience.

I am especially grateful to Wayne R. Kime, an old friend and fine scholar, for his thoughtful reading of several drafts of this study.

I was sustained by Cynthia in this, as in all things.

We certainly are not that class of beings which we vainly think ourselves to be . . .
(Hector St Jean de Crèvecoeur)

Introduction

To understand American literature, and indeed America, one must understand the Gothic, which is, simply, the imaginative expression of the fears and forbidden desires of Americans. The Gothic has given voice to suppressed groups, and has provided an approach to taboo subjects such as miscegenation, incest and disease. The study of the Gothic offers a forum for discussing some of the key issues of American society, including gender and the nation's continuing drama of race.

From the beginning, and to the present, some of the best and most revealing of our literary works have been Gothic, and many of America's finest authors have worked within this tradition: Hawthorne, Melville, Poe, Emily Dickinson, Henry James, Ambrose Bierce, Stephen Crane, William Faulkner, Cormac McCarthy, Toni Morrison, among others. The best-selling American novel before *Uncle Tom's Cabin* (1852), which has its own Gothic elements, was George Lippard's Gothic *The Quaker City; Or, The Monks of Monk Hall* (1844). Some of the most prolific and popular authors of the present, such as Anne Rice, Stephen King and Joyce Carol Oates, write within this tradition. American Gothic has, from the beginning, included works of high seriousness as well as genre works for the mass market, expressions of popular culture. We would now include *Noir* cinema within our definition of Gothic, some crime fiction (for example that of Ross Macdonald and James

Ellroy), as well as, of course, movies and television programmes about vampires, much science fiction (for example novels of William Gibson and the late Octavia Butler, and the *Alien* movies) and some graphic novels.

The Gothic is famously difficult to define, and the accepted definitions have shifted during the last few decades. Generally the category of Gothic, especially American Gothic, has broadened, and become more inclusive. Leslie Fiedler's landmark 1960 study *Love and Death in the American Novel* was a key work in creating the current definition. American Gothic is no longer defined as a narrow tradition bound by certain props (ruined castles, usually in foreign lands, and imperilled maidens). It is now usually seen as a tradition of oppositional literature, presenting in disturbing, usually frightening ways, a sceptical, ambiguous view of human nature and of history. The Gothic exposes the repressed, what is hidden, unspoken, deliberately forgotten, in the lives of individuals and of cultures.

In the United States, a belief in progress is almost an article of faith. The Gothic, however, is deeply sceptical that either individuals or societies can be perfected. The Gothic insists that humans are flawed and capable of evil, and that the stories we tell ourselves in our history books may leave out what is most important for us to understand. The Gothic patrols the line between waking and dreams, human and machine, the normal and the freakish, and living and dead. As a literature of borderlands, the Gothic is naturally suited to a country that has seen the frontier (a shifting geographical, cultural, linguistic and racial boundary) as its defining characteristic.[1]

The Gothic evokes emotions variously described as dread, horror, terror and the uncanny. Being frightened can be pleasurable, a strange fact of human nature that accounts for the popularity of roller coasters. Popular Gothic literature can indeed function like a thrill ride, with familiar conventions assuring the rider/reader of a safe return. More challenging Gothic works can be unsettling or intellectually stimulating. The theory of terror, from the beginning, was based on the stimulation of the imagination and intellect. Moreover, the reader's response to the Gothic may be seen as cathartic, a process of confronting fears and healing the injuries inflicted on individuals and societies by traumatic stress, change and rigid authority.[2]

Gothic backgrounds

The Gothic appeared in Britain in the eighteenth and early nineteenth centuries, and, as studied in detail elsewhere in this University of Wales Press series, includes as its early signature works Horace Walpole's *The Castle of Otranto* (1764), Ann Radcliffe's *The Mysteries of Udolpho* (1794), and M. G. Lewis's *The Monk* (1796). The Gothic, that is, was born on the cusp of the Neoclassical movement and Romanticism, a time that also witnessed the formation of the new United States.

Much critical debate concerns the relationship of the Gothic to the great intellectual currents that collided at the time of its birth. While the Gothic is often seen as a variant of Romanticism, or a subset within it, some early Gothic masterpieces (like Walpole's) actually appear in the Neoclassical period and precede the landmark works of early Romanticism. Perhaps it would be simplest to see all of the changes of the eighteenth and early nineteenth centuries as parts of one great tectonic shift in Western thought, from which the modern world emerges. It is convenient, however, to retain the traditional terms of Neoclassicism and Romanticism in making some essential points about this period of intellectual ferment in which the Gothic arose.

A new way of thinking rejects the old ways by distorting and parodying them. Like victors in a war, young people in a triumphant movement will write their own histories, and define the villains and monsters of the age they have defeated – and still fear. The Neoclassical period, marked by the Restoration and the Glorious Revolution in Britain, was also called the Age of Reason. Thinkers of this era saw themselves as throwing off the ignorance and superstition of the past, and they found a set of emblems for all they despised in the Middle Ages, and especially the medievalism of the Continent. The architecture of this earlier, ignorant time, churches and castles, was now scornfully called 'Gothic', and the name became associated as well with a new literature that was often set in the ruins of medieval castles and churches. Decadent monks and European aristocrats provided the villains for early Gothic novels.

These settings and character types continued as standard features (or clichés) in later Gothic literature, even though Romanticism brought new concerns and new villains. If the Age of Reason valued balance, symmetry, mature and rational thought, orderly gardens, law and well-designed institutions, the Romantics favoured individual freedom, untamed nature, disorder, emotion, dreams and innocent childhood. For the Romantics (the term was not their own, but given later in the Victorian period), the greatest evil is to be found in obsessive rationalism combined with authority. William Blake's magnificent poem 'London' (1794) captures this view perfectly, chanting the word 'charter'd' into an obscenity, describing the 'mind-forg'd manacles' that break the human spirit. In Victor Hugo's 1862 novel *Les Misérables* (a Romantic, though not a Gothic work) Jean Valjean and Inspector Javert represent the opposition of the Romantic spirit of freedom (Valjean) and the Neoclassical obsession with control (Javert), as the Romantics saw it.[3]

Thus, with the Romantic period a new kind of character enters Gothic literature, in three variants, all representing, like Inspector Javert, the abuse of knowledge and authority: the lawyer or judge; the schoolmaster; and the abusive scientist or doctor. This unholy troika continues into the present, demonstrating the continuance of Romantic ideas within the Gothic tradition.

Mary Shelley's *Frankenstein* (1818), a flawed work but a brilliant idea, has an enduring legacy because it embodies a deep anxiety, still with us, about the legitimate boundaries of scientific enquiry. While Victor Frankenstein is portrayed sympathetically, the scientists drawn by Hawthorne and Melville combine scientific skill with the cold hubris and disregard of human consequence that are the signature traits of the Gothic villain. Science fiction for most of the last century and a half has been filled with the questions evoked by Mary Shelley: what does it mean to create life, or intelligence, and what are the responsibilities of the creator? The movies *Blade Runner* (1982) and *AI: Artificial Intelligence* (2001) are among many evocations of this theme in movies.

Education and law, two traditions justified as protecting and nurturing, in fact are usually instruments of control. (These are meanings contained in William Blake's use of the word 'charter'd'.) A few examples show the endurance of villains in these roles. Judge Pyncheon in *The House of the Seven Gables* (1851) is an embodiment of the repressive Puritan tradition of New England. Judge Holden (usually simply called 'the judge') of Cormac McCarthy's *Blood Meridian* (1985), one of the great villains of recent literature, is such an enemy of freedom that he wants to put all wild animals in zoos. Toni Morrison's 'schoolteacher' in *Beloved* (1987), a character combining pedagogue and scientist, uses the bogus racist theories of the nineteenth century to justify slavery, and even conducts 'scientific' measurements on the slaves of Sweet Home plantation to prove their inferiority. 'Schoolteacher' uses both 'mind-forg'd' and literal manacles of oppression.

'*Schoolhouse Gothic*', as defined by scholar Sherry Truffin, has a long history.[4] The American tradition perhaps begins with Poe's 'William Wilson' (1839), and would include such diverse works as John Knowles's *A Separate Peace* (1959), Stephen King's *Carrie* (1974, Brian De Palma's film adaptation 1976), David Mamet's play *Oleanna* (1992), the movie *Heathers* (1989), and the television series *Buffy the Vampire Slayer* (1997–2003).

The sublime, the uncanny and the grotesque

As we develop and discuss a large literary idea such as the Gothic, we construct an eclectic vocabulary of useful terms, each of which has its own history. Three such terms are *sublime, uncanny* and *grotesque*: the first two are classical ideas, used in English by both critics and creative writers since the middle of the eighteenth century; the third, a concept from the writings of Sigmund Freud.

The Greek writer Longinus, about whom nothing is certain, wrote 'On the Sublime' sometime between the first and third centuries AD. His ideas were greatly expanded and modified according to eighteenth-century psychology by the English statesman and theorist Edmund Burke. In *A Philosophical Inquiry into the Origins of our Ideas of the Sublime and Beautiful* (1757), Burke defined the aesthetic and psychological response to a kind of beauty that is irregular, strange, disturbing and even frightening. This is not the beauty of a carefully planned garden, or symmetrical Neoclassical architecture, but that of a wild mountain panorama, for example, or of ancient ruins. The sublime replaces comfortable beauty with a beauty that mingles awe and even fear. Burke's ideas had a great impact on European art and literature, including the Gothic, and were assimilated into Romantic theory. The relevance of the sublime to Gothic literature, already invested, so to speak, in ruins, is obvious. Ann Radcliffe employs the term in *The Mysteries of Udolpho* (1794), and clearly draws on the aesthetic of the sublime in constructing her descriptions of castles and alpine scenery. The ability of her heroine, Emily, to appreciate sublime scenery is a mark of her superior sensibility.

The aesthetic of the sublime has surprising durability, persisting beyond the Romantic movement, through the nineteenth century, and to the present. We see it, for example, in the cityscapes of the 'ash-can' school of artists, as in the series of paintings by George Bellows in 1907 depicting the excavations for Pennsylvania Station in New York. The great gaping space of the excavation and the menacing power of steam-driven machinery all combine to create a response that an earlier painter like Frederick Church would have found in the wilderness, such as the grandeur of Niagara Falls. In contemporary Gothic, the aesthetic of the sublime extends even to scenes of post-industrial ruins in science fiction novels and movies, or the wrecked spacecraft in the film *Alien*.

The term 'grotesque', like 'sublime', has a tradition running back to the classical past. The root of the term is 'grotto', and it refers specifically to a style of decoration sometimes found in the excavated ruins of ancient Roman homes. The art-historical and literary uses of the term have diverged somewhat, and for our purposes 'grotesque' refers to the strange, distorted or monstrous, usually as applied to human characters. The silent dwarves encountered by Rip Van Winkle on the mountain are grotesque, as are characters in the works of (for example) Erskine Caldwell, Nathanael West and Carson McCullers. Grotesque characters are often found in Gothic fiction, but it must be stressed the terms are not equivalent. Grotesque characters can appear in non-Gothic works, even in comedy, while Gothic characters may appear completely normal.

While the terms sublime and grotesque have long histories, our critical use of the term 'uncanny' dates from the publication of Sigmund Freud's essay '*Das Unheimliche*' in 1919. Freud has been a favourite theorist among writers and artists, in part because he was interested in the arts and the creative process, and was himself an excellent prose stylist. Recent scholars of the Gothic have even claimed, more than half seriously, that Freud's *Civilization and its Discontents* (1930) is a Gothic masterpiece, and that Freud's notion of the superego is an internalized version of the Gothic villain, in his judge and schoolteacher role, imposing mind-forged manacles.

Freud draws his illustration for the uncanny (the English equivalent of the German '*unheimlich*') from a literary text, E. T. A. Hoffmann's story 'The Sandman', in which, among other odd events, a student falls in love with a professor's daughter, Olympia, who turns out to be a wind-up mechanical doll. The essence of the uncanny is a sense of weirdness, created when something that seemed safe and familiar suddenly becomes strange, or something that should have remained hidden is revealed. In German, the root of '*unheimlich*' is *Heim*, home. Thus Freud's term contains the idea of a haunted house: the place that should have been comforting, home-like, revealing something ominous or threatening. Freud lists several situations that can produce the uncanny, including coincidences, odd repetitions and doubling–all familiar devices of Gothic literature.

Subsequent theorists have debated and extended the implications of Freud's term. Hélène Cixous's feminist reading, in 'Fiction and its phantoms: a reading of Freud's *Das Unheimliche* ('The Uncanny') (1975)', turns her attention to the mechanical doll Olympia, whom Freud 'imprisons' in a footnote.[5] Joyce Carol Oates's story 'The Doll' (1994) is a kind of riff on 'The Sandman' and Freud's and other theorists' interpretations of it. Oates's protagonist is a feminist professor who encounters a house that mimics her childhood dollhouse, and at the end of the story is described herself as a 'precise clockwork mechanism, a living mannequin.'[6]

Romantic agony and villain-heroes

Romanticism offered the artist both freedom and impossible expectations. Gone was the view of artists as craftsmen, who might learn their trade by following mentors or earlier models, like village potters or weavers practising traditional patterns from their grandmothers, or Neoclassical poets carefully studying Horace. Artists were now prophet-like figures relying on inspiration, and the test was always originality. Behind this shift in the artist's role was a revival of Platonic philosophy during the Romantic period, which posited a world of pure and perfect forms, of which the world we inhabit is a poor and imperfect shadow. This view, that our world is unreal and insubstantial, is counter-intuitive but nonetheless one of Western philosophy's most enduring traditions. It is comprehensive, a theory that can explain everything. (Plato's student Aristotle rejected the whole package, and in many ways Western thought and culture are still a dialogue between Platonic idealism and Aristotelian materialism.) What is an artist? In Romantic – Platonic theory, the artist's vision can sometimes see beyond the flickering shadows of the cave in which we are chained, and glimpse the real world of perfect forms. The work of art, however flawed, contains this vision, and helps us, the audience, in our own quest for the good, the true and the beautiful.

But what happens when the vision of the artist falters? The romantic artist, a role having life beyond the Romantic period proper, extending at least though the age of Modernism, has a record of brilliant success and of dispiriting failure. Much Romantic literature records the dreary or frightening intervals between moments of inspiration, time spent during (in the words of the twentieth-century poet Sylvia Plath) 'The long wait for the angel / For that rare, random descent.'[7] With continuous pressure to be original, to make it new, it is not surprising that poets of the Romantic period, like contemporary jazz and rock musicians, their true heirs, sometimes turned to alcohol or drugs to stimulate, or simulate, inspiration.

This awareness of living in a flawed world, while tantalized by a perfect one just beyond our outstretched fingers, is the source of what is called 'Romantic agony', which, in turn, can be seen as

---

8

one impetus behind the Gothic. Gothicism records our disgust or rejection of a fallen, haunted, cursed or diseased world that we know should be something else. A creature of powerful intellect, suffering this Romantic agony, could be driven to misguided, cruel deeds, trying to set the world right, or to avenge a sense of outrage or betrayal.

Thus arose the Gothic villain-hero. The type has roots in earlier literature, especially in the Satan of *Paradise Lost* (1667), as the Romantics chose to misread Milton's epic, and in Shakespearean characters like Hamlet and Richard III. The Gothic villain-hero combines traditionally opposite roles, and brings great energy to ambiguous or destructive ends. Melville's Captain Ahab is a 'grand ungodly, godlike man', terms that would describe any number of European and American characters, from Emily Brontë's Heathcliff to William Faulkner's Thomas Sutpen.

The Gothic in the New World

At present, when British authors complain that they must satisfy book reviewers in New York, it is difficult to remember a time when the situation was reversed. But authors in the American colonies and the early republic struggled for many long and discouraging decades trying to find their audience, their material and their voice.

A difficult set of problems concerned artistic conventions brought from Europe, and their suitability to the subject materials of the new land. The poetic language of Neoclassical high seriousness, formed in imitation of Latin style by writers like Dryden and Pope, seemed very distant from the speech and concerns of everyday life in America: the problem is illustrated by the struggles of the freed slave Phillis Wheatley, probably the best Neoclassical poet in America, to match her language to her experience. Romantic theory, with its validation of common speech, was to prove liberating for American writers, producing, ultimately, the language of *Leaves of Grass* (1855) and *Adventures of Huckleberry Finn* (1885). But this would take many decades, and much longer still for the acceptance of Black American English as a literary language.

Moreover, the English novel, as masterfully developed by Samuel Richardson, Jane Austen and others, was essentially a series of variations on the Cinderella story (her triumphant marriage to the prince, or her rape and exquisite death), assuming a multi-layered class structure of servant girls and upper classes, with the middle-class reader sandwiched between. This model was a poor fit for the increasingly fluid sociology of America. The sentiment of the proverbial English prayer, 'God bless the squire and his relations / And keep us in our proper stations', was not often embraced on the other side of the Atlantic.

What then was an American subject? To the eyes of many writers and artists in early America, there was a paucity of material. Even the landscape seemed empty and raw. There were indeed plenty of trees, and wilderness vistas suitable for evoking a version of the sublime, as painters of the Hudson River school (Thomas Cole and his followers) demonstrated. However, there was a distressing lack of ruins, either for Gothic effects or for gentle, reflective melancholy. There was no Tintern Abbey to be viewed by moonlight; nor were there at first any country churchyards or deserted villages, though these would come in time. (The deserted villages of the Indians were not made of stone or brick, and seldom left a trace.) There seemed, to eyes trained in Europe, a lack of history in America. There was in fact almost too much history, but somehow it was difficult to see, or to see as suitably artistic. We may think of American literature as a process of learning to see American history, and the Gothic would play its part in making the invisible visible.

Hawthorne works the problem

Nathaniel Hawthorne is an instructive case, a major writer who seems to us both a visionary and a blind man. This is his notorious catalogue of the limitations of America as material for art, from his preface to *The Marble Faun* (1860):

> No author, without a trial, can conceive of the difficulty of writing a romance about a country where there is no shadow, no antiquity, no mystery, no picturesque and gloomy wrong, nor anything but a commonplace prosperity, in broad and simple daylight, as is happily

the case with my dear native land . . . Romance and poetry, ivy, lichens, and wallflowers need ruin to make them grow.[8]

The statement may be in part discounted as an apology for writing a romance set in Italy, rather than his dear native land. Still, much in this statement makes the reader of our time gasp with astonishment. Is he possibly being ironic? No picturesque or gloomy wrong? It is remarkable that any thinking American, then or now, could be oblivious to the wrongs suffered by Indians and enslaved African Americans. In 1860, the year *The Marble Faun* was published, the preamble to the Civil War was being written in a series of bloody skirmishes in Kansas, a conflict over the expansion of slavery initiated by the Kansas – Nebraska Act, which had been promoted by Hawthorne's Bowdoin College classmate Franklin Pierce, during his disastrous presidency. In the fall of 1860, of course, the election of Abraham Lincoln would precipitate the long-dreaded full-scale fratricidal war.

Yet Hawthorne already had written brilliantly of the American past, and gloomy wrongs, in a series of tales and in three Gothic novels.[9] He had also the example of intelligent forerunners such as John Neal and Charles Brockden Brown. Hawthorne and his predecessors will be discussed in some detail in the next chapter, but it is worth pausing here to look at an early story, 'Alice Doane's Appeal', for an example of an American writer of talent working the problem of how to recognize and use material for serious fiction in America. 'Alice Doan's Appeal' is in fact a self-reflexive story about writing the Gothic in a new land.

The tale was never collected by the author, and was published for the first time long after his death. Its complicated genealogy goes back to Hawthorne's extended apprenticeship, when, after graduating from Bowdoin College in 1825, he lived in his mother's house in Salem, Massachusetts, studied, wrote and tried to puzzle out his craft. During this period he completed a collection called 'Seven Tales of My Native Land'. Five of these he burned; a story called 'Alice Doane's Appeal' was one of the two that survived because they were in 'friendlier hands', presumably those of an editor.

However, the story that we have is not quite the story that escaped the fire. It is a narrative describing the earlier tale being read to an audience of 'two ladies'. Thus we have a 'frame story', a narrative device that is a particular favourite of American authors. In the frame, the narrator, who seems to be identical to the author, takes the two unnamed ladies on a walk to Gallows Hill, outside Salem. There, seated overlooking the town, the narrator entertains the women with a story he has written, the horrific Gothic tale of Alice Doane and her twin brothers. The story is partly directly quoted, partly summarized for us by the narrator. The tale involves a wizard, ghosts and demons in a graveyard, fratricidal murder and brother – sister incest (at least threatened, and possibly consummated). While the tale seems to frighten the ladies, the narrator tries to pile up one too many Gothic embellishments (telling his auditors that they are seated near the grave of the wizard), and they burst into laughter. The story has failed.

Chagrined, the narrator now decides to make a trial 'whether truth were more powerful than fiction', and tells the ladies of an event 'from old witch times'.[10] What follows is an actual episode from the witchcraft scare of 1692. In all, nineteen accused witches were hanged in Salem that year before the trials were discontinued in the fall. Another man had been tortured to death, crushed beneath heavy stones ('pressed for an answer', as the law allowed), when he refused to enter a plea. The event described by Hawthorne took place on 19 August 1692, when five convicted witches, four men and one woman, were hanged on Gallows Hill: the greatest number of deaths on any day of this prolonged tragedy. (Hawthorne's account is slightly inaccurate, since he describes two women walking in the procession to the gallows, whereas only one woman was executed that day, Martha Carrier.) One of the men hanged was John Proctor, whose tragedy is the basis of Arthur Miller's twentieth-century play, *The Crucible* (1952). But at the time, the drama of the day centred on George Burroughs, a former minister, since his speech before execution moved the spectators to sympathy, and nearly led to a spontaneous uprising against the hangings. Burroughs forgave his accusers, and concluded his address at the foot of the gallows by leading the spectators in reciting the Lord's Prayer. As one historian notes, this was 'something of a trick',[11] since in popular superstition witches said the prayer backwards during the Witches' Sabbath, and hence were unable to present it in its normal form without stammering. Burrows got through it perfectly. When the crowd seemed about to intervene, Cotton Mather, the celebrated Boston theologian, addressed the citizens from horseback, and insisted that the legally authorized executions go forward. So all five were hanged and hastily buried on Gallows Hill.

In his narrative Hawthorne describes the procession of the condemned, officials, townspeople and the 'afflicted', supposed victims of witchcraft whose testimony had convicted the accused witches. But in Hawthorne's telling, it is the witches who are the victims, and their accusers who are guilty:

> Behind their victims came the afflicted, a guilty and miserable band; villains who had thus avenged themselves on their enemies, and viler wretches, whose cowardice had destroyed their friends; lunatics, whose ravings had chimed in with the madness of the land; and children, who had played a game that the imps of darkness might have envied them, since it disgraced an age, and dipped a people's hands in blood.[12]

Hawthorne's greatest scorn is poured upon a mounted man following the crowd:

> In the rear of the procession rode a figure on horseback, so darkly conspicuous, so sternly triumphant, that my hearers mistook him for the visible presence of the fiend himself; but it was only his good friend, Cotton Mather, proud of his well won dignity, as the representative of all the hateful features of his time; the one blood-thirsty man, in whom were concentrated those vices of spirit and errors of opinion, that sufficed to madden the whole surrounding multitude.[13]

As Hawthorne begins to describe the gallows, his listeners, the two ladies, seize his arms, and he ends his tale: 'their nerves were trembling; and sweeter victory still, I had reached the seldom trodden places of their hearts, and found the wellspring of their tears.'[14]

The implications of this pair of stories within a story are clear. The materials for powerful art, especially Gothic art, are about us in abundance in the New World; there is no need to draw upon stale

European conventions for horrific events when our own history can provide them. This is a point we will see repeatedly in the following chapters. Notice that this conclusion completely contradicts what Hawthorne later wrote in the preface to *The Marble Faun*. American writers apparently have to keep rediscovering America as their subject again and again.

Before leaving Hawthorne's tale, we should note that it is an excellent example of the way Gothic literature often generates an 'excess of meaning', and allows, or even requires, alternate readings.[15] For example, the superiority of the second framed story, the account of the witch hangings, is in part undercut within the narrative: the two ladies in fact do not allow the narrator to conclude the story. 'Alice Doan's Appeal', then, is not a complete prescription for how to write Gothic in America: it dramatizes both the power of tragic stories in American history and the resistance of Americans to hearing them. Moreover, many readers have noted that the two framed tales of 'Alice Doane's Appeal' bristle with psychological and political implications, that while seeming quite different, even contradictory, they resemble each other on a symbolic level, that they interact with the framing story of the two ladies and the dramatized narrator, and that they both suggest issues with Hawthorne's own life. Without pretending to tease out all of these implications, we might observe that both of the framed stories contain tragic family histories: in the first, brother kills brother over the love of a sister, in a kind of retelling of the Rape of Tamar story from the Old Testament, while in the second, one of the condemned witches is denounced by her own son. We may wonder also about the relationship of the narrator to the two ladies: is one of them his sister, and what is his motive in telling her this story?

The powerful denunciation of Cotton Mather, moreover, is not as straightforward as it first seems. Mather's actions on that day in 1692 were about as Hawthorne describes them; however, in making him the chief villain of the witchcraft trials, Hawthorne was unfair, as he must have known, since he was a thorough scholar of local history. Mather was not an official at the trials, but, as the leading philosopher and theologian of New England, was used as a consultant. If his recommendations had been followed, the standards for conviction would have been higher, 'spectral evidence' (evidence of visions supposedly experienced by witnesses that could not be empirically tested) would have not have been allowed, and it is doubtful that the trials could have snowballed into the horror they became. More responsibility rests with the judges at the trial than with Mather. One of these, John Hathorne (as the name was spelled then), was Nathaniel Hawthorne's great great grandfather. The powerful 'darkly conspicuous' man on horseback is a stand-in for a figure Hawthorne is unwilling to confront directly.

Ultimately, all Gothic stories are family stories.[16]

Of borders and boundaries

The study that follows attempts to illuminate both of our key terms: Gothic and American.[17] However, some qualifications must be acknowledged at the outset, since the Gothic, a literature we have defined as one of crossing boundaries, is not always defined or confined by the nation state.

When Hawthorne titled his first attempted book 'Seven Tales of My Native Land', he was not referring to the United States: he meant New England. The best literature is often deeply rooted in particular regions, and this is true as well of the Gothic. National borders are the result of treaties between governments. Regions are produced by the interaction of human culture and landscape; lines arbitrarily drawn on maps do not define them. Thus, the Great Plains do not end at the Canadian border, and the culture of the Deep South has interacted throughout its history with that of the Caribbean. These qualifications, that literature is regional and local as well as national, and that regions cross borders, are restraints on our generalizations about American literature.

We should recall that borders do not restrain authors and ideas, either. Although American authors progressively moved from under the shadow of British literature, there never has been a complete separation of American literature from the rest of the world, and it would be a sadly diminished thing if there had been. American writers continue to be influenced by British authors, as we see in the long Gothic shadow of *Frankenstein*, and later in that of *The Strange Case of Dr Jekyll and Mr Hyde* (1886) and of *Dracula* (1897). The currents, of course, have not run just from the Old World to the New, but have been interactive. The influence of other literatures has been essential as well; for example French (especially in the late nineteenth century), Latin American and, more recently, Japanese and Chinese. Authors, also (as well as film directors), often move from country to country, and resist categories: recall Hector St Jean de Crèvecoeur (the 'American Farmer' who was a Frenchman), Lafcadio Hearn (who was born to Irish and Greek parents, but ended his life a Japanese citizen) and Henry James (claimed by both Britain and the United States).

This study, then, like all critical enquiries, is part of an ongoing dialogue that can never be complete, to which the reader will bring new questions and answers.

1

American Gothic to the Civil War

ஒ

In the decades between the American Revolution and the Civil War, the nation grew from a narrow strip of land along a largely unexplored landmass to a continental power. Nature was tamed, the frontier pushed far to the west. These accomplishments, celebrated by most Americans still, led to an optimistic belief in progress: the lives of Americans inevitably improved because of democratic values, righteousness, education, technology and the free markets of an expanding nation. American Gothic presented a counter-narrative, undercutting the celebration of progress, inquiring about its costs and the omissions from the story. Gothic writers persisted in asking troubling questions about Americans and wilderness, and about Americans' belief in themselves.

First frontiers and colonial Gothic: wild beasts, devils and wild men

The roots of these questions run deep into the period of exploration and early settlement of the continent, and can be illustrated by works written by three men of different culture and temperament who were trying to make sense of life in the new world. William Bradford's *Of Plymouth Plantation* records the arrival of the *Mayflower* pilgrims in New England and their subsequent struggles, triumphs and, as he saw it, spiritual decline.[1] A few decades later, Cotton Mather's *Wonders of the Invisible World* (1692) describes the terrifying outbreak of Satanism in Salem, Massachusetts. On the eve of the American Revolution, in a completely different social and intellectual climate, Hector St Jean de Crèvecoeur's *Letters from an American Farmer* (1752) celebrated the success of the new culture, but also discovered its Gothic undertow.

When the first British colonists arrived in North America in the early 1600s, the boundary between what was known and unknown to Europeans was the beach. William Bradford, leader of the 'Pilgrims' who settled Plymouth Plantation, recalled in later years the appearance of the landscape confronting him from the deck of the *Mayflower*:

> . . . what could they see but a hideous and desolate wilderness, full of wild beasts and wild men—and what multitudes there might be of them they knew not. Neither could they, as it were, go up to the top of Pisgah to view from this wilderness a more goodly country to feed their hopes, for which way soever they turned their eyes (save upward to the heavens) they could have little solace or content in respect of any outward objects. For summer being done, all things stand upon them a weather-beaten face, and the whole country, full of woods and thickets, represented a wild and savage hue.[2]

This is a masterful passage of plain but nuanced English prose, filled with echoes of the Book of Exodus. Bradford presents a model, a way of looking at the strange and threatening landscape, and making sense of it. The words wilderness, wild and savage are entirely negative here, unlike their later revisions in the Romantic period. This is a hostile place, like the wilderness in which the Children of Israel wandered for years before reaching the promised land of Canaan. Or perhaps it is worse. Moses, at least, was granted a vision of Canaan from Mount Pisgah; Bradford, the Pilgrim leader, cannot even find the mountain. But for the Pilgrims, as for the Israelites, the wilderness will be a place of hardship, where their faith, as they expect, will be tested and justified.

For Bradford, as for later Christian settlers, the great threat posed by this wilderness was not starvation or torture by Indians. It was losing one's faith. To lose one's faith meant to lose one's identity and hope of salvation, and to become like the 'other', beastlike: a fear that would be reinforced by direct or second-hand observation of frontier life and a sense of one's own repressed impulses. Early accounts of life in remote settlements, as well as Indian-captivity narratives, are filled with glimpses of Europeans not only degenerating to crude and savage creatures, but even crossing the line and joining the Indians. Puritans endured hardship with the belief that the testing was for their benefit, part of a divine plan. The Indians might seem devils, but God was still in control. This belief sustained Mary Rowlandson, wife of a Puritan minister, held captive in the Massachusetts woods by Indians during King Philip's War; her captivity narrative (1682) was one of the first best-selling works by an American author.

Yet one's faith could also fail. Bradford began writing *Of Plymouth Plantation* to chronicle the struggles and triumphs of his fellow adventurers, many of whom died from disease or malnutrition in the first years after the colony was founded in 1620. The survivors felt that they were blessed and their faith vindicated. But twenty years later, Bradford records an outbreak of 'wickedness' in Plymouth: 'Not only incontinency between persons unmarried . . . but some married persons also. But that which is worse, even sodomy and buggery (things fearful to name) have broke forth in this land oftener than once.'[3] Shortly afterward, the manuscript of the history ends.

Bradford may seem a Malvolio figure here, outraged that the colonists will have their cakes and ale, or a prototype of the Puritan leaders who persecuted Hester Prynne. In context, however, we understand the ageing hero's sadness and even horror. The Puritans had met the challenge of the 'Starving Time' and yet failed to maintain their original ideals; many had lost themselves in this wild place. They were not, after all, who they thought they were.

In *Of Plymouth Plantation* we see an early representation of ideas that are central to American literature and American Gothic. The concept of wilderness is among the most complex in the national culture, and retains, even to the present, traces of the demonology we see in Bradford, though the landscape has been largely conquered and tamed. As a repository of our fears, wilderness is still Gothic territory.

In 1692, the dominion of Puritans over the new land remained tenuous. That year's witchcraft panic in Salem, Massachusetts, was an event that still shadows American history and literature. Like the eruption of 'wickedness' recorded by William Bradford, the witchcraft trials disrupted the narrative of progress in which New Englanders wished to believe. Even now, after over three hundred years, it is difficult to explain what happened, and historians continue to assess the mixture of fraud, hysteria, opportunism and perhaps genuine witchcraft, that led to the execution of nineteen men and women (and one dog), and the death of another man under torture.

There are good reasons why these events should not have occurred. New England in the seventeenth century had much more enlightened laws about witchcraft than did European countries. The accused, for example, had the right to trial in an open court, had a reasonable chance of being acquitted, and, if acquitted, could even sue accusers for damages. Witches had been convicted and hanged in New England before 1692, but these were rare and usually isolated events.

In that year, when several girls and young women, from eleven to nineteen years old, began to display symptoms we would now call hysterical, authorities at first proceeded cautiously. Apparently the girls had been experimenting with fortune-telling and folk magic. It was believed that these pursuits made them vulnerable to witchcraft, and that witches were tormenting them. The girls, and a slave woman from the Caribbean named Tituba, were questioned. A circle of accusations began to spread. The leading authority on witchcraft, Cotton Mather (1663–1728), was contacted and gave measured advice.

Mather was not the narrow zealot that later Americans (including Nathaniel Hawthorne) have envisioned. The most accomplished intellectual of his generation of Americans, respected in Britain, he was not only a theologian and historian, but a scientist with training in medicine. He was among the first to urge general inoculation with the newly developed smallpox vaccine. Mather believed that there were witches who entered into compacts with Satan, but he also understood that both the presumed victims of witchcraft and their judges could be mistaken in their perceptions about what had occurred. He had successfully treated afflicted girls in the past with a combination of prayer and, as we would call it, counselling. He wrote about these cases in *Memorable Providences Relating to Witchcrafts and Possessions* (1689), just a few years before the Salem episode.

In a letter to Salem judge John Richards, Mather urged caution in the matter of 'spectre evidence'. As noted in the previous chapter, if this advice had been taken, testimony about ghosts of the dead and phantoms of the living would have been disallowed, and it is unlikely that the tragedy would have unfolded as it did. Nonetheless, when the accusations in Salem radically expanded, until dozens of men and women were under indictment, he supported the judges, men of his class who clearly had permitted events to spin out of control. Mather wrote his *Wonders of the Invisible World* (1692) to demonstrate that witchcraft did exist in Salem, and to defend, in general if not in every particular, the witchcraft trials there.

Mather builds his narrative around the trials of five witches: G.B. (George Burroughs, who recited the Lord's Prayer before his execution), Bridget Bishop, Susanna Martin, Elizabeth Howe and the most notorious, Martha Carrier, whom Satan had promised to make Queen of Hell. All entered pleas of innocence, but Mather and the judges believed that their guilt had been proven, and that a coven of witches did exist in Salem. The case was built largely through the testimony of confessed witches, who by their testimony escaped punishment. Witches met in the forest, they testified, celebrated the 'black mass', and tried to recruit new members to their fellowship. Many citizens of Salem also reported that witches repaid grievances with curses that sickened or killed cattle and sometimes people; and that witches would torture God-fearing victims to induce them to sign the Devil's book. Under this weight of evidence, all five accused witches were convicted. Some were hanged on the day commemorated in Hawthorne's 'Alice Doane's Appeal'.

For Mather, the witchcraft episode brought to light a counter attack by Satan against the progress of New England civilization. As the title of Mather's most ambitious book, *Magnalia Christi Americana* (1702) suggests, he saw American history as the epic of Christian people in the new world; but of Christians settled in land that had once been 'the *Devil's* Territories'.[4] Witches were part of the 'Army of *Devils*' sent to take it back.[5]

The legacy of the year of witchcraft, as recorded by Mather, is enduring, powerfully disturbing and contradictory. Americans still respond to Mather's Manichaean, paranoid vision of evil hidden beneath the surface of comfortable American life. (See, for example, the 1982 movie *Poltergeist*.) The name of Salem still evokes fear of the supernatural, and has been so used by writers from Hawthorne to Lovecraft and beyond. Mather's *Wonders of the Invisible World* can still be read, as it was by Irving's Ichabod Crane, as an anthology of horrifying supernatural events. Ira Levin's *Rosemary's Baby* (1967, movie 1968), though set in Manhattan, uses the details of coven and black mass fixed in our imagination by Mather.

An opposite view of the events in Salem began even as the trials were still in progress: that they show a community maddened by fear, vindictiveness and fanaticism. In this view the real villains were the judges, Mather himself, and much of the craven community that cooperated with them. Possibly the 'bewitched' girls should also be included in this indictment, a charge made by Hawthorne and, in the twentieth century, by Arthur Miller in *The Crucible*. When Americans speak of a search for scapegoats in a climate of fear as a 'witch-hunt', it is the legacy of Salem that is being distantly evoked. Whether one locates the evil of Salem in the witches or in their persecutors, the events of 1692 were truly Gothic, demonstrating what Melville would later call 'The Power of Blackness'.

We are not the beings we think ourselves to be . . .

By the late eighteenth century, the eastern seaboard had been settled, and the frontier was the Appalachian Mountains. Hector St Jean de Crèvecoeur was a French immigrant who had lived in Canada, was a veteran of the French and Indian Wars and was wounded in the epic Battle of Quebec of 1757, in which the British forces under Wolfe battled French forces commanded by Montcalm for control of the continent. Crèvecoeur would die in France in 1813. However, as a naturalized citizen of the English colony of

New York, and writing in English just before the Revolution, he asked the central question of the emerging American experience: 'What is an American?'

In the twelve epistles of *Letters from an American Farmer*, Crèvecoeur presents the reflections of 'John', a fictionalized version of himself, about the life of his fellow citizens in a new land. Anticipating Frederick Jackson Turner's 'Frontier Thesis' by more than a century, Crèvecoeur proposed the social importance of a landscape passing from wilderness to frontier to farmland. In the farming communities of the colonies a new society is created, in which there is no great distance between the richest and poorest in a neighbourhood, and simple democratic values prevail: 'We have no princes for whom we toil, starve, and bleed; we are most perfect society now existing in the world. Here man is free as he ought to be, nor is this pleasing equality so transitory as many others are.'[6]

In this new land people intermarry with neighbours who are emigrants from other countries, and old national differences disappear:

> Here individuals of all nations are melted into a new race of men, whose labours and prosperity will one day cause great changes in the world. Americans are the western pilgrims who are carrying along with them that great mass of arts, sciences, and industry that began long since in the East; they will finish the great circle.[7]

These views are the earliest full articulation of the optimistic creed of American progress and exceptionalism that underlies the actions of Americans, and America, to the present day. American values are inherently virtuous, carry with them all that was right in earlier European culture, while purged of European error and corruption. The triumph of American values is inevitable and right. Note that Crèvecoeur reached this belief even before the United States existed as a nation.

Yet Letter IX is filled with bitter reflections that overturn the cheerful progressive ideas of the earlier letters, and replace them with a Hobbesian vision of universal war and cruelty: 'The history of the earth! Doth it present anything but crimes of the most heinous nature, committed from one end of the world to the other? We observe avarice, rapine, and murder, equally prevailing in all parts.'[8] In such a world, it is folly to believe in progress, folly to believe that Americans are different from other peoples. Here is a sad renunciation of this illusion, the implied motto of many works that we will discuss in this study: 'We certainly are not that class of beings which we vainly think ourselves to be.'[9]

The occasion of John's bitter rant, which continues for several pages, is a discovery he makes in the woods, while visiting Charlestown, South Carolina. Seeing a cage in a tree covered with fluttering birds of prey, he approaches:

> I perceived a Negro, suspended in the cage and left there to expire! I shudder when I recollect that the birds had already picked out his eyes; his cheek-bones were bare; his arms had been attacked in several places; and his body seemed covered with a multitude of wounds. From the edges of the hollow sockets and from the lacerations with which he was disfigured, the blood slowly dropped and tinged the ground beneath . . . I found myself suddenly arrested by the power of affright and terror, my nerves were convulsed; I trembled . . .[10]

This is a true Gothic moment. The vision of horror in the woods strips away John's illusions, and leaves him shaken, unable to view the world or himself in the same way again.

The reality of slavery had been everywhere around John in the New World, but, paradoxically, it took a dying man whose eyes had been pecked out to make him see it. In this study we will find repeated examples of the racial horror of America breaking through the wilful blindness of white characters; and we will see the emergence of black and other silenced voices, for which this nameless slave stands as a prototype.

And we will see repeated over and over, in different contexts, Crèvecoeur's horrified discovery. We are not who we believed ourselves to be. We are something else.

Founders: Charles Brockden Brown, George Lippard and John Neal

The first professional authors of American Gothic were political reformers and social activists. Probably none of them would have been comfortable with the term Gothic. Charles Brockden Brown, in the introduction to his novel *Edgar Huntly*, wrote of the need to abandon the conventions of European Gothic and to find appropriate American settings for 'engaging the sympathies' of readers: 'Puerile superstition and exploded manners; Gothic castles and chimeras, are the materials usually employed for this end. The incidents of Indian hostility, and the perils of the western wilderness, are far more suitable . . .' [11] Brown emulated the novels of William Godwin, an English Gothic writer who avoided the conventions of the Ann Radcliffe school. John Neal also considered that he was not writing English Gothic, but something opposed to it. Like George Lippard, Neal did not need the supernatural to shock and terrify. It says something of the underlying Gothic sensibility of Lippard and Neal, however, that they both understood the troubled genius of Poe, and befriended and supported him.

Brown's Gothic woods and urban wilderness

America's first Gothic master, Charles Brockden Brown (1771–1810), pioneered, in a brief, brilliant career, many of the issues and techniques used by his successors. Though he was the best writer of fiction the new country would see for many years, he was financially unsuccessful, and died of tuberculosis before his fortieth birthday. His best novels, *Wieland* (1798), *Arthur Mervyn* (1799), and *Edgar Huntly* (1799) written in a short burst of creative energy, are foundational works of American fiction, and of American Gothic.

From Brown onward, the Gothic would be an engine of technical innovation in American literature, and especially in fiction. Brown's experiments in ambiguity and narrative unreliability would be extended by writers such as John Neal, Poe, Nathaniel Hawthorne and Herman Melville, and later by Henry James. They anticipate some of the devices of modernism in the twentieth century.

Brown's innovations may be sampled in his story 'Somnambulism: A Fragment' (1805). Many of his favourite patterns are on display, including a nightmarish night journey into a forest, graphic violence, and confused events with differing possible interpretations. We know that a young woman, Constantia Davis, was shot to death in the darkness, after being separated briefly from her father. The events are reconstructed by the narrator, a young man who was in love with Constantia, from the testimony of her father and other witnesses to parts of the night's events. Was the killer a retarded 'monster' named Nick Handyside, who lurked in these woods? Brown plants clues to suggest that, alternatively, the narrator unwittingly may be the murderer. He had warned father and daughter against the night journey, and then dreamed that he was in the woods with them, trying to protect them. When he awakens in the morning, not in bed but in a chair, he remembers dreaming that he had fired a pistol at someone who had assaulted Miss Davis. One can thus assemble the pieces of the puzzle to conclude that the narrator, who is known to suffer from sleepwalking (somnambulism), has acted out what he has dreamed, and killed his love-object while imagining that he was defending or avenging her. Or was he punishing her for having rejected him? (She was engaged to another man.) The forest of this story, Norwood, becomes a murky realm where (to adapt terms from Bradford's history), the wild beasts and wild men may turn out to be ourselves. The discoveries in this fictional wood are profoundly upsetting to our Enlightenment assumptions. We want to believe that the world can be known through our senses and understood by our reason. We do not wish to discover that our senses cannot be trusted, or that we cannot tell dream from reality, or (now to echo Crèvecoeur) that we are not the people we thought we were.

Such ambiguity informs Brown's novels as well. *Wieland* is the most read of his novels, probably because it is the shortest. Often considered his masterpiece, it suffers from the improbability of its main plot device (deception by ventriloquism), and it could be argued that Brown's characters and settings, nominally American, seem lifted from the England of William Godwin's fiction. Nonetheless, the novel has real power as it traces the degeneration of the title character to madness and murder.

In the first half of *Edgar Huntly*, a novel filled with doubles and doubling, Brown sensibly places the most British elements in Britain, in the retrospective narration of the immigrant character Clithero. The American hero, Huntly, is in many ways a counterpart of Clithero, and the subsequent plot intertwines their lives in many ways. The second half of the novel moves into the indisputably American terrain of the forest. Huntly, like Clithero a somnambulist, awakes to find himself in the total darkness of a cavern. Before the night is over, he will kill a wildcat and eat it raw, escape from the cave into the woods and kill four Indians, in an escalating series of violent scenes on the frontier. The action sequence in the woods is told with a narrative skill not matched until Cooper, if then. In this night of violence, a nightmare version of *A Midsummer Night's Dream*, the civilized man becomes indistinguishable from the savage: Huntly and a party of his friends even fire on each other in the darkness. Brown himself is shaken by the brutality emerging in his character. Though the novel ends with apparent conventional resolution, there is enough ambiguity, as in 'Somnambulism', to allow alternative readings. Some readers suspect Huntly himself of an earlier murder that is attributed to Indian raiders.

In *Edgar Huntly*, Brown pushes far into the terrain of wilderness Gothic. *Arthur Mervyn*, set in Philadelphia, is the first major American urban Gothic novel, and Brown's most complex experiment in narrative ambiguity.

Arthur Mervyn seems to be a classic *Bildungsroman*, with Gothic overtones created by the presence of a Gothic antagonist, the English criminal Welbeck, and also by explicit, horrifying descriptions of the yellow fever epidemic that ravages Philadelphia. The protagonist first falls under the influence of the evil Welbeck, then catches the fever. He finds a worthy mentor in Dr Stevens, who provides both medical care and moral counsel. After numerous adventures, in which Mervyn follows his innocent good intentions (a phrase repeated with variations throughout the novel), he is rewarded by marriage to a prosperous and nubile English widow. 'My behaviour', Mervyn proclaims, ' . . . was ambiguous and hazardous, and perhaps wanting in discretion, but my motives were unquestionably pure.'[12]

But were they? While certainty eludes us in *Arthur Mervyn*, there is ample reason to distrust the narrator-protagonist's claims of the purity of his motives. In fact, dissenting witnesses testify repeatedly that Mervyn is a fraud, a lecher, a horse thief, a confidence man and a son who would cheat his own father. A careful reader will find many inconsistencies in his narrative, and note how often his interventions in the lives of others are disastrous for them, profitable for him. One way to read the novel, indeed, is as a duel between the old-world villainy of Welbeck and the new-world villainy represented by the slippery Mervyn. In this contest, Welbeck is hopelessly outclassed by the new-style American model, whose Gothic villainy lurks beneath his assumed mantle of innocence and good intentions.

Brown has thus explored the character of the same 'new man' we saw in Crèvecoeur's *Letters*, a type later to be called the American Adam, and has revealed its Gothic potential.[13] A character who never reflects, never doubts, never considers consequences for others, but rushes ahead to solve the problem as he sees it, Mervyn leaves destruction in his wake, and is responsible for several deaths (as well as the complete ruin of the overmatched Welbeck), all the while professing his good intentions. This is a type prophetic of much in American culture and politics.

George Lippard and the city gothic

The epidemic of yellow fever in *Arthur Mervyn* is a metaphor for the corruption of Philadelphia and its mercantile culture. A generation later, George Lippard made the corruption of the metropolis the theme of *The Quaker City; Or, the Monks of Monk Hall* (1845) and dedicated the book to the memory of Charles Brockden Brown.

The novel is a sprawling, ramshackle affair, with three intertwined primary plots, each involving rape or seduction. It surely is one of the most sexually explicit novels legally published in English in the nineteenth century. Most of the action is set inside the building of the subtitle, which is a gambling and opium den and brothel, serving as both a secret men's club for the city's elite and a hideout for its criminals. Monk Hall, with its many stories and subterranean passageways, is a double for the novel itself. At the centre of both the Hall and the book is Devil Bug, who has been called 'perhaps the most gleefully evil, sadistic character in American literature.'[14] Devil Bug is a deformed monster with a single eye, a torturer and murderer, a sometime hangman, and master of ceremonies in Monk Hall.

And yet, though Devil Bug is morally abhorrent, he serves as an honest observer (with his one eye). He enjoys hanging an English sailor, in an episode he narrates, but it is clear to him and to us that the condemned man is innocent (the episode, as Lippard's note explains, was based in fact). Devil Bug's account of the execution exposes the injustice and hypocrisy of the city's legal system, its clergy (represented by the chaplain at the execution, whose mind is on his supper) and the howling mob that comes to enjoy the spectacle. Paradoxically the lurid Gothic tale, as is often the case, reveals the moral earnestness of the author.

John Neal (1793–1876) had a long and financially successful career as a writer of fiction, drama and criticism, though little of his once great reputation remains. He is remembered, with Lippard, as one of the few American men of letters of the time who understood and defended Poe. His immense, sprawling novel *Logan* (1822) has drawn attention again recently as a failed masterpiece, a book that somehow *ought* to have been great, since it had a great subject: the Mingo chief who had befriended settlers, but led a war of revenge after his family was slaughtered by whites in 1774. Neal's short story 'Idiosyncrasies' shows his powers of technical innovation, in a chilling account of a man's destruction of his loving family. The story is told to a framing narrator by a madman who insists, like several of Poe's narrators, that he is not mad at all. As with so many American stories, 'Idiosyncrasies' takes its characters into a natural setting, in this case a winter excursion up a mountain by the narrator, his wife, son and daughter, which results in fatal harm to the little boy. At every step in the story we see the insane stubbornness of a man who insists that his behaviour is entirely reasonable and justified, though it leads, ultimately, to his wife's suicide as well as his son's death.

Irving's (almost) Gothic

Washington Irving (1783–1859) was an immensely talented and popular author who, among other achievements, exerted great influence on the American short story. He established a set of conventions that were used by later writers of ghost stories on both sides of the Atlantic. Henry James's long story or novella *The Turn of the Screw* (1898) may be considered an evolution of Irving's technique of the embedded narrator. Irving established a recognizable tone, comfortable and avuncular, that was infectious and much imitated, but, as feminist scholars began to assert in the 1970s, has proved confining to women authors and readers.[15] Like Hawthorne's 'Alice Doane's Appeal', many of Irving's stories explore the Gothic potential of North American and European subjects. Yet, while his stories are often *about* the Gothic, depicting Gothic settings and events, or characters telling Gothic tales to one another, they are usually not Gothic in their effect on the reader. Irving's tales make the reader feel comfortable, amused, sentimental or nostalgic, all states of consciousness that undermine the Gothic.

'The Legend of Sleepy Hollow' (1820) begins with an epigram taken from James Thomson's 'The Castle of Indolence' (1748), and the story extends that poem's mood of relaxed reverie. Irving's narrator Diedrich Knickerbocker had hunted in the woods around Sleepy Hollow as a boy, views it with affection and nostalgia, and imagines himself retiring there. The superstitions of the region are, for Knickerbocker, part of its charm. The Sleepy Hollow farmers and their wives tell stories of ghosts and goblins, of the headless horseman, and of the unfortunate Major André, who was arrested near the tree now haunted by his spirit, and executed for his presumed part in Benedict Arnold's conspiracy.[16]

The schoolmaster Ichabod Crane avidly hears these local stories, and repays them with tales of Salem witchcraft from his treasured copy of Cotton's Mather's 'witchcraft book' (presumably *Wonders of the Invisible World*). But these stories – both those from Sleepy Hollow and from Salem – are only summarized; Irving does not allow them to trouble the reader. When Crane walks or rides through the woods trembling with fear after these ghost-story sessions, he is feeling emotions we do not share. Nor are we frightened with him on his wild ride from Major André's haunted tree to the bridge, since we understand from Irving's winks and nudges the real identity of the Horseman, who throws not his head but a pumpkin at the careening pedagogue.

Around the margins of 'The Legend of Sleepy Hollow' we glimpse an African American presence that for another author, or in another age, would have evoked the Gothic of race. The abundant harvests of the Van Tassel farm were made possible by slave labour (still practised in New York at this time). A black messenger brings Ichabod the invitation to the party at the Van Tassel home. An 'old grey-headed negro'[17] plays his fiddle for the dance, while black faces watch from the doors and windows as Ichabod dances, their ambiguous grins indicating admiration, or more likely derision. We cannot know, but may imagine, that among the tales of witches and ghosts told in the home of the slave-owning Van Tassels may be some that passed through the imagination of black storytellers.

'Rip Van Winkle' (1819) is a gentle version of wilderness Gothic. Rip's journey up the Catskill Mountains and his return to his Hudson Valley village twenty years later conform to the classic pattern of a transforming experience in the wilderness. While it is too sunny and genial for true Gothic shadows, the story does have a genuine uncanny moment when the bewildered Rip encounters his grown son and his grandson, each bearing his own name:

> God knows . . . I'm not myself. —I'm somebody else—that's me yonder—no—that's somebody else got into my shoes—I was myself last night; but I fell asleep on the mountain—and they've changed my gun—and every thing's changed—and I'm changed—and I can't tell what's my name, or who I am! [18]

Rip's transformation turns out to be not so painful after all, since, freed of his nagging wife, he is able to pass from a prolonged adolescence to a comfortable retirement, having skipped most of the stress and inconvenience of adult life.

In 'Rip Van Winkle', the woods are presented like those in a European folk-tale; not surprisingly, since Irving in fact had adapted a German source. Rip tells neighbourhood children 'long stories of ghosts, witches and Indians' as well as teaching them about kites and marbles.[19] Likewise, Irving entertains us with a story that is meant to please but not really threaten. Other writers, however, would present the American wilderness as more disturbing and menacing.

31

Into the wild

In the first decades of the nineteenth century, American writers continued to explore the potential of the wild landscape as a zone of imaginative liberation or of terror.

Following the example of Brown in *Edgar Huntly*, many writers of the early nineteenth century found the wilderness an appropriate stage for adventure stories in which the brutal interaction of settlers and Indians could cross the line into the Gothic. James Kirke Paulding, for example, was a sometime collaborator with Irving. Paulding ridiculed the European Gothic in his critical work, yet there are Gothic elements, based on American conditions, not haunted castles and ghosts, in his fiction. He used the woods as the site for the madness of his hero in *Westward Ho!* (1832). Robert Montgomery Bird's *Nick of the Woods* (1837), a considerably darker work, is a revenge story in which the protagonist, a Quaker named Nathan, transforms himself in the woods into an Indian-killer feared by the Indians as an evil spirit called the 'Jibbenainosay'. The double life of sober frontier-citizen and remorseless Indian-killer was apparently well known on the frontier, at least in legend. Melville would tell another such story in the chapter 'The Metaphysics of Indian Hating' in *The Confidence-Man* (1857).

The most popular writer of wilderness adventures in the pre-Civil War period, of course, was James Fenimore Cooper. Each of the five novels in the Leatherstocking series contains Gothic elements, and *The Last of the Mohicans* (1826), at least, could be described as a Gothic romance. The narrative is based on historical events of the French and Indian Wars, and its centrepiece is the massacre of English soldiers and their dependants after the surrender of Fort William Henry in 1757. Against the background of these epic events, Cooper places characters derived from Romantic and Gothic convention. The Gothic villain is played by Magua, a brooding satanic figure whose 'fatal and artful eloquence'[20] incites the orgy of slaughter, and who attempts to make one of the Colonel's daughters, Cora, his concubine. Other Indian antagonists in Cooper's fiction, such as Rivenoak in *The Deerslayer* (1841), share his Gothic-villain qualities.

The colonel's daughters, Cora and Alice, half-sisters, are themselves types from European convention: the dark heroine, of exotic background, intelligent, sensual and rebellious; the light heroine, pure, innocent, religious, and usually the winner in the competition with her dark counterpart. Rowena and Rebecca in Scott's *Ivanhoe* are an example of this pairing. Both figures, and especially the dark heroine, will see evolution in the works of later American writers such as Hawthorne and James.

Cooper's most memorable creation, Natty Bumppo, does not derive, at least not obviously, from Gothic models. He has been much discussed not only as the centre of the values of the Leatherstocking series, but also as a prototypical American hero. D. H. Lawrence summarized his character thus: hard, isolate, stoic and a killer.[21] He is an intuitive man of action who never agonizes over moral choice. Though presented favourably by Cooper, this is the character type whose disturbing potential Charles Brockden Brown portrayed in *Arthur Mervyn*.

The Last of the Mohicans (and the Leatherstocking series generally) reveals the cultural ambiguity many scholars have located in the Gothic tradition. Are Gothic tales subversive, or do they reinforce the values of the dominant culture? Cooper presents the collapse of Indian culture as sad but inevitable. He depicts Indians through the conventional stereotypes of noble savage (Chingachgook and Uncas) or demonic savage (Magua). Massacres by Indians are shown in graphic detail, while massacres of Indians by British and Americans (as at the end of *The Deerslayer*) take place off-stage. The cumulative effect of the series, an epic of Western expansion, is to reinforce the dominant national narrative of settlement and progress.

And yet, at the core of the story are Natty and Chingachgook, who hate the settlements. Does this relationship represent an alternative to the dominant vision of progress? Or is it simply a fantasy escape from it for the reader, like a weekend camping trip at a national park?

Cooper's ambivalence toward these issues, and toward the wilderness, may be seen in his portrait of other frontiersmen, such as the Bush family in *The Prairie* (1827). They are a clan of brutish, 'wasty people', who are first seen chopping down one of the few trees in the prairie landscape. In many ways they represent the author's fear of degeneration on the frontier; yet they are capable of patriarchal, Old Testament forms of honour and justice. In chapter 32 of *The Prairie*, the family patriarch, Ishmael Bush, avenges his son's death by executing the murderer, who is Ishmael's own brother-in-law. This Gothic sequence is a nightscape suggesting the darker paintings of the Hudson River School, like those of Cooper's contemporary Thomas Cole. A dead tree, a symbol of mutability for Romantic American painters, is illuminated by moonlight. Bush leaves his brother-in-law, Abiram White, balanced on a thin shelf of rock beneath this willow, the noose around his neck tied to a branch; he returns later to find the moon breaking through the clouds and revealing the taut rope and the hanging body. Ishmael digs a crude prairie grave while his wife mumbles prayers over her brother's corpse. The description evokes awe and surrounds the events with a primitive dignity. There is a rudimentary sense of justice and family honour here, the elements of a society, though one that Cooper clearly fears and disdains.

Cooper was a patrician but had been born in a frontier town founded by his father, and which bore the family name (Cooperstown, New York). Most descriptions of frontier life in the period between the Revolution and the Civil War were written by people (usually men) who, if not professional authors like Cooper, were journalists, lawyers, politicians or others who were distanced by class and education from their subjects. One category of writing, inadequately called 'Old Southwest Humor', written about backwoods life in the frontier South, was considered unsuitable for general publication then, and was often published in a magazine for men called *The Spirit of the Times*. Rough, often obscene and bawdy, its sexual humour partly disguised with phonetically spelled dialect, this energetic fiction would influence major American writers from Melville and Clemens to Faulkner and Cormac McCarthy.

The stories of 'Old Southwest Humor' are often very funny indeed, in a rough back-country sort of way. But in their grotesqueness, violence and racism they sometimes cross the Gothic frontier.

Racial swamp, black masks

Henry Clay Lewis's 'A Struggle for Life' (1850) is a case in point. The story describes a backwoods doctor summoned by a slave to treat a sick planter. The slave, a dwarf with a harelip and protruding teeth, leads the doctor on a short-cut across a swamp: the familiar pattern of a journey into the wilderness. Wading through the rising waters, the doctor makes the mistake of offering the slave brandy as a remedy against the cold and wet; but the guide becomes drunk, loses his way in the swamp and, at nightfall, as they prepare to camp, he attacks the doctor with a savagery and strength that the latter cannot resist. The strangled doctor loses consciousness, believes that he is dead, but revives later to find that the dwarf, 'maddened by the spirits, had rushed into the flames' of the campfire, and burned himself to death. The next morning the doctor finds his way out of the swamp, but 'I would not for the universe have looked again upon the place'.[22]

'A Struggle for Life' begs for interpretation as a fantasy of slave rebellion, the inner fear of all white people in the slave-owning South. The grotesque dwarf seems to arise directly from the subconscious of the doctor, compounded of all of the repressed guilt and terror of his class. The rebellious slave is a powerful figure, one of the most potent, indeed, in American culture of the time, because he is based on a fear understood by both black and white Americans. Thus, he can be used to great effect even by a minor writer like Henry Clay Lewis. As we saw in Crèvecoeur, the rebellious slave strikes through the conventions of race enforced by the masters: slaves must appear to be happy, content and respectful; at least, they wear a mask that conveys this, and never speak their true thoughts. The slave in 'A Struggle for Life' drops the mask. Though Lewis, a brutal racist, as his other stories show, would never have admitted this, the grotesque features of the dwarf represent the terror of the master at being confronted with the reality behind the illusion he has created. We will see this dwarf again.

Mystical blackness

The period known as the American Renaissance, between, roughly, the publication of Emerson's *Nature* in 1836 and the Civil War, marked the high tide of Romanticism in the United States. (It had peaked earlier in Britain.) The major writers of this period shared Romantic traits: they valued the individual, distrusted authority, favoured organic forms over artifice, and so on. They disagreed sharply over questions of good, evil and human nature. The writers of the time can be defined by their agreement with or dissent from the ideas of Ralph Waldo Emerson, its central thinker, or at least disseminator of ideas. Emerson recorded his insights first as aphorisms in his journal, which he embedded in his lectures and essays. It would be easy to capture the essence of his philosophy in a few of his Orphic pronouncements. For example:

> In the woods is perpetual youth ... In the woods, we return to reason and faith. (*Nature*)

> Good is positive. Evil is merely privative, not absolute: it is like cold, which is the privation of heat. ('The Divinity School Address')

> Let me admonish you, first of all to go alone; to refuse the good models, even those which are sacred in imagination of men, and dare to love God without mediator or veil. ('The Divinity School Address')

> On my saying, 'What have I to do with the sacredness of traditions, if I live wholly from within?' my friend suggested— 'But these impulses may be from below, not from above'. I replied, 'They do not seem to me to be such; but if I am the Devil's child, I will live then from the Devil'. No law can be sacred to me but that of my nature. ('Self-Reliance')

> Standing on the bare ground ... all mean egotism vanishes. I become a transparent eyeball; I am nothing; I see all; the currents of the Universal Being circulate through me; I am part or parcel of God. (*Nature*)

Emerson sees human nature as basically good, though people are damaged by society, and by their separation from Nature. He encourages a life spent recovering this natural goodness. This philosophy is essentially Platonic; one can ascend to a realm of the good, true and beautiful and gain contact with the divinity in all things, which Emerson calls the Oversoul.

The writings of Poe, Hawthorne and Melville record their disagreement with these views. Since the three were not a movement (and Poe did not know the other two personally), they collaborated on no manifesto. However, Melville's review 'Hawthorne and His Mosses' (1850) defines their Gothic position:

> For spite of all the Indian-summer sunlight on the hither side of Hawthorne's soul, the other side—like the dark half of the physical sphere—is shrouded in a blackness, ten times black. Whether Hawthorne has simply availed himself of this mystical blackness as a means to the wondrous effects he makes it to produce in his lights and shades; or whether there really lurks in him, perhaps unknown to himself, a touch of Puritanic gloom,—this, I cannot altogether tell. Certain it is, however, that this great power of blackness in him derives its force from its appeals to that Calvinistic sense of Innate Depravity and Original Sin, from whose visitations, in some shape or other, no deeply thinking mind is always and wholly free.[23]

No prose passage written by an American in this period has had greater resonance in later critical discourse. Besides being the sharpest insight ever written about Hawthorne's art, we are also at the heart of Melville's own convictions. Poe likewise inhabited this world of 'mystical blackness'.

Despite efforts of some theorists to assimilate all use of the work 'black' to the racial issue, Melville is not speaking specifically about race. (Of course, the crime of slavery is contained within the larger category of human 'Depravity'.) Nor is he really talking about Puritanism. While Hawthorne considered himself a Christian (though not a Puritan), Melville, by this time in his life, did not. But he did accept the basic premise of the doctrine of Original Sin: all humans are flawed and capable of evil. Where Emerson considered evil merely 'privative', the absence of good, Hawthorne, Melville and Poe, like all true Gothic writers, believed that evil was real and an active force in our lives.

The difference between the Transcendentalists and these dark Romantics is signalled by the images they favoured. The writings of Emerson and Thoreau are filled with light and with circles:

Emerson's transparent eyeball, Thoreau's clear Walden Pond. But opposed to the Transcendentalists' circles and light are the dark Romantic's emblems of darkness, disunity and ambiguity: the globe of the world half shrouded in darkness; the two sides of the turtle, one bright, one dark; the two eyes of the whale looking in opposite directions; the dark waters of Poe's silent seas and mist-covered tarns; Hawthorne's twilights and shadows and moments between waking and dreaming. The world is much more 'belittered' (Melville's term) for the dark Romantics; moving in a straight line through it is difficult. There is real evil here, and in us. The challenge is to recognize the evil, and yet not go mad.

Poe's Gothic

In a very literal sense, Edgar A. Poe gave a face to American Gothic. An 1848 daguerreotype of Poe is one of the best-known American portraits of the century. It is often difficult to untangle Poe's life and achievement from popular culture, parodies and theories about his death. He has had a great influence on French readers and writers, who know him through the brilliant translations of Charles Baudelaire. In France, Poe is known (like Baudelaire) as a supreme *poète maudit*, a courageous and self-destructive outsider artist dedicated to the purity of his art. Native English-speakers may be less impressed by Poe's occasional heavy-footed June / moon rhymes and his shameless self-promotion. James Russell Lowell's estimation of Poe, 'Three-fifths of him genius, and two-fifths sheer fudge', seems about right.[24]

Nonetheless, Poe's accomplishment and influence is immense in several areas: in detective fiction, a genre he virtually created, in the theory of short fiction, and in creating an eerie dreamscape (sometimes called the Poescape or Poeland) that is instantly recognizable. He pushed farther than anyone, even his friend John Neal, in experiments with unreliable or mad narrators. He repeatedly explored the uncanny effects of doubles, and gave his own stamp to the Gothic devices of the revenant (the soul returning from the dead) and the haunted house. He was one of the inventors of the sea Gothic, a form soon to be extended by Herman Melville.

Present-day Gothic master Joyce Carol Oates defines Poe's influence as 'incalculable', and asks, rhetorically, 'Who has *not* been influenced by Poe?'[25]

Poe tried to build his fiction and verse on universal fears such as darkness, falling and claustrophobic confinement, and of violation of such taboos as cannibalism and incest. Yet many details of his personal disasters are echoed in his work, as well as the common anxieties of Americans of his time.

Poe's Romantic agony

Poe shared with other Romantics a Platonic belief in the gap between our world and the barely glimpsed realm of the true and the beautiful. Poe's 'Romantic agony' over the unbridgeable distance between ideal and reality was intensified by the notorious circumstances of his life: his early loss of parents, his estrangement from his foster father, James Allan, his inability to escape poverty, his alcoholism and the early death of his child-bride and cousin, Virginia Clemm. The great themes of his work are mutability and loss, the desire for and fear of what has been lost, and the divisions within the human mind. The past haunts us, and we haunt ourselves.

In his poem 'Israfel' (1831), Poe contrasts an ideal artist, the angel Israfel playing his lyre above the stars, with the situation of the earth-bound poet:

> Yes, heaven is thine: but this
>> Is a world of sweets and sours;
>> Our flowers are merely—flowers,
> And the shadow of thy perfect bliss
>> Is the sunshine of ours.

If 'I', Poe, the earthbound poet, could live in Israfel's starry realm, he could produce a 'bolder note'; and conversely, Israfel, were he in our world, 'Might not sing so wildly well'.[26]

Poe could envision Israfel's realm of the ideal, as indicated, for example, in his prose sketch 'The Domain of Arnheim' (1864), in which an artfully perfected landscape becomes the equivalent of a

Platonic heaven. In 'To Helen' (1831), one of his most celebrated poems, Poe transmutes his beloved from a real woman into the realm of myth, art and ideal beauty: one of the standard Romantic responses to mutability, loss and death. However, most of his poems and stories deal with the sublunary world, a world of 'sweets and sours', in which everything and everyone is imperfect and temporary, and often terrifying.

Imp of the Perverse

Poe's story 'The Imp of the Perverse' (1845) articulates his theory of flawed and divided human nature. The narrator appeals to everyone's experience: why do we often postpone tasks that we know need to be done? What counterforce within us blocks our will to begin? He extends this very familiar pattern to a terrifying one in which 'We stand upon the brink of a precipice'. Of course we wish to 'shrink from the danger'. But something paradoxically draws us to the edge. (Poe in fact had dramatized this scene in *The Narrative of Arthur Gordon Pym*.) 'If there be no friendly arm to check us, or if we fail in a sudden effort to prostrate ourselves backward from the abyss, we plunge, and are destroyed'.[27]

'The Imp of the Perverse' seems at first to be an essay, but the reader learns that the author of this disquisition on perversity is a murderer who was moved by the spirit of self-destruction – not to commit the murder, which he regards as rational and defensible – but to confess his crime in public.

The psychology of 'The Imp of the Perverse' fuels much of Poe's writing. In story and poem we encounter the psyche divided against itself. As the narrator of 'The Imp of the Perverse' reveals his crime, in public and again to us, other narrators, as in 'The Black Cat (1843)' and 'The Tell-Tale Heart' (1843), reveal what should be kept secret. Poe's conflicted narrators insist on their rationality, while their tales reveal that they are barking lunatics.

Doubles

In other stories, such as 'William Wilson' (1839) and 'The Cask of Amontillado' (1846), pairs of mirror-image characters represent the conflicted mind. The two stories themselves are doubles, parallel tales in which narrators tell of their long-ago vengeance against their tormentors, each ending in an Italian carnival season with the masked and costumed narrator killing his opposite.

The setting of 'William Wilson', perhaps Poe's most celebrated study of the double, or *doppelgänger*, is drawn in part from the author's childhood memories. His largely happy recollections of his two years at the Manor House boarding school at Stoke Newington, outside London, provide the background for Wilson's account of life at Dr Bransby's School. There Wilson is surprised to learn that another student bearing his name, and even his birthday, enrols at the same time. Poe gives an allegorical slant to this pairing, making the second Wilson a projection of the narrator's conscience. Wilson's double follows him from Dr Bransby's to Eton and to Oxford, and then to cities on the Continent, always appearing at moments in his moral decline. They meet for the last time in Rome, during Carnival, that time of masked faces and unmasked inhibitions. The two duel with swords, and Wilson destroys his conscience, watching the second Wilson die as if he were looking into a mirror.

'William Wilson' is perhaps the earliest example of American Schoolhouse Gothic, and the relation of the two William Wilsons prefigures later relationships, like that of Gene and Finny in John Knowles's *A Separate Peace* (1959).

'The Cask of Amontillado' is a briefer story on the same theme of a man and his double. Stripped of the allegory of 'William Wilson', of any 'back-story', even a clear motive, we have only the narrator's (possibly dying) confession of his revenge on his rival, long ago, at Carnival time. The closeness between Montresor and his victim becomes uncannily apparent as the masonry wall rises before the chained Fortunato, and he begins to scream: 'I replied to the yells of him who clamored. I re-echoed—I aided—I surpassed them in volume and in strength. I did this, and the clamor grew still.'[28] The two screaming Italians on opposite sides of the half-finished wall recall the mirror images of the Wilsons in their final encounter.

We do not know what Montresor has become since disposing of Fortunato. The older Montresor, in a familiar pattern, addresses his confession to a barely suggested interlocutor who is scarcely distinguished from the reader: 'You, who know so well the nature of my soul'. [29] Thus we are made into Montresor's priest, or perhaps his accomplice. The story displays candidly the pleasures of revenge (which the reader will understand) while hinting at the resulting corrosion of the spirit.

She came and departed as a shadow

The borders of Poe's dreamscape are madness and death; his works always inhabit these frontiers. Poe's murderers are madmen, but he also indicates – in 'Eleonora' (1841) for example – his Romantic–Platonic belief that on the borderland of madness are to be found 'in snatches' glimpses of a world beyond. Beyond death, likewise, may be a world of perfection, like the lost 'Valley of the Many Coloured Grass' inhabited by Eleonora. But death also brings physical corruption, and no American Romantic gave such attention to rotting flesh as Poe. In 'The Facts of the Case of M. Valdemar' (1845), Poe imagines a man hypnotized at the moment of death, so that the body remains intact until the hypnotist releases the subject, after *'nearly seven months'* [30] and the corpse instantly collapses into 'a nearly liquid mass of loathsome—of detestable putridity'. [31] This is the epitome of gross-out Gothic, to which film-makers have aspired endlessly.

Poe famously said, in 'The Philosophy of Composition' (1846), that the most poetic of all subjects is the death of a beautiful woman. [32] Beauty and decay, timelessness and loss: such is the range of Poe's sad music. The most celebrated of his works, such as 'The Raven' (1845), are based on this master subject. So is Poe's favourite among his stories, 'Ligeia' (1838).

Like most of Poe's stories and poems, 'Ligeia' seems set in a landscape drawn from nightmare, or filtered through the consciousness of a deranged narrator. The 'old, decaying city near the Rhine' appears to have no name, and might as well be on the

River of Silence in 'Eleonora'. The narrator claims never to have known the family name of Ligeia. The story's logic is that of dream, not of memory. The raven-haired Ligeia, the perfect woman, seems both lover and mother as seen through the eyes of a small child: one who knows and teaches everything, provides for all needs. After her death from a wasting disease, the narrator moves to Britain, and brings his new bride Rowena to his English Gothic castle. The struggles between Ligeia and Rowena over the body of the new bride encapsulate the endless contest between light and dark heroines seen throughout Romantic literature. The story ends with Ligeia's raven-black tresses spilling from the cerements that had enclosed the blonde locks of Rowena, a sudden disclosure of what had been anticipated, desired and feared, as in the quick revealing close-up that is the pay-off in a horror movie. The moment combines triumph and horror, beauty and deep taboo, like the return of Madeline Usher: an amplified version of the Romantic sublime that is the core of Poe's aesthetic.

Poe's apparent fascination with disease, death and decay, like most elements of the Gothic, involves only a slight exaggeration of the everyday reality of his time. Childhood diseases were endemic, as was tuberculosis. Since bodies were customarily prepared for burial in the home, nearly everyone had more direct experience of death and corpses than is the case in prosperous Western societies today. Tuberculosis, the disease that took Poe's wife Virginia, was especially cruel, draining the strength of its victims, turning them into pale shadows. It may be, in fact, that persistent TB contagion is responsible for a native vampire tradition in New England in the early and mid nineteenth century.[33] Poe's story of the revenant Ligeia may be read, with typical Gothic ambiguity, as a story of the triumph of the human spirit over death, or the triumph of disease over life, taking one strong young woman after another.

'The Masque of the Red Death' (1842), another story of disease, looks forward to Jack London's *The Scarlet Plague* (1912), to an episode in Thomas Pynchon's *V* (1963), and any number of recent apocalyptic novels and films. It is both a fantastic, carnivalesque allegory, and an accurate account of the way people may respond to an uncontrollable epidemic. (In *The Peloponnesian War*, Thucydides describes the careless hedonism of Athenians during a time of plague.) Prince Prospero and his nobles retreat from the contagion into a pleasure palace, only to find that Death is the unwelcome guest at their revels. At the end, the only sound in the seven rooms of the imperial suite is the ticking clock, symbol of inevitable change and loss.

Revenge of the dwarf

'Hop-Frog' (1849), published the year of Poe's death, is woven from several of his favourite themes: a corrupt royal court, a masquerade and revenge. The story reflects Poe's circumstances and, covertly, the fears of his age.

A brutal king and his court abuse the dwarf court jester and his beloved Trippetta. Hop-Frog tricks the king and his seven courtiers into dressing as 'Eight Chained Ourang-Outangs' for the masquerade, and burns them to death in their inflammable costumes. Inevitably, this revenge story could be read as Poe's comment on his own situation as artist and husband. Like Hop-Frog, whose king continually demands new ideas for entertainments, Poe is likewise a slave to the demands of his public and editors for new material. Even the king's cruelty in forcing Hop-Frog to drink alcohol, in spite of his aversion to it, reflects Poe's insistence that his own problem with alcohol was something imposed on him by circumstances. How satisfying it would be to call down fiery apocalypse on the whole system of torment and escape with his beloved, as Trippetta and Hop-Frog escape from the skylight of the palace.

And yet behind this story of the rebellion of the oppressed lurks another familiar pattern, that of the slave uprising. Poe was a Southerner, and a supporter of the slave system. Unlike Melville, he had not thought his way through to a rejection of the received ideas of his age on race and power. 'Hop-Frog', like 'A Struggle for Life' by his younger Southern contemporary, Henry Clay Lewis, draws on the dominant fears of the time, without exploring their causes. By not identifying Hop-Frog as a black man, but as another sort of slave, he freed his imagination and identified with the oppressed. Yet, typical of Gothic's ambiguity, an opposite reading of the story's climax is possible. Hop-Frog enacts a slave rebellion, but the burning alive of the king and his courtiers, bound and dangling from a chain, reverses this pattern and is 'a grotesque approximation to southern lynchings'.[34] Recall the dying slave in a cage described by Crèvecoeur.

Poe and the sea Gothic

The sea, like the forest, was a frontier for Americans, and thus a zone for encounters with the unknown. Poe's *The Narrative of Arthur Gordon Pym* (1838) stands at the beginning of a significant and continuing tradition of sea Gothic that would soon include Melville and would extend in later years to Jack London, and on to Robert Stone, Peter Matthiessen and Philip Caputo.

The Narrative of Arthur Gordon Pym might be dismissed as a combination of hoax and shaggy-dog story. Like its frontier equivalent, *The Journal of Julius Rodman* (1840), *Pym* is filled with plausible details and technical terms designed to gull readers into believing that they are reading a real account of a journey of exploration – a popular narrative form of the time. Moreover, the *Narrative* breaks off with the boat of Pym and Dirk Peters speeding toward a mysterious gigantic white figure looming in the mist over the South Pole. The reader is left frustrated, without explanation of the figure's significance or of the means of Pym's survival to tell the tale. (It is possible, of course, that Poe had planned a sequel.)

The adventures of Pym, nonetheless, may resonate in the reader's imagination. Pym is motivated by the Imp of the Perverse, repeatedly going to sea in risky circumstances that defy common sense. His initiation on the *Grampus*, as many readers have noted, can be read as a kind of death and rebirth into a new life: his confinement in the coffin-like box in the hold, his rescue, his impersonation of a corpse or ghost, the replacement of his friend Augustus by the half-Indian sidekick Dirk Peters. Ultimately he will resort to cannibalism to survive starvation before he and Dirk are rescued by the *Jane Guy*.

As with 'Hop-Frog', the *Narrative* is filled with images of slave rebellion. In the mutiny on the *Grampus*, an African American cook is the most brutal in his slaughter of resisting sailors and officers. The island of Tsalal, of course, is inhabited by people so black that even their teeth are black, and they are afraid of any object or creature that is white. The slaughter of the crew of the *Jane Guy* by the Tsalal chief Too-Wit, after they had been offered safe conduct, recalls various historical events, including a massacre of Romans described by Caesar in *The Conquest of Gaul* (which all educated men of Poe's generation had studied in school); but slave rebellion would have been the fear evoked in American readers of the time. Pym and Peters survive because they are trapped in the 'blackness of darkness' of a landslide, and are able to escape 'the most wicked, hypocritical, vindictive, bloodthirsty, and altogether fiendish race of men upon the face of the globe.'[35] Stealing a canoe, they are drawn by a current into a warm sea of white mists, toward a 'shrouded human figure . . . of the perfect whiteness of the snow.'[36]

While clearly evoking race, Poe's symbolism of black and white in *The Narrative of Arthur Gordon Pym* is no more coherent than the rune-like symbols Pym finds on Tsalal. They insinuate meaning without revealing it. But the play of light and dark in *Pym* would powerfully resound on the imagination of Herman Melville, who would draw on Poe without acknowledgment in *Moby-Dick* (1851) and *Benito Cereno* (1856).

Hawthorne and faith in the woods

Emerson had attempted to break free of the past, and especially of the legacy of his Puritan ancestors. When he wrote, 'In the woods we return to reason and faith', he was inverting the vision of the Puritans: for them, you bring your faith *into* the woods, and try to keep it.

Nathaniel Hawthorne's 'Young Goodman Brown', probably the best known of his tales, was published in 1835, the year before *Nature*, and serves as a brief counter-vision to Emerson's sunlit certainties. Hawthorne recreates the atmosphere of Salem on the eve of the witchcraft scare. His dark woodland, lit with flashes of lurid red flame, is an arena where the ambiguities of human psychology and those of nature interact. Goodman Brown both finds and loses his Faith in the woods. He finds the allegorically named Faith (perhaps) in the veiled figure by the altar; loses Faith because, in spite of his last-minute appeal to her to resist temptation, he can never again trust his wife, his fellow villagers or himself.

The celebrated ambiguities of Brown's experience body forth the key legal issue of the Salem witchcraft trials, that of 'spectral evidence'. Once such testimony was admitted, all hope of rational proceedings was lost. If you can prove that you were not near a witchcraft victim at a certain time, but testimony that your 'spectre' was there is accepted as valid, what defence is possible? In Hawthorne's tale, Brown sees the figures of townsmen and hears their voices passing by in the darkness, but cannot tell if they are real, or illusions created by his companion, the Devil. His virtue is weak because it is based on the example of others, and, aside from the spectres of deacons and pious old women who may be secret sinners, Satan has abundant historical examples of the sins of Brown's New England ancestors: persecution of Quakers, genocidal war against Indian tribes, participation in the slave trade. Brown's first steps in the margins of the woods are slow and tentative, but when even his Faith seems tainted (as the pink ribbon floats down from the 'black mass' of passing cloud), he runs madly toward the witches' Sabbath in the heart of the wilderness.

Though he awakens under a tree after crying out for Faith to resist temptation (did he dream the whole encounter in the woods?), his return to the village, unlike Rip Van Winkle's, does not bring reconciliation, but a life of doubt and suspicion. In traditional religious terms, the Devil has won. Brown's cloistered virtue has failed its first encounter with the morally ambiguous world outside the refuge of his home, and the refuge of his untested beliefs. Thus, Brown cannot lead a Christian life, and 'no hopeful verse' is carved on his tombstone. In a more psychological reading, which Hawthorne always invites, Brown fails because he does not recognize that every temptation he experiences, every one of them, comes entirely from within. In his conversation with the Devil, Brown in fact proposes every obstacle that the Devil must (easily) overcome. Since Brown sees all evil as located in others, he cannot recognize its real source and overcome it, or accept it. Thus, in this tale, the woods are not where 'we return to reason and faith'. Like all characters in Hawthorne's fiction, and in Gothic literature generally, Brown is unable to escape the past or himself.

This pattern of the failure of Emersonian nature in repeated in Hawthorne's most celebrated novel, *The Scarlet Letter* (1850). Chapter 18, 'A Flood of Sunshine', again presents the familiar journey from the settlements to the woods, where, for the first time since their love affair, Hester meets the Reverend Arthur Dimmesdale. It is never stated, but many readers will conclude that the wilderness clearing where they meet is the place of their romantic trysts in the past. The woods, in any case, are an escape from the Puritan restraints of Boston, and they are an equivalent for Hester's mind, which has never submitted to the restraints with which the authorities have tried to humble her.

When Hester and Arthur meet in the clearing, she urges him to leave the Puritan community, promises to go with him, takes the scarlet letter from her dress and removes her cap, letting her sensuous hair fall to her shoulders. The effect is as if we have been watching a movie in black and white, or sepia tones, which has suddenly turned to colour, while violins swell on the soundtrack:

> All at once, as with a sudden smile of heaven, forth burst the sunshine, pouring a very flood into the obscure forest, gladdening each green leaf, transmuting the yellow fallen ones to gold, and gleaming adown the grey trunks of the solemn trees. The objects that had made a shadow hitherto, embodied the brightness now.[37]

This is an Emerson moment, filled with Emerson's symbol of light, and it is urging an Emersonian moral: to go alone, to follow the law of one's own nature.

Unfortunately, the moment does not last; it provides no real guidance. This is Hawthorne's world, not Emerson's, and a Gothic novel. Hester and Dimmesdale, like all of Hawthorne's characters, are restrained by the past, by their own limitations and, one might add, by the author's priggishness. Little Pearl, surely one of the most annoying children in American literature, refuses to recognize her mother without the symbolic letter and modest cap. Hester replaces these symbols of Puritan repression, and the sunshine dies. Hester,

Pearl and Dimmesdale retrace their steps to the town, where they must resolve their destinies.

The Scarlet Letter is a major accomplishment in American Gothic, and has never been out of print since its publication in 1850. We recognize in it many of the conventions of the Gothic novel: the dark Romantic heroine, the villain plotting his revenge, family secrets, and considerable narrative and moral ambiguity. The villain, Chillingworth, embodying learning and authority used for destructive ends, is kin to the schoolteacher and judge figures we see throughout American Gothic. Though these characters and devices may be based on Gothic conventions, they do not seem stereotypes to most readers, because they are so deeply felt and imagined by the author. In 'The Custom-House', the preface that should be considered an essential part of the novel, the half-fictionalized author places the dusty scarlet letter, found with a bundle of manuscripts in the garret of the custom-house, on his own chest. He feels a burning pain because he identifies with Hester, his fellow artist. His pledge to tell Hester's story is an act of defiance against his Puritan ancestors, the Salem witchcraft judges (John and William Hathorne), whose legacy apparently haunted the author all his life.

Hawthorne was fascinated by the past and, in his obscure years after graduating from Bowdoin College, is said to have read every book on local history in the Salem public library. But he did not love the past, any more than Thoreau did. In some moods, at least, he was as willing as Thoreau, or his own character Holgrave of *The House of the Seven Gables*, to destroy the past, which 'lies upon the Present like a giant's dead body'.[38] Better to burn everything and start again.

The House of the Seven Gables (1851) is at once the most and least Gothic of Hawthorne's four romances. The Gothic elements of haunted house, sinister villain, concealed crimes, ancestral curse and hidden manuscript are familiar and conventional, but convincingly rooted in regional history. The house of the title was a real structure in Hawthorne's Salem (and is a tourist attraction today). The curse that Matthew Maule threw at the original Pyncheon, 'God will give you blood to drink',[39] while fictional, resembles actual events of the Salem witchcraft trials. Moreover, present-day readers notice an

African American presence around the margins of the story, from the 'Jim Crow' cookies in Hepzibah's cent shop to the black servants in the scenes set in the past. The Pyncheon fortune is founded on specific local crimes (the judicial murder of Matthew Maul, the false imprisonment of Clifford) and on the larger crimes of slavery and dispossession of Native Americans, as represented by claims on the eastern (that is, Maine) lands. The crimes of the Pyncheons echo the larger patterns of American history.

Within these shadows Hawthorne throws the gentle glow of his heroine Phoebe (a light Romantic heroine indeed, whose name refers to the moon) and her ancestress Alice. The hero, Holgrave, is a modern man, an artist in the new medium of photography. The marriage of Phoebe and Holgrave (who is a Maule) ends the long feud between the families, expiating not only old Colonel Pyncheon's crime against Matthew Maule, but also Maule's grandson's mesmeric abuse of Alice Pyncheon, which led to her death. At the end, an elegant dark-green barouche (the nineteenth-century equivalent, perhaps, of a Bentley), sweeps away Phoebe, Holgrave, Hepzibah, Clifford and Uncle Venner to a new home and a new life. The House of Seven Gables has been escaped; the Gothic novel named after it dissolves into a happy ending. All curses have been lifted. Light, Holgrave's medium (and Emerson's), has replaced darkness. Yesterday's gone, yesterday's gone.

And yet, to many readers this ending (like many of Hawthorne's endings) seems contrived, superimposed on a story that seems headed elsewhere. Certainly, the most memorable scene of the novel is not its honeymoon-photo conclusion, but the long chapter 18 in which the narrator mocks and taunts the dead Judge Pyncheon. This is a savage and strange scene, as dark and Gothic as anything Hawthorne wrote. Its very intensity suggests that it is near the book's and the author's imaginative core. Judge Pyncheon, a virtual reincarnation of his witchcraft-era ancestor Colonel Pyncheon, seems a stand-in for Hawthorne's own Puritan ancestors. While intended as an exorcism making possible the sunny conclusion, the corpse-bating sequence is an act of symbolic patricide, like the defiance of the Hathorne judges in 'The Custom-House'. It is by no means clear that Hawthorne has freed himself from his demons and the shadows of the past.

His next novel describes another attempted escape from the corrupt world. *The Blithedale Romance* (1852) is based on Hawthorne's own sojourn of several months at Brook Farm, a commune founded on Transcendentalist principles. Thus, the novel is Hawthorne's most explicit critique of Emerson's ideas. As in all of his romances, it is filled with references to the Eden story, appropriate to a book which questions whether people can regain lost innocence and a simple relationship to nature. And, as in all his other novels, there is an artist figure, here the poet Miles Coverdale. His actions suggest some of the issues about the role of the artist, and the psychological dangers of being one, that troubled Hawthorne.

Masqueraders

The Blithedale Romance is unfairly considered the weakest of Hawthorne's four Gothic novels, and was long thought to be incoherent. It is not: it is the most technically flawless of his novels, a skilful experiment in unreliable first-person narration. The novel's narrative complexities are a careful match to Hawthorne's vision of an ambiguous world.

It is not surprising that the experiments of *The Blithedale Romance* were understood and appreciated by the next generation of major American novelists. Henry James, the master of narrative theory, paid homage to *The Blithedale Romance* in *The Bostonians* (1886), W. D. Howells in *The Undiscovered Country* (1880).

In the first pages, Old Moodie, a seemly inconsequential figure, but in reality one of god-like power, approaches the narrator, Miles Coverdale, to ask for a favour. When Coverdale hesitates, betraying a reluctance to help, Moodie walks away: he will ask the favour of someone else (Hollingsworth). Coverdale's hesitation is typical of a man who is unwilling to commit to any action, a character trait critiqued by Zenobia in her 'Legend of the Silvery Veil', and effectively places him outside the story he is trying to tell. For the rest of the novel he will try to catch up with the evolving drama between Hollingsworth, Zenobia, Priscilla, Westerveldt and Old Moodie, often arriving just too late to catch the key moment of a scene, or missing an event altogether, reconstructing it after the fact.

The narrative is thus screened from the narrator, a strange circumstance that is echoed in imagery of masks, veils and costumes. Westerveldt's face (with false teeth and false hair) is a mask; even Old Moodie's eye-patch seems a mask, which, an alert reader will note, is sometimes over his right eye, sometimes the left. In chapter 24, 'The Masqueraders', this imagery erupts into a carnival-like sequence, followed by the unmaskings that lead to the novel's conclusion.

In the central section of the novel, between Coverdale's first meeting with Old Moodie and his final meeting with Hollingsworth, Priscilla and Zenobia at Eliot's Pulpit, the narrative divides between the surface events that Coverdale witnesses and what might be called the 'submarine plot', in which a half-dozen off-stage encounters, scenes that in a conventional novel would be shown in detail, move the plot forward. The two symmetrically placed fables, 'The Legend of the Silvery Veil' and 'The Story of Fauntleroy', are coded revelations of what is happening beneath the surface. Coverdale, and the reader, piece together the relationship among Moodie, Priscilla and Zenobia, learn of the betrayal of Priscilla to Westerveldt, and of the consequent intervention by Old Moodie that strips Zenobia of her wealth. Hollingsworth's actions, both off-stage and in the visible scenes, such as 'The Village Hall', reveal him to be so consumed by his single purpose, a scheme for prison reform, that he is blind to the betrayals he has committed. Behind this evolving story of the principal characters we see the old Eden fable, rewritten to include Lilith, the alternative Eve of rabbinical lore (a figure behind many Romantic dark heroines).

When Coverdale joins Priscilla, Hollingsworth and Zenobia at Eliot's Pulpit, the visible and submarine plots of the novel rejoin. The once reluctant Coverdale is soon capable of action. He had been enthralled through most of the narrative, rendered impotent by his complex emotional relationship to Zenobia and Hollingsworth (as his dreams reveal), and by his role as an artist-observer. Now he is freed by Zenobia's death. The midnight scene in which he directs Silas and the humbled Hollingsworth in dragging the pond for Zenobia's body is surely one of the most powerful prose passages in American Romantic literature. At the end, the brief Eden of Blithedale has collapsed, and its survivors return to our world, the world after the Fall.

The guilty artist

Hawthorne feared that there was something inherently compromised and guilty about a life of art. Perhaps he never escaped the weight of the Puritan disapproval toward art and storytelling he dramatizes in 'The Custom-House'. But the key problem is touched by Zenobia, after the wrenching scene of recrimination between her and Hollingsworth: 'Is it you, Miles Coverdale? ...Ah, I perceive what you are about! You are turning this whole affair into a ballad.'[40] The role of the artist is voyeuristic. If the most characteristic gesture in Hawthorne's fiction is stepping across a threshold (nearly every Hawthorne story or novel begins this way), the next most typical is peering through a window or other opening. Coverdale does this continually, as when he spies on the community from his secret lookout in the branches of a tree, or looks though the window of the apartment shared by Zenobia and Priscilla in the city. Trying to turn the affair into a ballad, he becomes a peeping Tom. Trying to learn the secrets of others, he comes to resemble the great villains of Hawthorne's fiction, like Chillingworth, peering into the recesses of the human heart.

The role of the artist, with its psychological dangers, is a recurring theme in Hawthorne's fiction. In several stories, artist and scientist are blended to reveal dangers of their common search for perfection. In 'The Birth-Mark' (1843), Aylmer tries to use his science to remove the only flaw in his wife's beauty. In 'Rappaccini's Daughter' (1844), Dr Rappaccini uses chemistry to create a new Eden for his daughter: a place that is perfect, intensely beautiful and poisonous, its Eve immune to its lethal vapours. Rappaccini's quest for perfection, like Aylmer's, ends in the death of the lady. Perfection cannot be achieved in a flawed world, and living beings cannot become works of art. Coverdale had once wished that Zenobia were a statue, so that he could admire her voluptuous body without sexual embarrassment. At the novel's end he gazes with horror at her rigid corpse, which preserves the twisted agony of her death in the pond.

The Italian setting of 'Rappaccini's Daughter' anticipates that of Hawthorne's last Gothic romance. *The Marble Faun* (1860) returns to the Catholic Europe favoured by early Gothic writers like Ann

Radcliffe, though the time is the present, and Hawthorne's characters are American artists working in Rome.

Hawthorne repeats several of the patterns of *The Blithedale Romance*, with less success. There is a quartet of major characters, duelling dark and light heroines, and a nearly continuous play of allusions to the Eden story. The novel, I suggest, exposes Hawthorne's residual prudishness, his discomfort with nudity and eroticism in European art. He may be drawn to the liberating possibilities of the life of a bohemian artist, but he insists on celebrating the cloistered virtue of the icy Hilda, remote in her tower studio with her white doves.

In 'Young Goodman Brown', Hawthorne recreated the Puritan fear of losing one's faith in the woods. *The Marble Faun* dramatizes the danger of losing one's faith while in Europe, the land and culture that the Puritans had fled. The final temptation offered to Brown by Satan at the heart of the forest was knowledge of the community's guilty secrets. Now, in *The Marble Faun*, in the museums and cathedrals of Italy, the temptations are again sexual, and prurient. At the centre of the maze, and the core of everything symbolized by Old Europe, is the figure of Beatrice Cenci, the young Renaissance noblewoman who was raped by her father, and who killed him in retaliation. Beatrice is beautiful but sinister, innocent but a patricide; she attracts and repels. Hawthorne gives an early chapter (7) to the confused response of his dark and light heroines, Miriam and Hilda, to Hilda's copy of Guido's painting of Beatrice. Hilda has somehow managed to forget this history of the subject, shudders when reminded of it, and thinks that Beatrice should 'vanish away into nothingness'.[41] Miriam, however, the Lilith figure, has a sympathetic impulse to 'clasp Beatrice Cenci's ghost, and draw it into myself!'[42] At the end they can only drape a cover over the frightening image. The artists cannot resolve their responses to Beatrice and the complex European heritage she represents, not here or elsewhere in the novel.

As in early British Gothic novels, the fear of continental corruption fills *The Marble Faun* with dread. Europe offers no energizing escape from a declining Puritan tradition. It would be left to another generation, and particularly to Henry James, to explore the further implications of the international theme opened by Hawthorne, and to show Europe as embodying both the threat of moral decay and the possibility of freedom and psychological enrichment. James's first novel, *Roderick Hudson* (1875), about an American sculptor in Italy, would be both a homage to and a movement beyond *The Marble Faun*.

Melville's Gothic

During Hawthorne's lifetime, his greatest impact was on Herman Melville. The younger author's catalytic encounter with *Mosses from an Old Manse* (1846), as recorded in 'Hawthorne and His Mosses', clearly was the most important event in his creative life. His discovery of the symbolic depths in Hawthorne's fiction emboldened him to rewrite *Moby-Dick*, then in progress, and to attempt a series of experimental Gothic works, such as *Pierre* (1852) and *The Piazza Tales* (1856), which included *Benito Cereno* and short pieces such as 'The Bell Tower'. The example of Hawthorne made Melville a major artist, but destroyed his reputation as a purveyor of marketable adventure stories.

Melville, like Hawthorne, saw the world as profoundly ambiguous. Like all Romantics, like his character Ahab, he desired to 'strike through the mask' and find the meaning behind appearance. Yet for him the world remained solidly physical, with pleasures like fish chowder, pipe tobacco or a warm bed on a bitter night. It also contained real peril. He had, after all, lived the rough life of a sailor, and had seen more of the world than any other American writer of his era. Nature for him was not Walden Pond, but the Seven Seas, and he rejected the optimism of the Transcendentalists, whom he parodied in the 'Mast Head' chapter of *Moby-Dick*. He understood the cruel side of nature, and the remote Galápagos Islands, as described in *The Encantadas* (1854), were as much a laboratory for him as they had been for Charles Darwin.

The challenge for Melville's life and art was responding to the world's ambiguity and evil without either going mad or numbing his keen intelligence. In the great 'Try Works' chapter of *Moby-Dick*, which in its imagery recalls Hawthorne's 'Ethan Brand' (1850), Ishmael weighs the options: look into the smoky fire too long, and become a monomaniac; live only in the gentle sunshine, and be placid and superficial. Ishmael is able to envision a balance between these alternatives, and symbolizes it in a 'Catskill Eagle' in some souls 'that can dive down into the blackest gorges, and soar out of them again and become invisible in the sunny spaces'. [43]

But for the commander of the *Pequod*, there will be no such compromise, no balancing act. Ahab, the 'grand, ungodly, god-like man', [44] has elevated his rage against a whale to a quest to right all the evils of the universe, embodied for him in Moby-Dick. Like all great villain-heroes of Gothic literature (and Ahab is one of the greatest), he combines powerful intelligence, charisma and strength of will. Like any successful demagogue, he offers his doomed crew an enemy and a crusade. His view of the world (perhaps like that in Tolkien's *Lord of the Rings*) is Manichaean. The universe is divided into forces of light and darkness. Evil radiates from a single source: join with me, he asks, in the holy crusade to destroy it.

Melville shares with Ahab a scorn for the 'lee shore' of safe and comfortable beliefs. Nevertheless, Ahab, like Hawthorne's Chillingworth and Hollingsworth, becomes a force for evil. He disregards human compassion, and is willing to sacrifice anything to his goals. His monster-slaying war destroys his knights and his Gothic castle (that is, his crew and the *Pequod*). Only Ishmael, possessing the balanced vision symbolized by the Catskill eagle, escapes Ahab's madness and his final encounter with his nemesis.

As Melville's imagination darkened and became more pessimistic in the years following *Moby-Dick*, he would never again envision the sane and open intelligence represented here by Ishmael.

Mystery of Isabel

Melville's next novel, *Pierre* (1852), is a Gothic *Künstlerroman*, or novel about an artist. It could be considered, in fact, a symbolic retelling of the imaginative origins of *Moby-Dick*. Pierre Glendinning's discovery of Isabel, probably, though not certainly, his illegitimate half-sister, blasts through the certainties of his life and opens his imagination to ideas that excite and frighten him. Isabel herself seems a kind of primitive creative force, who chants over her guitar (also named Isabel) and produces strange harmonic vibrations. It is not difficult to see this shock as echoing Melville's discovery of Hawthorne, first the writing (as recorded in 'Hawthorne and His Mosses'), then the man. Isabel lives in a little red farmhouse resembling Hawthorne's own home in the Berkshires near Pittsfield, Massachusetts, not far from Melville's Arrowhead Farm.

Pierre's decision to pretend to marry the dark Isabel (rather than his blonde fiancée, Lucy), in an attempt to shelter her and to protect his dead father's reputation, causes his mother to disinherit him. In the city with Isabel, living in drab rented rooms, Pierre feels contempt for 'the dreary heart-vacancies of the conventional life'. [45] He is no longer able to write reassuring literature for middle-class readers. His mind boils with new ideas that accompany his liberated creative process: 'that which now absorbs the time and the life of Pierre, is not the book, but the primitive elementalizing of the strange stuff, which in the act of attempting that book, has upheaved and upgushed in his soul'. [46]

This state of mind apparently echoes that of the author of *Moby-Dick*, which teemed with creative energy and strange and frightening thoughts. While Melville, like Emerson, believed that natural facts are symbolic of spiritual facts, he found that the meanings of the symbols were obscure or sinister. Pierre vows, using one of the dark Romantics' favourite images, that 'From all idols, I tear all veils; henceforth I will see the hidden things'. [47] The physical world, however, is represented for him by the Terror Stone and the enigmatic stone shape that suggests the Titan Enceladus. These seem hieroglyphics suggestive of great and terrible forces that are beyond the mind's power to decipher. When Pierre, after the revelation of Isabel, looks at the mountain near Saddle Meadows, he sees something much more sinister than the mountain in 'Rip Van Winkle', and indeed as nightmarish as any landscape in Poe:

> On both sides, in the remoter distance, and also far beyond the mild lake's further shore, rose the long, mysterious mountain masses; shaggy with pines and hemlocks, mystical with nameless, vapoury exhalations, and in that dim air black with dread and gloom. At their base, profoundest forests lay entranced, and from their far

owl-haunted depths of caves and rotted leaves, and unused and unregarded inland overgrowth of decaying wood ... from out of the infinite inhumanities of those profoundest forests, came a moaning, muttering, roaring, intermitted, changeful sound: rain-shakings of the palsied trees, slidings of rocks undermined, final crashing of long-riven boughs, and devilish gibberish of the forest-ghosts.[48]

Turning from the outer to the inner world (and, indeed, the above passage is already in the inner world), Melville and his hero again found mystery. Melville intends in *Pierre* to 'follow the endless, winding way, — the flowing river in the cave of man; careless whether I be led, reckless where I land'.[49] He thus claims the territory of what we now call the subconscious, hidden motivations and desires, as his territory. This subterranean realm was also murky and frightening. While Pierre attempts to order his life with the 'chronometics' of absolute truth, people's motivations, Melville realizes, are often 'secret from themselves'.[50]

Pierre's subconscious motivations are suggested, among other techniques, by a series of portrait paintings. Late in the novel, for example, after Lucy has joined Isabel and Pierre in the city, Pierre takes the girls to an art exhibition, where they find a portrait called 'The Stranger' facing a copy of Guido's portrait of Beatrice Cenci (the same picture featured a few years later in *The Marble Faun*). 'The Stranger' is a double of the portrait of Pierre's father that he had burned earlier in the narrative; now, uncannily, it has reappeared. The facing picture of Beatrice Cenci shows a beautiful woman who is 'double hooded', as Melville puts it, 'by the black crape of the two most horrible crimes . . . possible to civilized humanity—incest and parricide'.[51] Together, the pictures underscore two obvious running themes of the novel: Pierre's Oedipal relationship with his parents, and his sexual attraction to his putative sister. (Melville leaves unstated whether this attraction – clearly mutual – is consummated.)

Lucy's arrival in the city, where she will share the apartment with Pierre and Isabel, and practise her own art of crayon portraiture, raises briefly the possibility of a kind of healing balance, like that achieved by Ishmael at the end of *Moby-Dick*: Lucy standing for a rational, Apollonian art, Isabel the art of Dionysian instinct. However, the world will have none of it, seeing only a man living in a bizarre ménage with two women (or three, counting the maid, Delly). Lucy's arrival only hastens the novel's catastrophic conclusion, in which (like the last act of *Hamlet*, clearly an influence), bodies litter the stage: Lucy, Isabel, Pierre and Pierre's respectable double, Glen Stanley.

Like all the dark Romantics, Melville came to see art as both liberating and destructive, putting the artist at odds with society and loosing chthonic forces within his own soul.

Masked figures

Masks and veils are favourite images of Hawthorne and Melville, and are a common Gothic trope that we will see again. Two of Melville's shorter works of the late 1850s (both collected in *The Piazza Tales* of 1856) are built around this image. In 'The Bell-Tower', a masked figure is smuggled into the tower, and is revealed when the bells are first rung. In the novella *Benito Cereno*, masked figures are displayed on the stern of a distressed ship; on its prow a canvas conceals the figurehead.

'The Bell-Tower' is Melville's most Hawthorne-like work, adapting the Renaissance Italian setting of 'The Artist of the Beautiful' and 'Rappaccini's Daughter' (both 1844), as well as some of Hawthorne's narrative mannerisms. The villain-hero of the tale, Bannadonna, is both artist and scientist, the designer and builder of the highest bell-tower of his time, its great bell and the clockwork mechanism that will ring it. The draped figure brought into the tower is revealed only on the day the bell is first to be rung, when it is found standing over the corpse of Bannadona:

> It had limbs, and seemed clad in a scaly mail, lustrous as a dragon-beetle's. It was manacled, and its clubbed arms were uplifted, as if, with its manacles, once more to smite its already smitten victim. One advanced foot of it was inserted beneath the dead body, as if in the act of spurning it.[52]

'The Bell-Tower' has historical importance as perhaps the first robot story in English, and is thus the ancestor of all those stories, movies and television programmes in which machines rebel against their human masters: *I, Robot, Terminator, The Matrix, Battlestar Galactica*. But the implications of this fable are many, since Melville has poured over it many layers of allusion, perhaps too many, from his encyclopedic reading. We catch echoes of, for example, *The Autobiography of Benvento Cellini*, Spenser's *The Fairie Queene*, and the books of Genesis and Judges from the Bible. The robot is compared both to Jael, the Jewish heroine who killed the enemy general Sisera by driving a tent peg through his skull, and to rebellious African slaves. The masked figure is both an image of feminist defiance, and a symbol of black rebellion.

It is this fear that shapes *Benito Cereno*, which may be the most profound meditation on race relations in the Americas by a white author to this time, and one that sounds the racial possibilities of the American Gothic.

Yet to the point-of-view character, Captain Amasa Delano, it is not a Gothic story at all. Delano is a straightforward simple American man of action, of the sort we have seen prefigured in Arthur Mervyn. He is deceived at first by the charade staged by the Africans on board the *San Dominick*, who have taken over the ship, and killed the owner and much of the crew. The pageant devised by their brilliant leader, Babo, who pretends to be Captain Cereno's valet, is effective until Cereno escapes by leaping into the departing American captain's longboat. The American sailors subsequently storm the *San Dominick*, kill most of the Africans, and take Babo back to Lima for trial and punishment. The mysteries of the *San Dominick* are dissipated by the relentless clauses of the legal deposition: that . . . that . . . that. At the end, Babo is executed, his head displayed on a stake, and Captain Cereno is safe and free.

However, to Delano's surprise, it is not a happy ending:

> 'You are saved', cried Captain Delano, more and more astonished and pained; 'you are saved: what has cast such a shadow upon you?'
> 'The negro.'
> There was silence, while the moody man sat, slowly and unconsciously gathering his mantle about him, as if it were a pall.[53]

The Spanish captain has been traumatized by the violence he has witnessed, including the murder of his friend, Don Alexandro

Aranda, whose flesh was stripped from his skeleton. 'The negro' is, most obviously, Babo, the leader of the slave rebellion. But 'the negro' resonates with other meanings, in its literal Spanish meaning of black, blackness and, more broadly, the enslaved African people. The *San Dominick* is a kind of floating allegory of the tragic and brutal relationship of Africans and Europeans in the New World. Its original figurehead, that of Christopher Columbus, was replaced by the skeleton of the slave-owner Aranda, with the chalked legend '*Seguid vuestro jefe*', 'follow your leader'. The rebellion of the slaves recalls one of the most traumatic events of the Americas before the US Civil War, the rebellion of slaves on Haiti and their massacre of their French colonial masters. The stern-piece of the *San Dominick* shows the arms of Castile and Leon and 'groups of mythological or symbolic devices; uppermost and central of which was a dark satyr in a mask, holding his foot on the prostrate neck of a writhing figure, likewise masked'.[54] The masked figures prefigure not only the ambiguous situation on the ship, but the brutal realities of slavery wherever it is found. It does not matter who is on top and who is beneath the heel of the oppressor: both are equally degrading to humanity. But since enslavement of Africans was practised throughout most of the Americas at the time of *Benito Cereno*, the story cannot have a cheerful ending with the suppression of one slave rebellion, whatever the oblivious American Delano may think.

And what of Babo, who goes mutely to his death, like his literary prototype Iago? He gives literal mute testimony to the fact that his story is yet to be told. It would be another generation before his descendants in American literature would speak.

Woman in white

As much as Poe, Hawthorne or Melville, Emily Dickinson (1830 – 86) was an explorer of the haunted mind. Though she may not have read Melville, his description, in *Pierre*, of the 'heart of man; descending into which is as descending a spiral stair in a shaft . . . ' (402) might have appealed to her. Dickinson herself, a famous recluse customarily dressed in white, seems a character out of a Gothic novel: like Bertha, perhaps, Mr Rochester's first wife, secluded upstairs in his mansion, in Charlotte Brontë's *Jane Eyre*. Dickinson, however, chose this life deliberately, a seclusion in which she was defended by her brother, sister and sister-in-law (and her family's prosperity), in order to create a space, a room of her own, in which her rich imagination could flourish.

She was aware of the dangers of eccentricity, and this is one of the reasons she chose to publish almost none of her poems. Her view of art was Platonic, and she knew that the poet returning from visions of blazing truth and beauty would be considered mad. Society enforces its view of normalcy:

> Assent—and you are sane—
> Demur—and you're straightway dangerous—
> And handled with a Chain—(poem 435)[55]

Dickinson's imagination was Gothic.[56] The poet's inner and outer worlds (an often difficult distinction) were filled with dread. Her poem 670 begins with the comparison of mind and house that had been used by Poe in 'The Fall of the House of Usher' (1839):

> One need not be a Chamber—to be Haunted—
> One need not be a House—
> The Brain has Corridors—surpassing
> Material Place—
>
> Far safer, of a Midnight Meeting
> External Ghost
> Than its interior Confronting—
> That Cooler Host.
>
> Far safer, through an Abbey gallop,
> The Stones a'chase—
> Than Unarmed, one's a'self encounter—
> In lonesome Place—
>
> Ourself behind ourself, concealed—
> Should startle most—
> Assassin hid in our Apartment
> Be Horror's least.

The poem runs through a series of familiar Gothic situations, rejecting each as inferior to the horror generated by an encounter with one's self. By the fourth stanza, we have uncanny doubling – self lurking behind self – in a scene recalling Poe's 'William Wilson' and looking forward to James's 'The Jolly Corner' (1908).

Eeriness and dread can be found in the external world as well, as in the simple act of looking into a well. This act gives one the sense of an 'abyss', a frequent image of horror in Dickinson's world, and of the essential foreignness of nature:

> But nature is a stranger yet;
> The ones that cite her most
> Have never passed her haunted house,
> Nor simplified her ghost. (1400)

Dickinson, like Hawthorne and Melville, does not see Nature as a site where we return to reason and faith, but rather as one where we are reminded of our alienation. While she was sensitive to the beauty of nature, as her great poems of landscape and season show, there is always the separation from landscape, not the Transcendentalists' sense of merging with a greater spirit. And any separation can serve as a comparison for the last inevitable separation:

> There's a certain Slant of light,
> Winter Afternoons—
> That oppresses, like the Heft
> Of Cathedral Tunes—
>
> . . .
>
> When it comes, the Landscape listens—
> Shadows—hold their breath—
> When it goes, 'tis like the Distance
> On the look of Death— (258)

This distance was one Dickinson had measured. The 'look of Death': the appearance of the dying face, or the face of Death himself. Either way, Dickinson's gaze had not flinched. She is a great poet of death and dying, recalling for us a time when women cared for the dying in the home, and prepared their bodies for burial. She inventories the emotions of the survivors and even, in one startling poem, crosses into the mind of a dying person to record the shocking incongruity of the 'Blue—uncertain stumbling Buzz' of a fly as the last sensation recorded by a fading consciousness (465). These poems bring us closer to the emotions of such scenes than any amount of the sentimental verse typical of her time.

In the middle of the nineteenth century, Emily Dickinson's work demonstrates again that the Gothic was an engine of technical innovation in American literature, and that it offered a voice to emotions, writers and disenfranchised groups that would otherwise have been silenced. As it was, Dickinson's 'postcard to the world' would wait several generations to find its readers.

2

Realism's Dark Twin

భ

The tragedy of the American Civil War was followed by a period of great change, stress and paradox. The most characteristic and successful writings of this period were in the modes of realism (and its successor, naturalism) and the Gothic. Realism and the Gothic seem opposed, contradictory, but they responded to the same issues, and often were created by the same authors. The Gothic of this time was realism's shadow or dark twin. In a period of national growth and faith in progress, the Gothic continued to confront the nightmares in the shadows of American life, and continued its role as the engine of innovation in American literature.

The village graveyard

Transitions are seldom as sharp as historical labels suggest. No one rings a bell to announce the end of a cultural era or movement, and, though the great upheaval of the Civil War is a useful marker, the roots of late nineteenth-century realism are intertwined with earlier Romanticism, and the Gothic with both.

The stories of Alice Cary (1820–71) illustrate this knotted transition. Cary was only a year younger than Melville and Whitman, the last great American Romantic writers. Known in her own time primarily as a poet (and praised by Poe and Whittier), her short fiction has been rediscovered recently, and two volumes, *Clovernook* (1852) and *Clovernook, Second Series* (1853), are now seen as important early examples of what is now called women's regional realism, which is often Gothic.[1]

The Clovernook stories share a common narrator, who offers episodes in her growth from childhood to adulthood in rural southern Ohio. In 'The Wildermings', this narrator describes the mysterious arrival and departure of a family who lived briefly near an overgrown graveyard.

The cemetery is believed to be haunted by uneasy spirits of local wrongdoers, including Mary Wilderming, 'a fair young girl who died, more sinned against than sinning'. Her ghost 'had been heard to sing sad lullabies under the waning moon sometimes, and at other times had been sitting by her sunken grave, and braiding roses in her hair, as for a bridal'[2] – though the narrator has never seen or heard the ghost. When a new family – a young girl, a handsome man and an older woman – arrive to occupy the cottage near the graveyard, the narrator attempts to greet and befriend them, but fails to penetrate their distant courtesy. The man is sometimes heard playing his flute by Mary Wilderming's grave. After a few months the girl dies, and the family departs. The narrator learns that the 'stranger child' has been buried next to Mary Wilderming.

The eeriness of this story rests in its omissions. We witness a continuing family tragedy as if through a pinprick or a keyhole. Clearly, the narrator and her nameless housekeeper know something of Mary's story, only hinted at, which must have involved Mary's Wilderming's seduction and abandonment, and her death after bearing a child. Since the golden-haired stranger child is buried next to Mary, and the story is titled 'The Wildermings' (plural), we infer that she is Mary's baby. But who is the old woman? And is the flute-playing man the child's brother (half-brother?), as the narrator assumes, or perhaps her father? If the latter, the narrator's own evident interest in the flute-playing man, whom she considers 'handsome'[3] links her sympathetically to Mary, who evidently thought the same. For all our attempts to explain these events, however, the uncanniness of the story remains.

'The Wildermings' shows that materials for the Gothic can be found in apparently mundane small towns and rural communities.

To the outsider, only the boring details of everyday life are visible. Any long-time resident, however, knows many stories of strange events, tragic accidents, hidden bits of family history, and crimes. These stories are the heritage of any writer who has lived in such a place, and the realism of the commonplace and the Gothic are never far apart.

The tradition of women's regional realism nurtures one strain of indigenous female Gothic that continues through the nineteenth century, and reaches its pinnacle in the fiction of Sarah Orne Jewett, Mary E. Wilkins Freeman and Kate Chopin.

Freeman and Jewett were the leading authors of women's regional realism in the last decades of the nineteenth century, Freeman writing for *Harper's Monthly*, and Jewett for *The Atlantic*. Their stories depict the long sad saga of rural New England's decline, a process that had begun with the War of 1812, and had been accelerated by the movement of populations away from exhausted, marginal farmlands to eastern factory towns or to the west. New England, through this period and to the present, continues as a major site of American Gothic. No longer the empty wilderness described by William Bradford, it was now dotted with abandoned farms and deserted villages, the melancholy subjects once sought by English Romantic poets.

Jewett's best-known stories of the Maine coast concern a fishing village called Dunnet Landing. Most of these pieces were collected in *The Country of the Pointed Firs* (1896), a story cycle like Chesnutt's *The Conjure Woman* (1899) or Sherwood Anderson's *Winesburg, Ohio* (1919). All of Jewett's Dunnet Landing stories are built on the interaction of an unnamed vacationing writer, who is the narrator, and Elmira Todd, her local landlady. These tales have the double perspective, insider and outsider, typical of regional realism. Many are frame stories (that characteristic American form), tales told by Mrs Todd to her summer tenant.

Mrs Todd is a richly imagined character, an intelligent, kind-hearted woman who knows the history of every family in the village. And, though Jewett never quite says it, she is a witch. Like the *curandera* of the Hispanic south-west, she is a healer, as opposed to the *bruja*, or evil witch. In local parlance, Mrs Todd is a 'yarb' (herb) woman, dispensing remedies made from plants she grows in her garden or collects in the woods. Jewett invests her with a magical aura, comparing her to a sibyl or an enchantress,[4] and suggesting that she possesses primitive, elemental wisdom.

Witch stories

'The Foreigner' (1900) is a Dunnet Landing tale published in the *Atlantic Monthly* four years after *The Country of the Pointed Firs* had appeared, and never collected by the author. It is one of the richest and most Gothic of Jewett's stories.

When the narrator observes that Mrs Todd has never told her a ghost story, her landlady remarks that the storm raging outside reminds her of the night Mrs Tolland died, long ago. Her apparently rambling account of her friendship with the French woman brought back by Captain Tolland from the Caribbean seems irrelevant to the narrator's request, until, after circling several times around the events of Mrs Tolland's death, we finally meet the ghost.

'The Foreigner' is less a ghostly tale, however, than a women's initiation story that links witchcraft and feminism. The foreign woman was of dubious and obscure origins. She was found in Jamaica, singing in what was, in the most charitable interpretation, a tavern. She was shunned by the women of Dunnet Landing, except by Mrs Todd's broad-minded mother, who placed upon her daughter the Christian injunction to 'neighbor' with the captain's wife, who was alone while her husband was again at sea. In the brief interval before the foreign woman learned of the captain's death and died of grief, Mrs Tolland taught her new friend the lore of cooking and of herbs. She opened her mind to the world beyond Dunnet Landing, and, though the point is only suggested, tutored her in witchcraft. This knowledge was the real legacy that Mrs Tolland left Mrs Todd, far more important than the house that burned or the chest of treasure that was never found. 'The Foreigner' is a story of female power and solidarity, and explains how Mrs Todd came to be a good witch.

Mary E. Wilkins Freeman's 'Old Woman Magoun' also describes a vigorous older woman in a remote village, a woman who knows something of cooking and wild plants, and who is in many ways a counterpart to Jewett's Mrs Todd. While Jewett's story celebrates the possibility of sisterhood, Freeman's story is much darker: an inverted fable of Progress, a feminist rewriting of 'Rip Van Winkle', in which happy endings are undercut by masculine sloth and decadence and entropy. 'Old Woman Magoun' is a naturalistic story in which no connections between people, even well-meaning women, can survive the impact of inexorable destructive forces.

The setting of Barry's Ford is in mountainous New England, perhaps the Berkshires, but it could be any remote rural setting where once self-reliant frontiersmen have settled into a listless backwater existence. As Freeman tells us, it is 'Barry's Ford' because the leading family, now in decline, is named Barry, and Ford because the Barry River may be forded there, except in high-water season.

Mrs Magoun shames the lazy men of the town into building a bridge, and brings about tragic consequences. The bridge represents change, progress, in contrast to the inertia and degeneration of the mountain village. But the building of the bridge brings Magoun's pretty granddaughter Lily to the attention of her neglectful father, Nelson Barry. Barry, Magoun's antagonist, plans to deliver the girl to a kinsman in payment of a gambling debt, a betrayal combining paedophilia, rape and incest – all that the masculine gender represents in the story. The bridge then becomes a potential avenue of escape, as Magoun attempts to have Lily adopted by a decent lawyer in a neighbouring town. When that appeal fails (for the best male character is still inadequate), there is but one option left, and Magoun looks aside as Lily innocently eats poisonous sumac berries that have grown together with wild blackberries.

As is typical of Gothic villain-heroes, Magoun's actions are morally ambiguous. She has deliberately murdered her granddaughter, for she knows exactly what will happen when Lily stops near the seductive berries. Her motives, however, are understandable, and involve her in a tragic struggle with great forces she cannot defeat. Ultimately, her enemies are time and the reproductive instinct. She tries to keep her granddaughter pure (as her name indicates) and a child. When adulthood threatens, in the form of Nelson Barry's knock on the door, she must ultimately send Lily to the only sure refuge, the changeless realm of gold, unfading flowers and angel-mothers she describes to the dying Lily.

While Magoun's actions are monstrous, they are understandable in the world Freeman envisions, in which sexuality is entirely an evil male instinct, and no man is credited with a generous action.

Freeman's 'Luella Miller' is another eerie tale of a woman who is believed by her small-town neighbours to be a witch, who arouses 'wild horror and frenzied fear'.[5] She seems to be, rather, something of a succubus or vampire, a beautiful young and apparently helpless woman who sucks the life out of a series of victims, male and female. When no one in the town is left who is willing to assist her, for she will do nothing for herself, not even make coffee, she dwindles away and dies. Her house is believed haunted, and a woman who later tries to live in it speedily declines and dies, as if drained by Luella's ghost.

Luella's passivity and her blank insensitivity to her effect on her victims enrage the narrator, Lydia Anderson, though even she almost falls under the spell. Luella is pink and blonde and lovely, and is compared to a 'doll-baby' that was 'comin' to life'.[6] Her emblem is the 'helpless trail of morning glories' that grows in the ruins of her house after it burns years later. She has literary precedents in the mechanical doll in E. T. A. Hoffmann's 'The Sandman', in such pale Romantic heroines as Hawthorne's Priscilla in *The Blithedale Romance*, who is also symbolized as a clinging vine, and in European female vampires such as Le Fanu's Carmilla. The feminist point behind Freeman's story is that attractive women were, and perhaps still are, programmed by our society to accept tribute and to assume a passive role. The issue is posed differently in Charlotte Perkins Gilman's 'The Yellow Wallpaper' (1891), which describes the agonies of an intelligent woman who does not wish to be reduced to a mechanical doll.

Gothic room of her own

Madeline Yale Wynne's 'The Little Room' (1895), an elegant, long-neglected Gothic tale, is also set in rural New England.[7] The room of the title is in a Vermont house built by an old sea captain, who had come originally from Salem. The naming of the Massachusetts town is a discreet hint that witchcraft may lurk in the house.

Over the years the house is home to, or is visited by, a series of relatives, who encounter either the little room of the title, or, in its place, a built-in china-closet. In no instance will the spinster daughters of the captain, Hannah and Maria, admit that the house ever had a different layout. Eventually the house burns, and the mystery cannot be resolved. The story is a perfect illustration of what Freud meant by the uncanny, or *unheimlich*. The safe and familiar home refuses to be stable, mutates and shifts, violating our comfortable sense of reality. The house built by the old Salem sea captain is an antecedent of several shape-shifting houses of later fiction, including that in Mark Z. Danielski's *House of Leaves* (2000).

Many readers have noted that while both men and women visitors to the house have seen the china closet, only women and girls have seen the little room. The room and its decor are distinctively feminine, and its chief treasure seems to be a rather suggestive pink seashell. These details imply an inner refuge, a woman's room of her own, and a space that must not be violated. 'The Little Room' is a masterful example of the Gothic as a covert expression of women's unacknowledged needs.

Atlantic crossings

Both realism and American Gothic have deep sectional roots, and we will return to the Gothic of the South and other regions. Yet many American writers of this period were world-ranging cosmopolitans, in literary taste or actual residence, who blended European and American traditions, and often employed European settings.

That great site of the English novel, the country estate, continued to appeal to American writers, both from the direct experience of travellers or expatriates (like Henry James), or from novelistic traditions going back as far as Richardson and Fielding. When Louisa May Alcott began practising her craft, first using pseudonyms, she constructed narratives from the parts bin of the Great Tradition. 'Behind the Mask' (1866) is a Gothic tale about a governess – an idea that would occur later in a much more famous American novella.

Alcott's protagonist, Jean Muir, is a divorced actress, an impostor, a gold-digging adventuress and a witch. She is, as other characters sense immediately, uncanny. Remarkably, Alcott lets the reader see 'behind the mask' almost immediately in this transformation at the end of her first day at the Coventry estate:

> Still sitting on the floor she unbound and removed the long abundant braids from her head, wiped the pink from her face, took out several pearly teeth, and slipping off her dress appeared herself indeed, a haggard, worn, and moody woman of thirty at least. The metamorphosis was wonderful . . . [8]

Although the witch is not an innocent girl of nineteen but an old hag of thirty,[9] Alcott clearly wishes readers to give their sympathies to Jean Muir's attempts to trap one – any one – of the family's eligible men into marriage. The plot has many twists and hairbreadth escapes, and a bundle of incriminating letters threatens to expose her past and her schemes. We applaud when the witch-heroine manages to outwit her detractors, and lands the best of the available Coventry men – best in terms of wealth, status and power, which are her goals – though he is an elderly man in his fifties.

Jean Muir boasts of her power as a witch, yet her witchcraft seems ultimately to consist mostly of strength of will, shrewd intelligence – canny rather than uncanny – and skilful use of cosmetics. The Gothic elements of the story serve to highlight the common situation of women in her culture, who must, in some way, bewitch men in order to survive.

The novella presents itself as a work of British fiction, and is itself something of a masquerade, for the themes of the work are clearly American. The tradition of British fiction does indeed allow for women to ascend the social scale, and, as noted earlier, Cinderella is the foundation story of the English comic novel. However, Cinderella-Pamela must embody innocent virtue, her nobility of character substituting for nobility of birth in the judgement of her gentleman lover, and she does not scheme to bring this about. The adventuresses, the masquerader, the woman with a sexual history, are inevitably expelled in English fiction. Moreover, English culture does not esteem the self-made man or woman. Bringing oneself up by one's bootstraps, making something of oneself: these are positive American qualities. In British fiction and movies such social climbers are portrayed as boors or intrusive schemers, even now. Thus, American and British readers might have differing responses to Jean Muir, the witch who lived happily ever after.

Louisa May Alcott, like Freeman, had known poverty in her life, and at one time the future best-selling author of *Little Women* had worked as a domestic servant. She must have felt wicked pleasure in constructing this vengeful Cinderella who could play a game of wits against the world of male privilege, and win.

Lessons of the (Gothic) Master

Like most professional writers of the late nineteenth century, Henry James wrote in many modes, and included ghost stories or 'supernatural tales' in his repertory. He also blended Gothic elements into some of his realistic fiction, so that, for example, a ghost appears briefly in *The Portrait of a Lady* (1881), a work some would consider the finest of his realistic novels. James was the most cosmopolitan of American authors, fluent in Italian and French, famously a long-time expatriate on the Continent and then in England, becoming a British citizen during the First World War. His literary acquaintances included Turgenev, Flaubert, Stevenson and Conrad. But he also drew upon the traditions established by his American predecessors, especially Washington Irving and Nathaniel Hawthorne, and even published a study of Hawthorne (1879).

In his preface to *The American* (1877), James defines his work as a 'Romance', thus deliberately evoking the prefaces to Hawthorne's four long narratives, and claiming, as Hawthorne had done, the freedom to range beyond the light of common day and into an imaginative shadowland. *The American* begins in the most conventional of tourist destinations, the Louvre,[10] but James gradually ushers his readers into other realms, as if, as he said in his preface, he was slowly extending the line tethering their balloon, and then craftily cutting it free. Before the novel ends, we are deep in Gothic territory: an old aristocratic family with dark secrets, a night scene with an elderly family retainer revealing crimes and suspicions, a manuscript exposing a long-hidden murder, a duel, a beautiful heroine locked in a medieval convent. These are familiar notes on the organ-keyboard of the Gothic, played here to virtuoso effect.

James's most studied work, and one of only two best-sellers in his lifetime, was his tale of a haunted English governess, *The Turn of the Screw* (1898). In this *amusette*, as he deprecatingly termed it, James adopts the inherited form of the frame story, popularized by Washington Irving and a favourite of the regional Realists, and pushes it into one of the English language's most famous experiments in narrative ambiguity. Instead of a single framing narrator introducing a second storyteller, as in, for example, Jewett's 'The Foreigner', we have layers and layers of time and of narrative voices, like nesting Russian dolls, each adding its level of uncertainty, and all surrounding a core story with an unreliable narrator. The resulting epistemological puzzle has evoked scholarly discussion, as well as several film and television adaptations, and even a wonderful counter-narrative by contemporary author Joyce Carol Oates, 'Accursed Inhabitants of the House of Bly', which turns the story inside-out and retells it from the point of view of the Governess's ghostly antagonist, Miss Jessel.[11]

The most insistent critical controversy over *The Turn of the Screw*, which may have exhausted itself after several decades, concerns the reliability of the Governess as narrator. She is of course naive, the daughter of a poor provincial clergyman, who has never travelled and has gained many of her ideas from fiction, including Gothic novels. But is she to be trusted in the main details of the story, her account of the ghosts of Peter Quint and Miss Jessel? Or is she a madwoman, who hallucinates these apparitions, and thus is herself the source of the spreading evil that ultimately destroys her pupils?

A strong case can be made for another approach, which begins with the assumption that the Governess's tale of what happened at Bly was never intended to be taken as 'true'. (When discussing James one inevitably falls into his coy use of 'quotation marks'.) Even Douglas, who reads the Governess's manuscript to an audience in an informal ghost-story contest, never claims that it actually happened, but only that it is spooky. The ur-narrative of

The Turn of the Screw was an oral account told to young Douglas long ago by his sister's governess when he was home on holiday from Cambridge. (She later wrote down the story for him.) According to Douglas, the Governess told of events that happened ten years earlier, when he and his sister would have been exactly the ages of Miles and Flora in the narrative. This is a first hint that the Governess invented the tale to suit her auditor. But, in any case, it is simply incredible that the Governess could have been at Bly as described and again at the Douglas home.[12] It seems much more likely that the Governess invented the tale to entertain and possibly both titillate and warn off the infatuated undergraduate: see what I can do to clever boys.

As we experience the Governess's tale, we are continuously screened from the implications of what has happened at Bly by her own innocence ('a young woman privately bred'), the reluctance of Mrs Grose to talk about the past, and by Victorian proprieties. The story is based precisely on everything Victorians were uncomfortable talking about, or pretended did not exist. The Governess clearly understands from Mrs Dean's guarded confidences that Miss Jessel left Bly because Quint had impregnated her, and we assume that Jessel died from suicide or a botched abortion. But what is comprehended by Mrs Grose's statement that Peter Quint had his way 'with all of them?' And why was young Miles expelled from school? Surely the speculation that he 'took things' is hopelessly lame.[13] The story's blank spaces necessarily tempt readers to construct their own narratives, probably involving paedophilia and night revels between angelic-looking children and evil spirits. The story's implied events are indeed 'quite too horrible',[14] and the nastiness at its core comes from Victorian repression and the reader's own dark imagination and fear. James's *'amusette'* strikes at the root of the Victorian world's carefully constructed vision of childhood innocence.

During the Victorian era the interest in and re-invention of childhood was a social phenomenon on both sides of the Atlantic. Among its contributing causes was the development of what philosopher George Santayana (1863–1952) famously labelled the 'Genteel Tradition'.[15] By this Santayana meant the separation of private and public spheres in the privileged American classes, the walling-off of the home, the realm of childhood, women and high culture, from the rough world of business and politics and the language of the street. At the same time, great changes in all aspects of American life created a sometimes illogical nostalgia for childhood as it was remembered to have been earlier in the nineteenth century. Living in a world of steamboats, railways and telegraph, of new industries and new fortunes and swollen cities, American writers looked back at their simpler, sometimes barefoot, youth before the Civil War, and wrote works of autobiography and fiction with titles like *The Story of a Bad Boy, A New England Girlhood, Little Women, The Adventures of Tom Sawyer, A Boy's Town, A Small Boy and Others*. In many of these works a powerful nostalgia is balanced by a desire to portray accurately the childhood of that lost era. Thus, boy books and girl books in the post Civil War period are an important part of the realistic movement in American fiction, leading, for example, to *Adventures of Huckleberry Finn* (1884). And yet, the great changes of this era produced a sense of dislocation and strangeness, even uncanniness, and Gothic images often occurred to writers evoking their childhoods. When W. D. Howells returned in middle age to the mill in Ohio where he had played as a child, he found that it

> was sadly dwarfed, and in its decrepitude it had canted backwards, and seemed tottering to its fall. I explored it from wheel pit to cooling floor; there was not an Indian in it, but ah! what ghosts! ghosts of the living and the dead; my brothers', my playmates', my own! [16]

The object of nostalgia has turned into a kind of haunted house, inhabited by ghosts of the past. Change and its disorientations, then, are an impulse behind both Gothic and realism in this era.

Similarly, rapid change can produce a sense of dislocation from the present. Familiar settings that defined one's life are swept away by the new and unfamiliar – by progress – and the effect is uncanny. This sense of the strangeness of the present underlies Henry James's *The Jolly Corner* (1908), a story of a man who is haunted by his own alternative self.

Returning to the United States after thirty-three years in Europe, Spencer Brydon finds New York 'monstrous', a place where 'proportions and values were upside-down'.[17] As he explores the empty house of his childhood, which he has inherited, he finds himself fascinated, then haunted, by the idea of the person that he might have become had he remained in this monstrous, money-driven society, instead of living a dilettante's life in Europe, and fought his way up the ladder of rough-and-tumble American capitalism. As Brydon walks night after night through the big old house, the alter ego becomes palpable. He stalks it; it stalks him. The details of the setting subtly reinforce the theme: the corner location suggesting divergence and convergence, the checkerboard black-and-white tile squares of the entry hall. At last the two Brydons face each other. The stranger appears, clad in formal evening clothes, his hands spread over his face: 'one of these hands had lost two fingers, as if accidentally shot away'[18] Then the alter ego drops his hands and advances, and Brydon, horrified at what confronts him, faints.

Later, coming to consciousness with his head pillowed on the lap of his friend Alice Staverton, Brydon protests that he could not recognize himself in the 'awful beast' that he saw. But Alice, who has seen the double herself in a dream, replies that she has accepted this version of Brydon as a rugged millionaire.[19]

In later twentieth-century literature, the figure of the double or alter ego is often conceived as a Jungian shadow-self, which is an alternative personality formed in the subconscious from elements that have been repressed by the conscious mind. In Ursula Le Guin's *A Wizard of Earthsea* (1968), for instance, the apprentice wizard Sparrowhawk conjures an adversary, a monster, into existence, and only understands at the end of a prolonged narrative of flight and pursuit, as they close in combat, that the enemy has emerged from his own subconscious. In recognizing and accepting the antagonist as himself, he conquers it and incorporates its power, and thus becomes the greatest wizard of his age. Whether Brydon's double is read as anticipating a Jungian shadow or not, it is clear that his inability to recognize and accept it (as Alice does) is a failure. Brydon is one of James's ineffective males, like John Marcher in *The Beast in the Jungle* (1903). He fails to gain strength or self-knowledge from this encounter, and will remain an effete dilettante, and a victim of the rough forces of change of the modern world, a kind of ghost.

Gothic Dean

William Dean Howells would have been one of the most important literary figures of the age even if he had written no fiction, poetry or drama. As an editor, first of the *Atlantic Monthly*, then of *Harper's Monthly*, he was a powerful force for four decades, and many of the writers discussed in this chapter benefited from his encouragement. The breadth of his tastes could be measured by his championing of both Henry James and Samuel Clemens (and his friendship with each man), two writers who could not abide each other's fiction. He was also a prolific author, by general agreement today just barely missing the highest rank. As an editor and as a writer, by example and precept, he championed the cause of realism in American letters. His editorial columns were a running seminar on the theory of realism, even as the pages of the magazines he edited introduced works of American realism to his readers.

But there also was a Gothic side to the Dean. In his introduction to *Shapes that Haunt the Dusk* (1907), co-edited with Henry Mills Alden, Howells wrote: 'The writers of American short stories, the best short stories in the world, surpass in nothing so much as in their handling of those filmy textures which clothe the vague shapes of the borderland between experience and illusion.'[20]

Howells's evocation of this 'borderland' of the psyche, as well as the very title of the collection, is intended to recall the imaginary landscape of Hawthorne 'somewhere between the real world and fairy-land, where the Actual and Imaginary may meet'[21] Howells, like James, revered Hawthorne, and when he sought techniques to explore territory beyond his usual light of common day, he turned to the earlier master.

Though Howells seemed a practical, down-to-earth man in his daily life, he had wandered the psychic borderlands. He was raised in a family of Swedenborgians (a background he shared with Henry James), adherents of a faith that valued mystical experience. Growing up in rural and small-town Ohio, he was terrified of ghosts until at least the age of fifteen, as he later described in *My Year in a Log Cabin* (1893) and *Years of My Youth* (1916). Moreover, Spiritualism, in its folk-cult version, was rampant in these communities, and it seemed that every other household harboured someone, usually a young woman, who was or pretended to be a medium. Spiritualism, indeed, was a nearly continuous fixture in Howells's life, and he would occasionally attend seances as an adult. His novel *The Undiscovered Country* (1880), a largely realistic work that is nonetheless indebted to *The Blithedale Romance*, is set in the milieu of mesmerist performances and seances.

Howells suffered disturbing dreams all of his life, and he devoted considerable thought and study in an effort to understand them. He wrote of his dream life with surprising candour. In an essay in *Harper's Monthly* he published five years after *The Shadow of a Dream*, Howells reveals what may have been the germ of that novella. After acknowledging that he has experienced the nearly universal dream of nakedness in public, he goes on to mention, but in guarded terms, dreams that are even more disturbing:

> One may easily laugh off this sort of dream in the morning, but there are other shameful dreams, whose inculpation prolongs itself far into the day, and whose infamy often lingers about one till lunchtime. Everyone nearly, has them . . . During the forenoon, at least, the victim goes about with the dim question whether he is not really that kind of man harassing him, and a sort of remote fear that he may be.[22]

We understand the issue here as one of repression. The waking Victorian suppresses his passions (for sex, for violence, for anarchic freedom) and pays in guilt when these impulses reassert themselves in his sleep. The 'dim question' Howells mentions is a fear underlining much Gothic literature. We are not what we thought we were. We are what we feared. These are the issues of *The Shadow of a Dream* (1890).

Howells's most successful Gothic novella was published the same year as one of his best realistic novels, *A Hazard of New Fortunes* (1890). The works even share Basil and Isabel March, recurring characters based on Howells himself and his wife Eleanor, who appear in many of Howells's works. Here, in *The Shadow of a Dream*, the Marches serve as normative characters, the kind of sensible outsiders who often appear in Gothic fiction to establish a baseline and represent the values of readers as they enter the Gothic narrative.

It is a technically complex story, complex in the innovative ways we expect of the best American Gothic. While Basil March is a reliable primary narrator, he stands at the edge of the action, and information often comes to him at second hand, in a way that anticipates, for example, the narrative techniques of *The Great Gatsby* (1925). The essential story is a love triangle: Faulkner, his wife Hermia and his long-time friend Nevil, an Episcopalian minister. By the end of the story the three are dead, all because of the dream of the title: an ugly recurring dream experienced by Faulkner, of which we never have a first-hand account. Various narrative turns keep the dream from Basil and the reader, while allowing its influence to spread.

Basil March notes, after Faulkner's death, that 'There had never been any doubt with us as to the nature of Faulkner's dream', only about its specifics.[23] The reader, too, must speculate. Late in the story Basil hears a version of the dream from Faulkner's mother, but, like the explanations for little Miles's expulsion from school in *The Turn of the Screw*, it seems disappointingly lame: a surreal ceremony blending Faulkner's funeral with the wedding of Nevil and Hermia. The dream comes to us at fourth hand, and we are invited to believe that our own 'gross and palpable', that is, graphically erotic, conjectures may be more accurate.

However the contents of the dream may be imagined, the novella is a notable study in repressed sexuality and the interpretation of dreams. The presence of a character, Dr Wingate, who is a psychologist, and a discussion of the ideas of Théodule-Armand Ribot (whose work influenced Freud), marks a growing interest among American writers in clinical psychology and the subconscious.

The psychology of this tale, in fact, may not be exhausted by our understanding of Faulkner's jealousy over a possible attraction between his wife and his best friend. We are given more than one hint that Faulkner's relationship with Nevil is too close. Mrs March, for example, distrusts it, and asserts that Faulkner's inability to give up his intimate relationship with Nevil is proof that he is 'a kind of weakling'.[24] One critic has read the novella as a 'homosexual tragedy', with the unacknowledged love between the two men its real psychological centre. In this view, the truth revealed by the dream is that 'Faulkner unconsciously sees his wife as a rival for the love of his friend, not his friend as a rival for the love of his wife'.[25] Certain knowledge of Faulkner's dream and its significance has been placed outside our reach, but the Dean's surprisingly provocative 1890 novella nonetheless presents another example of the Gothic's power to suggest topics hidden from the public discourse of the age.

Howells also wrote short stories exploring memory, dreams and occasionally ghosts. Collected in *Questionable Shapes* (1903) and *Between the Dark and the Daylight* (1907), both Hawthornian titles, these tales continue Howells's experiments in narrative ambiguity. Several of the stories in *Questionable Shapes* have a common frame, a setting in the 'Turkish Room' of a men's club, and a group of storytellers including a novelist, an artist and a psychologist, allowing differing interpretations of the stories told. One of the tales in the second collection, 'A Sleep and a Forgetting', concerns the love between a young woman suffering from amnesia and the psychologist who treats her. This situation, so familiar in twentieth-century literature and film (recall Fitzgerald's *Tender is the Night* and Hitchcock's *Spellbound*), was new territory when Howells explored it, though his innovations have not been acknowledged often since.

Double Twain

Samuel Clemens derived his famous pen-name from the call of Mississippi steamboat crewmen taking soundings with a lead-weighted line. 'Mark twain' means a river depth of two fathoms, or twelve feet, safe water (barely) for a steamboat. The name carries the connotation of doubling, and this is appropriate for a writer who was fascinated with twins, doubles and alter egos. He shared with his friend Howells an interest in dreams and memory, and, like him, read the work of William James and other current psychologists. Like many of his time, he suspected that personality or character was not simple or stable. Though in some sense a Realist (a term, by the way, he never used), and committed to an accurate depiction of language, custom and region, he still harboured a

Melville-like suspicion that 'reality' was a mask concealing something formless, chaotic, sinister and Gothic.

Clemens drew on memories of his childhood games in *The Adventures of Tom Sawyer* (1876), but these were only a part of an early life filled with violence and ghosts. Hannibal was a rough slave-holding river town that retained much of the flavour of the frontier. Among many horrors, young Sam saw a slave killed with a lump of iron ore, was haunted by the screams of a tramp burning to death in the city jail, and apparently witnessed, through a window, the autopsy performed on his own father. A manuscript he composed in the 1890s, known as 'Villagers 1840–43', lists a series of people and families from Hannibal, each followed with a brief note. The memories are bits of hidden village life, the stuff of the Gothic. For example, the family named Ratcliffe that was cursed with a strain of recurring insanity:

> One son lived in a bark hut up at the still house branch and at intervals came home at night and emptied the larder. Back door left open purposely; if notice was taken of him he would not come.

> *Another son* had to be locked into a small house in corner of the yard—and chained. Fed through a hole. Would not wear clothes, winter or summer. Could not have fire. Religious mania. Believed his left hand had committed a mortal sin and must be sacrificed. Got hold of a hatchet, nobody knows how, and chopped it off.[26]

With such memories as material, Clemens's Gothic side perhaps is less surprising than the endless summer of *Tom Sawyer* – though even in *Tom Sawyer* there are a haunted house, a midnight visit to a cemetery, and a near-death experience in a cave.

Mark Twain's Gothic writing draws upon folklore sources, on European and American literary conventions, and on his own innovations. As a child Sam Clemens had heard ghost stories told by enslaved African Americans, such as the elderly 'Uncle Daniel' on the farm of his uncle, John Quarrels. Throughout his life he would draw on this tradition, and his stage performances often included 'The Golden Arm' as he had heard it as a boy. Clemens also read widely, more so than generally credited, both in serious literature and popular or, as he called it, 'wildcat' literature. His skilful use of Gothic conventions can be seen in the tale he inserted in Chapter 31 of *Life on the Mississippi* (1883), a revenge story that takes us from the great river to a morgue in Bavaria. But Clemens mistrusted all conventions, literary and otherwise, and he often included a Gothic sequence in a novel only to deflate it, as with the story of the 'Haunted Barrel' in the 'Raftsmen' chapter of *Huckleberry Finn*, where the ghostly tale is followed by the derisive hoots and insults of the listeners.[27]

Clemens's most powerful Gothic writing is based on the enduring American tragedy of race, and on his own tormented philosophical speculations during the last, unhappy, fifteen years of his life.

Pudd'nhead Wilson (1894) is a book about racial identity using the motifs of twins and doubling. The book is a kind of twin itself. Clemens had originally imagined a grotesque comedy about a pair of conjoined twins of radically different temperament. When Clemens introduced the changeling plot, with the slave Roxie switching her own son and that of her master, the story took a new direction, and Clemens eventually performed a 'literary Caesarean operation', separating *Pudd'nhead Wilson* from what became *Those Extraordinary Twins*. The original Siamese twins become the ordinary twins Luigi and Angelo, and the centre of the plot shifts to the two boys exchanged in the cradle, Tom and Chambers, their subsequent lives and their relation to Chamber's enslaved mother, Roxie, and the investigations of David Wilson that result in his dramatic courtroom unmasking of the false Tom as a murderer and slave.

The ending resonates with ironies. False Tom's fate is exactly what Roxy's tragic scheme tried to avoid; yet it is appropriate for the man who once sold his own mother down the river. False Tom is both a cruel slave-owner and a murderous rebelling slave, and is punished as both. Still, there is something wrong in making one person a surrogate and scapegoat for an evil system that survives untouched. Dawson's Landing believes that justice has been served. Only the chapter epigrams from Pudd'nhead Wilson's calendar reveal Clemens's cold cynicism. This is the last of these epigrams: '*October 12. —The Discovery. —*It was wonderful to find America, but it would have been more wonderful to miss it.'[28]

The racial labels of the slave-owning South were arbitrary, so that a light-skinned person might be assigned an identity as either white or black. The ambiguous identity of the mixed-race African American is the basis for the theme of the 'tragic mulatto', explored by both white and black American writers. Roxy and False Tom are examples of this type. For Mark Twain, as for other writers, the tragic mulatto theme can suggest broader questions about identity. Can we really know what or who we are? Such questions are the basis of an increasingly pessimistic body of writing from Clemens's last years, most not published until long after his death.

Samuel Clemens's later life was bitter, though the public continued to witness the popular amusing writer and stage personality. His speculation in a typesetting machine that he expected would make him wealthy bankrupted him instead, and shortly after this wound came one far worse, the death of his favourite daughter, Susy. Clemens's response to these and subsequent outrages at the hands of what seemed to him a capricious and sadistic fate was to vent his anger in a series of fantastic, fragmentary writings, most probably never intended for publication. A group of these manuscripts has the premise of waking from one nightmare into another, with the dreamer unable to tell what is dream and what is reality. In one of these stories, perhaps indebted to Poe's *Narrative of Arthur Gordon Pym* and to Fitz-James O'Brien's story 'The Diamond Lens' (1858), a man and his family sail endlessly though a nightmare sea that is a drop of water on a microscope slide. In another, recalling *Pudd'nhead Wilson* and echoing Melville's *Benito Cereno*, a white Southerner is blackmailed and enslaved by his own servant, who knows of a crime committed by the master.

The best known of Clemens's late manuscripts, *The Mysterious Stranger*, was first published in an editorial abridgement by Alfred Bigelow Paine, his literary executor, in 1916. The story actually exists in three versions, one set in Hannibal, two in medieval Austria. In all of them a magical stranger, variously known as Little Satan, Number 44 or Philip Traum, appears to a boy and instructs him in a series of ultimate truths. The last lesson (in one version) has the boy and the stranger alone in empty space:

It is true, that which I have revealed to you: there is no God, no universe, no human race, no earthy life, no heaven, no hell. It is all a Dream, a grotesque and foolish dream. Nothing exists but You. And You are but a Thought—a vagrant Thought, a useless Thought, a homeless Thought, wandering forlorn among the empty eternities![29]

This is the other side of Samuel Clemens, Realist. In an ultimate uncanny moment, not just the familiar home but reality itself is dismissed and dissolved.

Conjuring race

The issue of race, largely but not entirely that of African slavery and its legacy, continued to occupy the attention of white writers throughout the century. Most importantly, black American writers began to emerge, and the resulting dialogue of black and white is one of the distinguishing facts of American literature. For both black and white writers, the Gothic was a natural form for this discourse.

Emergence of a black Gothic began before the Civil War, in the writing of escaped slaves. *Narrative of the Life of Frederick Douglass's* (1845) could not be described as a Gothic work, but Douglass's great autobiography has powerful Gothic elements. The pattern of captivity and escape, after all, is a Gothic staple. When Douglass describes his introduction to slavery, the moment of his childhood when he became aware of what it meant to be a slave, it is a Gothic scene of sexual sadism:

> I have often been awakened at the dawn of day by the most heart-rending shrieks of an own aunt of mine, he used to tie up to a joist, and whip upon her naked back till she was literally covered with blood. No words, no tears, no prayers, from his gory victim, seemed to move his iron heart from its bloody purpose. The louder she screamed, the harder he whipped; and where the blood ran fastest, there he whipped the longest . . . I remember the first time I ever witnessed this horrible exhibition, I was quite a child, but I well remember it. I never shall forget it whilst I remember any thing . . . It was the blood-stained gate, the entrance to the hell of slavery, through which I was about to pass.[30]

The wielder of the bloody lash was not only Douglass's master, but also probably his father. In Douglass's life, as in much American racial Gothic, the facts of genealogy were concealed.

A most remarkable document in the history of slavery and of African American literature is *The Bondwoman's Narrative* by Hannah Crafts, recently discovered and published by Henry Louis Gates, Jr. We know little about the author of this apparently autobiographical novel, which, as Gates establishes, must have been written in the last years of the 1850s, about the time of Douglass's *Narrative*. She presumably wrote under a pseudonym, since she could have been seized and returned to her former owner under the infamous fugitive-slave laws, so we do not even know her real name. The author had become literate despite laws forbidding it, perhaps being taught by a sympathetic neighbour, as indicated in the novel, and clearly was familiar with Romantic literature, especially Dickens, from whom several passages are lifted. The novel is a hybrid of sentimental and Gothic traditions.

The Bondwoman's Narrative describes Hannah Crafts's life under slavery and her escape to freedom in the North. In this it follows the pattern and conventions of the escaped-slave narrative established by Douglass, Harriet Jacobs and others: this is a form, like the Indian captivity narrative, that was invented within American literature, and is one of the foundations of African American narrative. We can easily imagine that this large story arc of *The Bondwoman's Narrative* is true to the author's life. Within this frame are several subsidiary stories involving women of mixed race, 'tragic mulatto' stories, such as the tale of Hannah's unnamed 'mistress', who believes that she is white until her true heritage is uncovered by the novel's villain, the lawyer Trappe (an obviously allegorical name). There is also a cluster of stories involving the fate of mixed-race women kept as concubines by their masters. These stories may not have been witnessed directly by the author, but could have been based on real events and oral tales encountered throughout the South.

While Crafts sometimes stretches the reader's patience with outrageous coincidences, she is a writer of real narrative skill and some subtlety. The racial reassignment of her mistress by Trappe, for example, is echoed later in the novel by the comic episode in which another mistress, Mrs Wheeler, is mistaken for an African American when an unexpected chemical reaction turns her expensive French face-powder into blackface. Both episodes comment on the arbitrary quality of racial labels in America.

Crafts's novel is remarkable for its anticipation of Gothic devices used by later American authors (black and white) in racial narratives. In *The Bondwoman's Narrative* we encounter, for example, the story of free and slave children exchanged at birth that Mark Twain would use in *Pudd'nhead Wilson*, of a father selling his own mixed-race son (used by Charles Chesnutt, among others), and of a mother killing her child rather than allowing it to be enslaved (used with variations by Kate Chopin in 'Désirée's Baby' and by Toni Morrison in *Beloved*). Crafts's comic transformation of an arrogant slave-owner into a Negro is echoed by Chesnutt in 'Mars Jeem's Nightmare'; so too is Crafts's haunted tree as an emblem of the curse hanging over a slave-owning family ('The Marked Tree'). None of these authors was influenced by Crafts, since her novel was neither published nor, as far as we know, circulated in manuscript. Later writers discovered for themselves the paths through the tangled American racial Gothic travelled earlier by their forgotten foremother.

Haunted trees, haunted houses

In the years after the Civil War, Southern apologists fought a rear guard action to defend and idealize the values of the slave-owning South. In literature, this enterprise produced the 'Plantation School' or 'School of Southern Nostalgia', as represented by the fiction of Thomas Nelson Page (1853–1922). The view of the Old South promoted in this literature was that of the pre-war songs of Stephen Foster (1826–64). Slavery was not the horror painted by abolitionists, but was more like an extended caring family.[31] After the war, it was claimed that former slaves longed for the simple life on the old plantation, as in Page's popular story 'Marse Chan' (1884).[32] Such sentimental works might seem harmless, and even appear sympathetic or affectionate toward former slaves, but they portrayed black Americans as child-like and incapable of competing in the modern world. The other side of this racist coin was the image of former slaves as criminals and rapists. Together, these stereotypes were used to strip African Americans of civil rights after the controversial election of 1876, and to install a system of segregation, the so-called 'Jim Crow' laws.

A contrary strain of American writing, by both white and black authors, showed an anti-nostalgic, realistic view of race in North America. As we recall from Hector St Jean de Crèvecoeur's description of the slave hung in a cage in a tree while birds pecked out his eyes, realism and the Gothic are seldom far apart in the American racial scene. Like Mark Twain, many American writers after the Civil War returned to the era of slavery to expose its brutal realities, and followed its consequences through the post-war decades.

It is worth underlining the point that slavery and its aftermath are inherently suited to Gothic imagery and narrative. For example, the great African American historian and sociologist W. E. B. Du Bois describes the South as a black man travelling in a 'Jim Crow' railway car would see it. The black traveller sees old estates, each with its own complex family history:

> Here are the remnants of the vast plantations of the Sheldons, the Pellots, and the Rensons; but the souls of them are passed. The houses lie in half ruin, or have wholly disappeared; the fences have flown, and the families are wandering in the world. Strange vicissitudes have met these whilom masters. Yonder stretch the wide acres of Bilad Reasor; he died in wartime, but the upstart overseer hastened to wed the widow. Then he went, and his neighbors, too, and now only the black tenant remains . . . [33]

These are proto-Gothic stories, anticipating the novels of Faulkner. To tell the story of race in the South is to expose suppressed events, acts of violence and sometimes love, and to reveal the secrets of houses.

Slavery, that 'peculiar institution', was a *curse*: here is the master trope of the American racial Gothic. Writers explore the consequences of this curse for white and for black families. Since these families are often interwoven – a fact universally understood, but seldom acknowledged – a major theme of this literature is that of the suppressed genealogy. Sometimes hidden kinship will be revealed or exposed, but often it is only hinted at. Houses, then, in the two senses of the family and its home (as in Poe's 'The Fall of the House of Usher'), are central to many works of racial Gothic. Since racial Gothic is often about kinship and complex family-trees, literal trees (as in *The Bondwoman's Narrative*) often appear as emblems, shadowing houses. And since the literature of race is a literature of the taboo subject of race-mixing, the 'tragic mulatto' is a recurrent character.

Louisiana Gothic

While all regions of the United States have provided settings and subjects for Gothic literature, New England and the South have the deepest Gothic heritage. Each, for its own historical and demographic reasons, seems to cherish or brood over its past, and in each, traditionally, one finds a rich oral tradition. William Faulkner once said that it was not necessary for him to study Southern history to know it, but only to listen to old men sitting on benches in front of the county courthouse.

Within the South, Louisiana is in several ways unique, and especially suited to Gothic narrative. Its historic cultural centre, New Orleans, has some claim to be the capital of American Gothic, and (as shown in Anne Rice's novels) continues in this role to the present. The August 2005 destruction of much of New Orleans by Hurricane Katrina only confirms that the city has more past than future, that it has a strong heritage but a fragile reality, that it is a haunted place.

The racial heritage of Louisiana and New Orleans is even more complex than that of the rest of the South. While other slave-holding states had a binary racial system (a person was legally either black or white), Louisiana's laws long recognized mixed-race people as a separate category. Although the Southern binary system was finally imposed on Louisiana, the state, and especially New Orleans, remained more racially cosmopolitan than the rest of the South. In a system called '*plaçage*', wealthy white men chose concubines at formal 'Quadroon Balls' and sometimes raised parallel, separate white and mixed-race families.[34]

The complexity of race in Louisiana may be suggested by the word 'Creole', which changes its meaning according to context. It usually denotes white citizens descended from the original French and Spanish settlers. But it can also refer to a person of racially mixed background; the word is consequently nuanced and ambiguous, even dangerous. Its careless use by an outsider can be offensive, for it exposes the realm of hidden reality, things known but not spoken about, the realm of the Gothic.

One of the first writers to explore the Louisiana Gothic, George Washington Cable (1844–1925), had been a Confederate cavalryman and was wounded in combat. A white native of New Orleans, though not a Creole, Cable underwent a radical change of conviction after the war and dedicated himself to civil rights for former slaves. Most of the short stories collected in his first book, *Old Creole Days* (1879), explore the racial legacy of the Creole class. 'Jean-ah Poquelin' is a story of a haunted house and a family cursed and destroyed by slavery. The old slave-trader of the title retires after a trip to Africa, and his beloved younger brother is never seen again. Over the years his house acquires the reputation of being haunted, and its secret is revealed only after the old man's death. In a narrative rich with symbolism, the curse of slavery reveals itself as leprosy, a disease that in this instance has the paradoxical effect of turning a white man even whiter, a ghostly snow-white. The story could be considered, in fact, an exploration of 'whiteness'. One of the characters is even named Little White. 'Belles Demoiselles Plantation', another story from this collection, is the story of the fall of a house, which, as in Poe's tale, literally means the catastrophic collapse of the building, as well as the failure of the family line. 'Belles Demoiselles Plantation' presents a family with a white branch and one that is mixed with American Indian heritage. In Cable's first novel, *The Grandissimes* (1880), the parallel lines are white and black Creole, with racially different half-brothers bearing the same name. *The Grandissimes* has significant Gothic elements, including a curse on the Grandissime family by a dying slave, while at the same time it is, as Louis Rubin has claimed, one of the first American novels to deal realistically with racial relations in America.[35]

Cable's *Old Creole Days* received generally good reviews in the South, but as his views on civil rights became known, he was increasingly unpopular in his homeland, and eventually found it prudent to move to New England. A New Orleans contemporary, Grace King (1852–1935), actually became a writer out of anger at Cable's liberal racial views. King was not a Creole either, but closely identified herself with the old order of New Orleans, and was an admirer of such writers of the Plantation School as Thomas Nelson Page. Nonetheless, though beginning with motives that now seem ignoble and simply wrong, Grace King produced some sensitive and well-written fiction about Southerners of differing racial background. Her collection *Balcony Stories* (1893) were written within the tradition of women's regional realism, and are to be imagined as stories told among women sitting on New Orleans balconies on hot afternoons. 'The Little Convent Girl', from that collection, is an effective story in the tradition of the tragic mulatto. The girl of the title, whose name is never given, is in her teens but seeming younger (like the innocent Lily of Freeman's 'Old Woman Magoun'), and is plunged into the racial and sexual reality of the South when, returning to New Orleans after the death of her father, she learns that she is the child of a mixed-race mother.

Much of the emotional impact of 'The Little Convent Girl' comes from the girl's radical innocence. She has been so sheltered from the world that she has never even seen the stars, since she was not allowed out of her St Louis convent at night. The sympathetic pilot of the steamboat shows her the constellations, and she is delighted to learn that the theoretical knowledge of the sky she acquired in school is actually true. The pilot also tells her his theory of the river beneath the river:

> It was his opinion that there was as great a river as the Mississippi flowing directly under it—an underself of a river, as much a counterpart of the other as the second story of a house is of the first; in fact, he said that they were navigating through the upper story. Whirlpools were holes in the floor of the upper river, so to speak; eddies were rifts and cracks. And deep under the earth, hurrying toward the subterranean stream, were other streams, small and great, but all deep, hurrying to and from that great mother-stream underneath.[36]

This remarkable description of the shadow-self or dark twin of the river is an open-ended symbol, evocative perhaps of the mystery, power and menace of the great world that is opening to the girl's cloistered imagination, but still hidden from her. A month later, her future reduced to the sexual bondage that was her mother's life, the girl leaps into the river, perhaps to be carried by a whirlpool to 'that vast, hidden, dark Mississippi that flows beneath the one we see'.[37]

King's tragic convent girl is matched in 'Sister Josepha', a story from *The Goodness of St Rocque* (1899) by Alice Dunbar-Nelson (1875–1935). Like King, Dunbar-Nelson is writing within the tradition of women's regional realism; unlike King, Dunbar-Nelson was a mixed-race New Orleans Creole. Dunbar-Nelson's story uses the familiar Gothic pattern of the sexually menaced heroine trapped in a convent. The young nun of the title, whose birth name was Camille, had been placed as a small child in an orphanage run by nuns, and had become a nun herself after refusing adoption when the sexual leering of the proposed foster-father made her feel 'creepy'.[38] Now, at the age of eighteen, she plans to escape the convent, for the sight of a handsome young army officer in church has given her a revelation of life outside the walls, a life that is passing her by. However, an overheard conversation among the nuns in authority shows her the folly of her hopes:

> 'She is not well, poor child', said Francesca. 'I fear the life is too confining'.
> 'It is better for her', was the reply. 'You know, sister, how hard it would be for her in the world, with no name but Camille, no friends, and her beauty, and then—'.

The anguished thoughts of Camille (Sister Josepha) after hearing this exchange are shared by every character in the tradition of the tragic mulatto: 'Who am I? What am I?'[39]

Yet the key fact of Camille's life, her racial background, is never mentioned: it is the blank space following the older nun's words 'And then—', and it is obliquely referenced in the narrator's description of her dark beauty. Camille herself may not realize these racial markers, but she does finally understand that she would be a defenceless object of sexual predation outside the convent, which is both a trap and her only refuge.

Kate Chopin's 'Désirée's Baby' (1892) is perhaps the most complex and subtle of Creole Gothic tales. Chopin (1851–1904) was born and raised in St Louis, but was Creole on her mother's side, was bilingual, and married a Creole. Her writing career began after her husband's death in an epidemic. Living in rural Louisiana and then again in St Louis, she wrote of the range of ethnic and racial groups in the South, including the Creoles and the other French-speaking community in Louisiana, the Cajuns (Arcadians).

'Désirée's Baby' blends the tradition of women's regional realism (of which Chopin was a master) with European and American Gothic, and has the tight structure and narrative reversal associated with the French writer Guy de Maupassant, whom Chopin had read and translated. As so often with the best Gothic fiction, the story is innovative in its narration, using its time sequence and shifting points of view to create ambiguity. The revelation that Désirée's baby has an African background comes at different times to different characters: first (if we read carefully) to Zandrine, Désirée's servant; then to Désirée's adoptive mother; then to Désirée's husband, Armand; and at last to Désirée herself, who sees only her beautiful baby boy, not abstract characteristics of race.

Désirée was an abandoned orphan of unknown origin, thus opening the possibility of the racial heritage that Armand believes she has passed on to their child. Raised by the prosperous Valmondés, who had adopted her, she married Armand, even though he had a reputation of being a cruel master to his slaves and lived in a house whose 'roof came down steep and black like a cowl', surrounded by big oaks, whose 'thick-leaved, far-reaching branches shadowed it like a pall'.[40] Désirée brings light to this Gothic mansion, and her love for Armand has the effect of making him gentler and kinder – for a time. Désirée, in other words, believes that she is living a Gothic romance like Charlotte Brontë's *Jane Eyre*, in which the villain-hero, Mr Rochester, is transformed by love into an appropriate husband.

With the discovery of the child's race, however, Armand reverts to the monster he always was, and rejects his wife and child. Désirée takes the little boy and runs toward the swamp, where, presumably, she drowns both herself and the innocent child. The scene of Désirée fleeing the dark, brooding house, clad in her thin white gown, captures one of Gothic literature's enduring archetypes, one endlessly reproduced on the covers of present-day popular Gothic romances.[41]

Chopin's Maupassant-like twist at the end (which should not be spoiled for first-time readers) serves to heighten our sense of Armand's cruelty, since his rejection of Désirée and her baby contrasts so sharply with what we learn of the protectiveness of Armand's father, and his kindness to Armand's mother.

The theme of suppressed genealogy clearly is a major plot element, but most readers still miss how subtle and pervasive this theme is. There are strong hints that the little slave boy, son of La Blanche (whose name means the white one, or whitey), is also Armand's son. Thus, in the moment of epiphany, when Désirée looks back and forth between her son and the slave boy and recognizes their similarity, this similarity comes not just from both being racially mixed, but from the fact that they are half-brothers. Chopin makes a narrative device out of the silence of Southern society about the sexual subjugation of enslaved women, hinting at what must never be said.

Most of the fiction of Charles Chesnutt (1858–1932) explores the themes of 'passing' and suppressed genealogy developed in our reading of Chopin's 'Désirée's Baby'. Since both of Chesnutt's grandfathers were white slave owners, and his grandmothers slaves, the light-skinned Chesnutt knew something about life on the colour line. His early relationship with his audience, in fact, is a variation on the theme of passing. Though Chesnutt's editors at the *Atlantic Monthly*, then the most prestigious of American magazines, knew his racial identity, his first readers did not. His 'Conjure Woman' stories, collected in 1899, were seen as Southern local-colour dialect fiction in the tradition of Joel Chandler Harris. Chesnutt's Uncle Julius resembled Harris's Uncle Remus, a black teller of tales to a white audience, and readers were amused by Julius's antics and self-serving attempts to play upon the sympathies of his sceptical employer, John. Readers missed, or chose to ignore, the satire of white privilege and smugness that underlies all of these stories. Chesnutt tore off his mask and asserted his race when he published *The Marrow of Tradition* (1901), a novel based on the vicious race riots in Wilmington, North Carolina, in 1898. His white readers fled, and there was not a large enough black audience at this time to support him. Chesnutt, who was a lawyer, returned for his livelihood to his successful business of preparing legal documents, though he wrote four more novels (three not published in his lifetime), as well as short fiction, during his long literary eclipse.[42]

The stories in *The Conjure Woman* are all frame stories, in which the formerly enslaved Uncle Julius tells stories in dialect to his employer, John, and John's wife Annie. John intends to apply efficient Northern business values to grape growing in North Carolina. He is a representative of progress in the backward South. Here, progress is linked to assumptions of race as well as class, and, as always in American Gothic, the reader is led to distrust it. Julius tells stories that John smugly understands as transparent attempts to manipulate him. However, the stories contain implications that John cannot see, though his wife Annie, pointing the way for the reader, often does. Gradually we come to realize that Julius is a trickster figure, far deeper than John ever understands, and the oral historian of the region.

Representative of the 1899 volume is 'Po' Sandy', the second of seven stories. In this tale, John wishes to salvage lumber from an abandoned one-room school to build a kitchen, detached in the Southern fashion, for his home. Julius discourages John from this use, and tells a story to prove that the old building is haunted. While John is not in the least impressed by the tale, his wife Annie decides that she wishes to have her kitchen constructed of new lumber. Later John learns that Julius belongs to a church congregation that is holding services in the old school building. John is amused at being thus outmanoeuvred, while still feeling superior to Julius and his simple schemes.

Thus summarized, the story is comic in a minstrel-show sort of way, and is not at all Gothic. Gothic elements emerge, however, as we listen to the tale Julius tells, which John dismisses as simply preposterous: a slave man turned into a tree by his conjure-woman wife, Tennie, in an attempt to prevent his being hired out to a distant plantation; the tree being chopped down and sawed into lumber; the grief of his wife. (Of course, this is the very lumber used to make the building under dispute.) But John and his wife Annie react very differently to Julius's story:

> Annie had listened to this gruesome narrative with strained attention.

'What a system it was', she exclaimed, when Julius had finished, 'under which such things were possible!'

'What things?' I asked, in amazement. 'Are you seriously considering the possibility of a man's being turned into a tree?'

'Oh, no', she replied quickly, 'not that'; and then she murmured absently, and with a dim look in her fine eyes, 'Poor Tennie!' [43]

Julius's story is Gothic for Annie, comic for John. Probably most readers now would see Annie's point. Sandy's first wife had been sold away from him. His second wife uses conjure as an attempt to counter the power of the slave system, and brings about the very result she is trying to forestall, the loss of her husband, and she goes mad and dies of grief. While the story may be Julius's invention, it captures one of the central tragedies of a system that held people as movable commodities.

In 'Po' Sandy', Chesnutt makes a point upon which later black writers, most notably Toni Morrison, will insist. While the most common site of Southern Gothic is the decaying old plantation mansion (that Chesnutt, too, employs with great effect), little cabins and other structures throughout the country, built by black people and containing their stories, are also haunted. Here, Chesnutt surrealistically displays this haunting by having the schoolhouse constructed from the literal body and blood of a suffering black man, in which his grieving widow dies.

Two of the finest of Chesnutt's stories about John and Julius were not included in *The Conjure Woman*. 'The Dumb Witness' was excluded from the volume by Chesnutt's editor, apparently because no character in it uses magic, while 'The Marked Tree' (in which conjure is used) was written much later, and published in the National Association for the Advancement of Coloured People magazine *The Crisis* in 1924. Each story chronicles the decline of a Southern slave-owning family. Each is also a story of rebellion against the family, and contains a deeply submerged secret of kinship.

Tongues and silence

In an African American folk tale called 'Talking Bones' (not collected until 1967), a slave finds a hidden place in the forest where the bodies of murdered slaves are thrown. A skeleton opens its fleshless jaws and says to the slave, 'Tongue is the cause of my being here'. The slave runs to tell his master about the talking bones. But when the slave returns with several white men, the skeleton does not speak. The infuriated white men beat the slave to death, and leave his body by the skeleton. Then the skeleton speaks: 'Tongue brought us here, and tongue brought you here.'[44]

The story, presumably one used by slaves to school their children in survival, may suggest why so many stories about slavery have issues of speech and silence at their core. Don't tell them anything, the story instructs. Silence is resistance; silence is power.

In Chesnutt's 'The Dumb Witness' a slave owner named Murchison cuts out the tongue of his slave, mistress and kinswoman Viney, only to discover, too late, that she knows the location of documents essential to his estate. In the decades that follow, the plantation slides into poverty and neglect, while Murchison goes mad. His obsessive demands for the missing documents are answered by Viney's incomprehensible tongueless babble.

At the end, in a Maupassant-like reversal, we learn, after Murchison's death, that Viney was in fact capable of intelligent speech, and could have told her former lover at any time that the documents were hidden in his favourite chair.

'The Dumb Witness' is structured on an opposition of the written word – documents – and silence (or unintelligible nonsense, which is nearly the same thing). The Murchison family, like the nation they in many ways represent, draws its power from the written word, from texts. A Murchison had helped draft the Constitution of the United States, which legalized slavery. Murchisons had been lawyers in a slave state, creators of laws that defined people as free or enslaved. Opposed to this power is the silence of black people, who, without writing or even without a tongue, communicated to each other and kept their own history and culture alive. The story begs as well to be read in terms of the life of its author, who was a lawyer, a professional preparer of legal documents like wills, and also an author who gave voice to the hidden experience of African Americans.

'The Marked Tree' is another story with silence at its core, and a suppressed genealogy. One of only two stories in the John and Julius cycle to show magic used by slaves against their owners, 'The Marked Tree' describes the decline and extinction of a prosperous family named Spencer. When Aleck Spencer, the patriarch of the family, sells one of his slaves, Isham, who is subsequently abused and dies, the young slave's mother, Phillis, places a curse on the Spencer oak, the great tree that symbolizes the family's fortunes. Most of the remaining story describes the subsequent extinction of the Spencer family. One after another they die, each death associated in some way with the marked tree. Finally Aleck recognizes the connection, and calls the oak a 'upas tree', naming it after the legendary tree of death that destroys all life for miles around it. Aleck orders the tree cut down, and is killed in its fall. The few remaining Spencers subsequently perish in the fire caused when a burning log from the marked tree rolls from a fireplace. The upas tree here, of course, is another emblem of the curse of slavery.

Within the story of the fall of the house of Spencer is another tragedy, that of Phillis and her son Isham. The careful reader will discover what is not explicitly said: a familiar Southern story of unacknowledged kinship and of betrayal, and the full motivation for Phillis's curse.[45]

Weird tales: Bierce, Chambers and Hearn

The cold cynicism of Ambrose Bierce (1842–1914?)[46] probably was earned through his combat experience in the Civil War. It is difficult to draw the line between his tales of horror and his tales of war, since the glory of war was for him illusion, and nightmare its reality. 'Chickamauga' (1889), for example, one of his most anthologized stories, displays his characteristic shifting between subjective and objective reality, as we follow the adventures of a little boy playing in the woods and encountering strange beings and events he does not understand. Only at the end, as the child stumbles upon the ruin of his home and the mutilated corpse of his mother, does

Bierce step out of the child's mind and allow us to understand that the boy is deaf, and he has been an unwitting observer of one of the war's most savage battles.

Two stories by Bierce, 'The Death of Halpin Frayser' (1893) and 'An Inhabitant of Carcosa' (1887), though having some common elements, illustrate sharply different approaches to the Gothic tale, a split that will continue through and beyond the twentieth century. Both stories begin with a quotation from 'Hali' about corpses and revenant spirits, and each describes uncanny events in a graveyard.[47] The first retains the conventions of realistic fiction, so that part of the story, for example, is set in California's Napa Valley, with recognizable landscape features and vegetation, and names of towns (Napa, Calistoga, St Helena) that can be located on maps, and, indeed, visited today. There is a surreal section at the centre of the tale, in which Frayser, wandering in a wood, takes 'a road less traveled',[48] turns into a landscape dripping with blood, and encounters the dead body, or ghost, of his mother, who strangles him. But the narrator identifies this surreal sequence as the nightmare of Frayser, as he sleeps – and then dies – under a cedar tree. We are returned to the everyday world, as two rather bumbling normative characters, a policeman and a deputy sheriff, find Frayser's body in an old cemetery, near his mother's grave.

'The Death of Halpin Frayser' is in the tradition of Hawthorne's 'Young Goodman Brown', the classic American story of a nightmare encounter in the woods. Like Hawthorne's tale, it bristles with psychological implications. Bierce has constructed a kind of Oedipal tangle involving Frayser, his mother, his murderous stepfather and his poet great-grandfather, whose verse Frayser is channelling just before his death. As in Hawthorne's story, there are competing natural and supernatural explanations. Brown met the Devil in the woods, or he dreamed the meeting. Frayser was murdered by his mother's ghost, over her grave, or he was murdered by his fugitive stepfather, who had killed his mother. Or possibly Frayser strangled himself, while dreaming of his death. Various solutions present themselves, with typical Gothic ambiguity; yet each solution is a kind of trap, each contains a contradiction. We should recall that Bierce was also a master of the hoax, a literary form in which the reader is tricked into taking as fact something that is preposterous.[49]

In 'An Inhabitant of Carcosa', however, there is no possibility of a rational, materialistic reading of the story. The story is in the tradition of Poe, not of Hawthorne. The setting is fantastic, the speaker a ghost speaking through a medium, the language designed toward the single effect of weirdness or the uncanny:

> Over all the dismal landscape a canopy of low, lead-colored clouds hung like a visible curse. In all this there were a menace or portent— a hint of evil, an intimation of doom. Bird, best, or insect there was none. The wind sighed in the bare branches of the dead trees and the gray grass bent to whisper its dread secret to the earth; but no other sound nor motion broke the awful repose of that dismal place.[50]

This is the familiar Poescape. Bierce's half-personified landscape features (trees bend and whisper) and poetic devices such as alliteration ('low, lead-colored clouds') saturate the setting with menace and gloom. In it the speaker wanders, and comes to realize that he is a ghost, now inhabiting his long-destroyed city of Carcosa.

'An Inhabitant of Carcosa' probably is the most influential of Bierce's stories for later writers, and helped to establish the conventions of the 'weird tale' in the later nineteenth and twentieth centuries. The weird tale, which became a popular genre with dedicated pulp magazines, would continue in the line of Poe and Bierce to use fantastic settings and supernatural menace to produce the requisite chilling emotional response sought by the reader. Often considered, like pulp science fiction, a sub-literary form for adolescent boys, the weird tale would prove a training ground for many twentieth-century writers, and anticipated elements of later Gothic popular culture in radio serials, films, television and even electronic games.

The 'Carcosa' setting would be referenced, as a deliberate homage, by Robert W. Chambers and, later, by H. P. Lovecraft (who will be discussed in the next chapter).

Robert W. Chambers (1865–1933) took Bierce's lost city of Carcosa and transformed it, in four interrelated stories, into a sinister place in an alternative reality, ruled over by a King in Yellow.[51] Hali,

Bierce's sage, becomes the name of a lake, one of the features, like the overhanging black stars, often mentioned in Chambers's version of Carcosa.

Chambers's four Carcosa stories assume the existence of an ultimate Gothic text, a play called *The King in Yellow*. The play is so powerful that we receive only guarded generalities about it, and read only a few brief quotations. It is a literary masterpiece, but poisonous. Its effects are like a powerful drug, enslaving its victims and killing them or driving them mad. (Indeed, one could see in these stories a reference to late nineteenth-century abuse of drugs like chloral hydrate, opium and the newly synthesized morphine.) Moreover, reading the play can cause an irruption of the Carcosa-reality into our world, with strange figures like the watchman in 'The Yellow Sign' or the sinister organist in 'In the Court of the Dragon' preparing for the arrival of the King in Yellow himself. Of the characters in the four stories who read the play, only Alec and Geneviève (in 'The Mask') survive, Alec after two years of illness, Geneviève after an equivalent period frozen in stone before her Galatea-like transformation back into a living woman. Hildred Castaigne, of 'The Restorer of Reputations', a mad narrator in the tradition of Poe's, believes that he will become Emperor of America as the servant of the King in Yellow, and ends his life in an asylum.

Lafcadio Hearn's 'The Ghostly Kiss' (1880) is, like Bierce's 'An Inhabitant of Carcosa', a graveyard tale using the device of the narrator who discovers that he is a ghost. Hearn (1850–1904), of Irish and Greek ancestry, came to the United States in his teens, and worked as a journalist in Cincinnati and then for nearly ten years in New Orleans. 'The Ghostly Kiss' is a kind of surreal prose-poem, in which the narrator finds himself in a vast theatre, kisses the face of a lovely woman in the audience, and then finds that the theatre is a cemetery of white tombs. The setting may have been inspired by the extensive above-ground cemeteries of New Orleans that figure so prominently in later fiction set in that most Gothic of American cities.

After a brief period in the West Indies, Hearn settled in Japan in 1890. He became a Japanese citizen, took the name Koizumi Yakumo, and wrote several books based on Japanese material, often with supernatural elements. The title of his best-known collection of translated Japanese legends, *Kwaidan* (1910), means, as Hearn translates for us in his introduction, 'weird tales'.[52]

Hearn's career anticipates the globalization of literature we see in our own time, as stories, ideas and influences pass back and forth across the increasingly permeable membranes of national and linguistic frontiers. In one relevant example, consider the twentieth-century Japanese writer Edogawa Rampo (Hirai Taro, 1894–1965). The punning nom de plume is 'Edgar Allan Poe' said with a thick Japanese accent: Edoga Awaran Po. An influential author in Japan, Rampo was a Gothic writer whose stories have been turned into movies, and some translated into English (*Japanese Tales of Mystery and Imagination*, 1956). Thus American Gothic becomes part of a world-wide literature of the strange and terrifying.

The Gothic-naturalism paradox

As the nineteenth century ended, some of the most innovative American literature combined elements of Gothicism and a new literary movement called naturalism. This seems a paradox, a melding of opposites, given Gothicism's embrace of mystery, ambiguity and the supernatural. Naturalism claimed to bring a scientific approach to literature, and was influenced by Darwinian thought, especially as applied to social models by Herbert Spencer. For the naturalists, a proper literary text was a like a laboratory notebook. We put the rats in the maze, and report on their behaviour. Human beings, like other organisms, respond to stimuli, and to physical and biological forces. Because free will is an illusion, a naturalistic work will never invest with significance a character's struggle to make a moral decision; there are no real choices, only responses.[53] This point is the clearest distinction between the naturalists and their realistic predecessors, since the struggle to make a clear logical or moral decision is exactly what a realist novel (by Howells, for example) is always about.

The apparent distinction between Gothic tarns and castles and the laboratory of naturalism disappears with a closer look, since, in fact, the two apparently different approaches have a similar goal, a similar view of the world, and share favourite images and tropes.

Gothicism and naturalism are both devoted to shaking bourgeois complacency, revealing unsettling truths that society tries to conceal from itself. Each values extreme experience and emotion, and each envisions a universe of vast forces that can overwhelm and terrify the individual – though they may give the forces different names. Each explores the kinship of humans and beasts, and a common image in each is the cage in which they – we – are trapped. Consequently, naturalism and the Gothic often are indistinguishable.

Late nineteenth-century American naturalism was anticipated by such earlier works as Rebecca Harding Davis's novella *Life in the Iron Mills* (1861), which has its own Gothic elements. Most serious American writers at the turn of the century were influenced by naturalism, and most had read the major European models, Zola, the Goncourt brothers, Thomas Hardy and Henrik Ibsen (whose 1883 play *Ghosts* is a perfect illustration of the compatibility of naturalism and the Gothic). For writers who were born around 1870 the movement was especially compelling, and the reading of Herbert Spencer, the prophet of Social Darwinism, was often a kind of conversion experience. Seeing the truth, they set about preaching it in their writing. Of this generation, E. A. Robinson, Frank Norris, Stephen Crane and Jack London produced works that could be considered Gothic-naturalist hybrids.

Much of Robinson's best poetry chronicles 'Tilbury Town', a New England village based on his hometown of Gardiner, Maine. These poems recall the long economic decline of New England portrayed in the regional fiction of Sarah Orne Jewett and Mary E. Wilkins Freeman. Robinson's characters are defeated by economic forces, but most often simply by Time, which is Robinson's great theme. In the old flour mill of Robinson's 'The Mill' (1920), for example, 'there is the warm /And mealy fragrance of the past' because water-powered mills run by local artisans have been replaced by centralized steam-driven industrial mills.[54] Thus, the miller's last words, 'There are no millers any more.'[55] The miller's wife, finding his body hanging from a beam in the mill, drowns herself in the millpond. The poem's final lines are both lovely and cruel, reflecting (in naturalistic fashion) the cold indifference of nature to humans and their tragedies:

> Black water, smooth above the weir
> Like starry velvet in the night,
> Though ruffled once, would soon appear
> The same as ever to the sight. [56]

Robinson's Tilbury Town is filled with defeated characters and houses with ghost-like recluses, like the woman in 'Eros Turannos' (1916), who has been trapped in marriage by a fortune-hunting husband. Many of Robinson's poems record suicide, like 'The Mill', and in 'Luke Havergal' (1897), a poem surely the equal in eeriness to any by Poe, a ghostly voice beckons its hearer to 'the western gate':

> Out of a grave I come to tell you this,
> Out of a grave I come to quench the kiss
> That flames upon your forehead with a glow
> That blinds you to the way that you must go.[57]

While literary naturalists may profess scientific objectivity, in reality they often brood over their characters and evoke sympathy for them. Robinson's vanquished, ghost-ridden villagers recall those of the regionalists of a generation before him, and look forward in some ways to those of another writer about small-town Maine, the vastly popular Gothic writer Stephen King. King's story 'The Reach' (1981), in fact, is much like a Robinson poem, in its evocation of small and private lives swept by history into lonely and stubborn irrelevance.[58]

Degeneration

Frank Norris's first published work of fiction, 'Lauth' (1893) is set in medieval Paris. Though naturalistic in its attention to detail, graphic brutality and (rather specious) evocation of science, it has kinship as well to *Frankenstein* and such work of Poe as 'The Facts in the Case of M. Valdemar'. The body of Lauth, a student killed in a civil disturbance, is resuscitated by medical students. At first Lauth seems nearly normal, but then he becomes torpid, and ultimately resolves into a 'horrible, shapeless mass . . . upon the floor'.[59]

Degeneration, here seen in Lauth's body, is one of the terrors of the late nineteenth century. Lauth's metamorphosis is a reversal of evolution, a sinking back though stages of life to more and more primitive forms. The process is called *atavism*, a concept that the Social Darwinism of the day linked to social behaviour as well as biology. The Italian sociologist Césare Lombroso (1835–1909) taught that criminals were reversions to primitive stages of evolution, and that their facial and bodily features revealed their links with brutal ancestors. At a time of social unrest and fear of class warfare, the popularity of Lombroso's ideas reveals a middle-class anxiety that June Howard has dubbed the fear of 'proletarianization', or descent on the social scale.[60] The most common plot of the naturalistic novel, in fact, could be called the plot of the 'long slow slide', in which a once prosperous character (Hurstwood in Dreiser's *Sister Carrie*, for example) endures an agonizing descent until he finally becomes one of the unspeakable 'others' of the social lower depths.

Obviously this fear is close to the Gothic as well, as we see in Robert Louis Stevenson's *The Strange Case* of *Dr Jekyll and Mr Hyde* (1886), a story about the emergence of the hidden other or brute. The ancient legend of the werewolf, the human who is transformed into a savage predator, is also a vehicle for the terror the age felt at the prospect of atavism. Ordinary every day life may appear safe and stable, but who can know what chance event, infection or unchecked habit may trigger the emergence of the brute within us? Naturalism and the Gothic easily join to explore this nightmare.

Frank Norris's *Vandover and the Brute* is the classic illustration of Gothic-naturalist hybridization. *Vandover*, though drafted in 1894 and 1895 (when Norris was enrolled in Louis Gates's famous writing class at Harvard), remained unpublished at the author's death in 1902. The Victorian code forbidding references to syphilis still held. In 1914 the novel appeared, issued with some revisions by Norris's younger brother, the novelist Charles Norris.[61]

The eponymous hero is a young San Francisco artist of good family and social standing who succumbs to alcoholism and gambling addiction, contracts syphilis, and loses his social standing, his fortune and his talent. The typical naturalistic plot of the long slow slide allows Norris to depict settings and characters from top to bottom of the social scale of pre-earthquake San Francisco, from Nob Hill to the Barbary Coast. Several key scenes are set in restaurants with private rooms, a favourite contact zone for the city's fashionable sporting young men and the demi-monde of 'fast' girls. But as his descent accelerates we pass through cheap boarding-houses and bars and gambling halls, until at last the homeless Vandover is reduced to swabbing out filthy rental houses as a part-time worker for his former Harvard room-mate, who is now a wealthy real-estate lord.

Yet this typical Naturalistic plot also incorporates Norris's treatment of the werewolf legend. Vandover's temptation to vice is described as a beast within him that 'awoke and stirred'.[62] The beast may seem at first a moralistic figure of speech, but as Vandover's vice increases the beast grows and assumes physical control. Eventually Vandover suffers fits, in which he walks on his hands and knees, and snaps and snarls and howls. His doctor diagnoses 'lycanthropy', a neurological condition in which a person may mimic animal behaviour. Vandover's bizarre fits link the idea of atavism with the folk belief in the werewolf and an actual clinical condition, which here we are to understand is triggered by the venereal disease that has attacked his nervous system and also destroyed the coordination needed for him to practise his art.

The reader of *Vandover and the Brute* probably will finish it filled with awe, revulsion and dread. The world is less safe, and so are we, than we had hoped. Weakness, not evil, is punished. We know what morality is, and what ought to work; but it doesn't. The forces of justice do not rule here. The brute rules.

The monster of Whilomville

Stephen Crane's world is also cold, ironic and unforgiving. One of his poems, in fact, has the refrain 'God is cold'. His long story 'The Monster' is an account of the ways society expels the 'other', and anticipates in this respect Franz Kafka's 'The Metamorphosis' (1915). The central ironies of this story are that the monster of the title is acknowledged to be a hero, and that, because he is African

American, he is already seen as other, even before he loses his face and his sanity.

Dr Trescott's coachman, Henry Johnson, rushes into the burning Trescott home to rescue the doctor's little boy. He is trapped in the doctor's laboratory, where bottles of chemicals burn and burst with colours like gems or flowers. When he falls, Johnson is burned in a scene of surreal, horrifying beauty:

> ... a ruby-red snake-like thing poured its thick length out upon the top of the old desk. It coiled and hesitated, and then began to swim a languorous way down the mahogany slant. At the angle it waved its sizzling molten head to and fro over the closed eyes of the man beneath it. Then, in a moment, it moved again, and the red snake flowed directly down into Johnson's upturned face.[63]

The boy, who had been wrapped in a blanket by Johnson, survives, almost unharmed. But his rescuer lingers near death, his face eaten and mind destroyed by the burning chemical serpent. Dr Trescott's neighbour and friend, Judge Hagenthorpe, cogently predicts the outcome if heroic medical efforts save the coachman's life: 'He will be your creation, you understand. He is purely your creation. Nature has very evidently given him up. He is dead. You are restoring him to life. You are making him, and he will be a monster, with no mind.'[64]

The doctor, then, like Victor Frankenstein, must assume responsibility for his creature. With no face, Henry's one-eyed blank appearance horrifies everyone who looks on him, and even wrapping his head in a hood or mask fails to make him less frightening. When Henry wanders from confinement, he terrifies a little girl. Though the leaders of the community do not desert Dr Trescott, public sentiment turns against him, his patients leave him, the women of Whilomville no longer call on his wife, and he, like his monster, becomes a social outcast.

'The Monster' offers a model or test case of society's response to difference, the way it constructs the monster or freak, or the racial other. Henry, with his blank or shrouded features, provokes a response like that of the villagers in Hawthorne's 'The Minister's Black Veil', and becomes an object of their fears and anxieties. As a black man, of course, Henry was already at risk of rejection, but the citizens of Whilomville had accepted him through familiarity and knowledge of his role as Dr Trescott's coachman. After his face is burned away, the townspeople, though understanding rationally that he is still Henry Johnson, begin to project upon him their racial stereotypes. His frightening of a little girl provokes a near riot outside the jail where he is taken, as the townspeople begin to re-enact the pattern of lynch law that disgraced the nation in the 1890s.

Henry is just an invalid without a face. The monster is not, finally, Dr Trescott's creation, but the embodied fears of Whilomville, a town like ours.

Jack London and the Gothic

Jack London produced some fifty books and nearly two hundred short stories in his brief, intense career. One of the most popular of American authors internationally, he is still underrated at home, and usually represented in classrooms by two or three endlessly anthologized tales. But London was an inventive and rapidly evolving writer, who practised in many forms and traditions, and who made notable contributions to American Gothic.

Jack London was a scientific materialist who had read Herbert Spencer with attention. He was not very interested in the supernatural, though there was a mystic side to his character that would respond, late in his life, to the writings of Carl Jung. He found the popular occultism of Spiritualism and its associated fads, like palm-reading, distasteful and embarrassing. He had seen enough of this subculture while he was growing up in Oakland. The Bay Area's shabby social strata of frauds and fakes, which was rather affectionately recalled by London's older contemporary Gelett Burgess in his novel *The Heart Line* (1907), found its way into London's childhood home, as his mother was a devotee of the seance.[65] As a writer – and all experience is simply material for a writer – London would draw on this background for the character of the medium Mrs Grantly in 'Planchette' (1906), a competent Gothic tale about the revenge of a dead father upon his daughter's lover. He would use the idea of the transmigration of souls as the premise behind *The Star Rover* (1915), whose hero, Darrell Standing, while straitjacketed as a prisoner in San Quentin, enters a trance state that enables him to relive the previous lives of his soul. However, his novel *The Sea-Wolf*, the novella *The Scarlet Plague* and his short story 'The Red One' may illustrate the range of London's accomplishments in the Gothic. In these works, and others, the Gothic uncanny is found in human psychology and the material world, though London may extend the material world into the future, or include in it objects from space.

The Sea-Wolf (1904) is a flawed but challenging work, and London's most notable experiment in the Gothic-naturalist hybrid. As a sea Gothic, *The Sea-Wolf* is in the tradition of Poe's *The Narrative of Arthur Gordon Pym* and Melville's *Moby-Dick*. London, in fact, was one of the few writers (or readers, for that matter) at the turn of the twentieth century who still esteemed his fellow sailor-author Melville, then at the nadir of his reputation. London's Wolf Larsen may be a naturalistic *über*-dog, like Dreiser's caveman in a business suit, Frank Cowperwood, or London's own triumphant Buck, but he is also a Gothic hero-villain who identifies himself with the Satan of John Milton's *Paradise Lost*, and who owes something as well to Melville's grand ungodly god-like man, Captain Ahab.

Both naturalism and the Gothic are present from the beginning of the novel, when the ferry carrying Humphrey Van Weyden across San Francisco Bay collides with a tramp steamer. In an instant Humphrey's comfortable world and his mental assurance collapse, as he listens to the screaming of women passengers:

> I remember the scene impelled me to sudden laughter, and in the next instant I realized I was becoming hysterical myself, for these were women of my own kind, like my mother and sisters, with the fear of death upon them and unwilling to die. And I remember that the sounds they made reminded me of the squealing of pigs under the knife of the butcher, and I was struck with horror at the vividness of the analogy ... They wanted to live, they were helpless, like rats in a trap, and they screamed.[66]

This is textbook naturalism, with its insistent comparison of humans and animals and the ubiquitous naturalistic metaphor of the trap. But we are also told that Humphrey, a literary critic, has recently published an essay on Poe, and this reference may nudge us to remember the Gothic master's account of nightmare sea-voyages, as well as his stories of dying women told by hysterical narrators.

Humphrey is swept out to sea by the tide, and rescued by Wolf Larsen, captain of the *Ghost*. There his initiation into the law of club and fang begins.

Wolf Larsen is one of London's several attempts to envision a human equivalent to his wonder-dog Buck, as he is at the end of *The Call of the Wild* (1903), leader of a wolf pack, feared and honoured by the Yeehat Indians as the 'ghost dog'. Like Buck, Wolf Larsen can draw on both ends of the evolutionary scale: highly evolved and intelligent, he nonetheless has the elemental strength and energy of his primitive forebears. Wolf is an amoral, charismatic figure who dominates Humphrey as he does his crew. He is capable of cruelty, even savagery, but Humphrey reaches a qualified admiration, even love, for his rescuer, captor and mentor.

The novel becomes complicated and, most readers feel, weakened, when the *Ghost* rescues Maud Brewster, a woman of Humphrey's 'own kind', and a poet. The threat of rape hangs over Maud while she is on the *Ghost*, while at the same time Maud and Humphrey behave like potentially rebellious siblings with a dominating father. There is a psychological undercurrent of incest in the relationship of Humphrey and Maud, and it is perhaps appropriate that the pair occupy primly separate huts after they are stranded on an island together.

Wolf's decline into paralysis and death at the end, while Humphrey and Maud (vampire-like) grow in strength, has always seemed an arbitrary intervention of the author in his plot. His brain tumour may be a stand-in for the unmentionable disease that haunted the Victorian period. Wolf Larsen is often seen as London's version of the Nietzschean *übermensch*, and Nietzsche himself, notoriously, had died a scant six years before the publication of *The Sea-Wolf*, after a period of paralysis believed to have been caused by syphilis.

Another disease drives the plot of *The Scarlet Plague* (1915). An incurable epidemic sweeps the country, leaving only a handful of survivors, who unaccountably are immune. The novel is set in California, and early in the story a group of 400, university faculty members and their families, seal themselves with supplies in the Chemistry Building, hoping to escape infection. The novel, as this episode reveals, looks back to Edgar Allan Poe's 'The Masque of the Red Death'. But it is also the first in the tradition of the post-apocalypse novel, a tradition that would include Stephen King's recent *The Cell* (2006) and Cormac McCarthy's *The Road* (2006). The story of what happens when civilization ends has always been especially appealing in California, whose collective imagination seems to swerve between visions of utopia and dystopian collapse, and *The Scarlet Plague* anticipates such golden-state works as Matheson's *I Am Legend* (1954) and its film adaptation, *The Omega Man* (1971), Aldous Huxley's *Ape and Essence* (1948), Ursula K. Le Guin's *Always Coming Home* (1985), Carolyn See's *Golden Days* (1987) and Octavia Bulter's *Parable of the Sower* (1993).

As in Poe's story, the Red Death enters the building, and the barricaded scholars and their families begin to succumb. The narrator and protagonist of *The Scarlet Plague*, James Howard Smith, describes how he leaves Berkeley, one of a group of now forty-seven survivors, fleeing the burning city in a caravan of automobiles. In a few days Smith, somehow immune, is alone. It is the year 2013, and as far as Smith can tell, he is the last man on earth. After three years of living alone on the supplies of the hotel in Yosemite Valley, he wanders back to the coast and finds a handful of survivors living a tribal life, the old social order now inverted, the wife of an industrialist now forcibly mated to her former chauffeur.

The Scarlet Plague is narrated in 2073, decades after civilization's collapse, in response to a group of boys who ask Smith to 'tell us about the Red Death', and that long ago time of cities and electricity, which to them is fabulous, not really to be believed.[67] In a time of tribal life, of herding goats and sheep and living in huts, Smith sees only loss. A Berkeley professor – a type London first introduced to American literature – he still longs for the privilege, libraries and mayonnaise of his lost America. Yet the final scene of the novel – with wild horses playing in the surf at sunset, an image worthy of a Robinson Jeffers poem – suggests that the cataclysm may bring with it renewal as well as loss.

London's 'The Red One' (1916) is a horrifying adventure story set in Melanesia that is also a 'first contact' science-fiction tale. Written in the last year of his life and published posthumously, it is rich with biblical, literary and mythological allusions, and apparently reflects London's recent reading of Sigmund Freud and Carl Jung.[68]

The story also references Robert Browning's 1855 surreal poem 'Childe Roland to the Dark Tower Came', and like it is the narrative of a dubious quest through a hostile and ugly landscape.[69] London's protagonist, Bassett, is a naturalist exploring the beach of the Melanesian island of Guadalcanal when he hears a beautiful tone from the island's interior. Like a sailor from Greek mythology seduced by the Sirens' song, he strikes into the interior in search of the sound's origin. Many weeks later Bassett is in the grassy interior of the island, but is racked with disease, and living among cannibals. He had fought his way through the jungle, surviving attacks of hostile warriors only because of his ten-gauge shotgun. He remains alive now only because of the care of a repulsive native woman and a 'devil doctor'.

The beautiful sound continues to toll from the interior of the island, and Bassett, though slowly dying of fever, is still drawn to it. It is produced, he learns from the shaman, by something called The Red One, among other names, but it is a holy thing and Bassett is forbidden to see it. However, he visits it twice, first by bribing his infatuated native protector, Balatta, with an offer of marriage, then by offering the devil doctor the opportunity to cut off his head as an offering to the holy object, which is a red sphere, 200 feet in diameter, apparently left by space aliens.

Since the sphere never reveals its secrets, 'The Red One' is a truly ambiguous tale, and has engendered many interpretations. One approach would see it as a restatement of the 'Romantic agony' discussed in chapter 1. London's tale records disgust with the mutable world. Nature is presented here in Hobbesian terms, and life is short, nasty and brutish. Love is reduced to sex in its most repellent aspect in Balatta. The Red One, in contrast, is beautiful and apparently imperishable. It calls with its lovely sound, and allows Bassett to approach, and even ring its surface with his knife. But, though the glowing sphere may be packed with wisdom and truth from the stars, he cannot enter it, cannot obtain what is within or share in its perfection. Bassett, then, represents the scientist, artist or other seeker of the good, the true and the beautiful, who has a glimpse of what is sought, but can never attain it, except perhaps in death.

Summing up a tradition: Edith Wharton and Charlotte Perkins Gilman

The life of Jack London, former child cannery worker, teen age oyster pirate, hobo and true Westerner, could hardly have been more different from that of Edith Wharton. An aristocrat in all but title, first cousin of President Theodore Roosevelt, Wharton lived much of her adult life on her estates in France and, sharing the certainties of Old New York, saw no point in anything west of the Hudson River, and never went there. Yet, demonstrating the power of genre, their Gothic works have much in common. Wharton, like London, wrote Gothic tales, and novels that blend naturalism and the Gothic, and we find this amalgam in some of her most powerful works. She was deeply read in the works of her predecessors, and often in dialogue with them, so that much of her Gothic fiction can be seen as a summing up and amending of the tradition of Irving and Hawthorne.

Wharton saw the ghost story as a minor form, but ghost stories are enmeshed with her own early life. In 'An Autobiographical Postscript' to *The Ghost Stories of Edith Wharton*, the author recalls a near fatal typhoid infection when she was nine years old. When she began to recover, her parents, in spite of their general disapproval of 'silly books', gave her a book to amuse herself. The volume contained 'tales of robbers and ghosts', and the terror of the stories induced 'a serious relapse' in the young patient.[70] Wharton records that for the next seven or eight years she lived in a state of chronic terror. The threshold of her home was the site of a particular fear: she could not tolerate waiting for the door to be unlocked, since 'It' might catch her there before she could enter. Until she was twenty-seven or twenty-eight, Wharton claimed, she could not sleep in a 'room with a book containing a ghost story', and 'frequently had to burn books of this kind, because it frightened me to know that they were downstairs in the library'! [71]

Other clues to the origins of Wharton's Gothic imagination also involve books and libraries. As a small child, not yet able to read, little Edith Jones would walk back and forth carrying a book, pretending to read, but actually making up stories of her own. She already understood the disapproval of her parents for frivolous literature, but the book she carried was by Washington Irving, a friend of the Jones family and, as a member of their social class, exempt from their general condescension toward the profession of letters. Later, Edith would share her father's library as a refuge, and was allowed to read as she liked, though she continued to feel the family's disapproval of fiction. [72]

Many readers have noted the importance of library scenes in Wharton's fiction, and have speculated about their possible implications for her relationship with her father, who died while the author was in her teens. Certainly, the ghost story 'Mr Jones' (1928), in which the antagonist is a ghost with the same name as Wharton's father, begs for an autobiographical reading. The title character, the head butler of an aristocratic British family, was responsible, in the nineteenth century, for keeping the lord's young wife a virtual prisoner. She was deaf and dumb, and could express herself only by writing letters. In the present, the early twentieth century, the ghost of Mr Jones still exercises tyrannical authority, which is even worse than when he was alive, because, as a servant explains, since he is dead, he cannot be contradicted. Mr Jones conceals important documents that contain family secrets (a frequent Gothic pattern), and even kills a disobedient servant, but he is challenged, as the story ends, by the family's new heir, the modern young woman, Lady Jane.

Wharton's New England suite

In a group of novellas and stories set in New England, Wharton explored issues of gender and American cultural and narrative traditions, often offering oblique references to her own life. Not surprisingly, one of her novellas describes a young librarian trapped in her library.

Edith Wharton drew her vision of Gothic New England from her reading and from observation of the countryside and villages around her estate in the Berkshires. This territory is her fictional kingdom, with towns and villages (like Starkfield) whose names reappear from one text to another. As in nearly all New England Gothic, local traditions of witchcraft are in evidence here, and strange events and family horrors that are kept guarded from outside eyes. In 'Bewitched' (1925), a late revisiting of this landscape, we find a use of the regional tradition of vampirism, which seems based on the long miserable tuberculosis epidemic that gripped New England through the nineteenth century.[73] In this story Sylvester Brand must track and destroy his own dead daughter, who has returned to the living world and now draws the life from her former sweetheart, Saul Rutledge. But the emotional core of the story is less in the hunting of the vampire than in the reflections of the point-of-view character, Orrin Bosworth, a young man who has spent time in larger towns (like Starkfield) and has some sense of the world outside this remote outpost. He is a normative character, that typical Gothic device, and accepts the secular and rational outlook probably shared by the reader. But his involvement in the case of Brand's revenant daughter strips away his modernity and forces him to remember episodes of his earlier life, such as being taken to visit a mad aunt who was kept behind bars, and the horrifying moment when the mad woman kills a canary brought to her as a gift. He was cautioned by his mother never to tell anyone about the caged aunt.

> He remembered the scene now, with its deep fringe of mystery, secrecy and rumor. It seemed related to a great many other things below the surface of his thoughts, things which stole up anew, making him feel that all the old people he had known, and who 'believed in those things', might after all be right.[74]

In this remote place Christianity is but a thin veneer over the 'old ways'. 'Deacon Hibben believed' in the old ways, Bosworth realizes;[75] that is why he has been summoned by Rutledge's wife to destroy her rival, the vampire Ora Brand. But in this cold and inbred community, so 'far away from humanity',[76] even the 'normal people', like Mrs Rutledge, with her marble-like eyelids, seem little better than zombies.

In 'Bewitched', as in her other New England Gothic works, Wharton pays tribute to Nathaniel Hawthorne, her great predecessor. The name Brand here recalls Hawthorne's 'Ethan Brand', and Deacon Hibben recalls both Hawthorne's Deacon Gookin in 'Young Goodman Brown' and Mistress Hibbins from *The Scarlet Letter*. The influence of Hawthorne is even more apparent in her pair of New England Gothic novellas, *Ethan Frome* (1911) and *Summer* (1917).

Ethan Frome begins with a visitor, the narrator, stumbling on to a mystery surrounding an enigmatic, powerful, solitary person – in Melville's terms, an 'isolato'.[77] Frome is easily the most impressive man in Starkfield, though he is maimed, branded with a scar on his forehead, and walks with a limp 'like the jerk of a chain'.[78] The novella is the answer to the narrator's question, 'how could any combination of obstacles have hindered the flight of a man like Ethan Frome?'[79]

The question is phrased in naturalistic terms, and the novel indeed inventories many forces, beginning with the brutal weather that leaves the inhabitants like the survivors of a siege at the end of each winter. New England's long-declining rural economy also has trapped subsistence farmers like Frome, whose family tried to run a local sawmill as well. The failing fortunes of the Fromes were accelerated by the senile extravagances of his father, and by his mother's last illness. We observe Ethan's futile struggles against narrowing options, and fate seems to mock his plans to escape Starkfield for a new life with Mattie. The naturalistic plot of the long slow slide is compressed in this novella into a few weeks. It is accelerated by an apparently trivial event, the breaking of the red glass pickle-dish, and gathers momentum into the rush down the hill on the sled, with an oak tree waiting at the bottom.

The story's naturalistic plot outline does not account for its uncanny power, however. At the centre of the story's weirdness, like a spider in her web, is Ethan's wife, Zenobia (Zeena). Her presence is in a literal sense *unheimlich*: when she leaves the Frome house, 'it was surprising what a homelike look the mere fact of Zeena's absence gave it'.[80] Zenobia replaces the safe and familiar sense of home with her dark cold negative energy. Zenobia is a succubus or vampire. While she had appeared a 'genius of health'[81] when she came to nurse Ethan's mother, in fact she draws strength from the illnesses of others. She, not the New England weather, is the source of the numbing cold that permeates the novella. She is Dame Van Winkle with evil power.

However, it is reasonable to object that this Zenobia is the vision of the narrator, who has extrapolated the story of Zeena, Mattie and Ethan from mere scraps of information provided by Mrs Hale and Harmon Gow, his local informants. The rest is his invention. There is almost no real evidence in the frame for the sad, tentative love affair of Ethan and Mattie, none at all for the key scene of the novel, their night alone when Zeena goes to Bettsbridge to consult her doctor. The narrator's imagination suffuses the scene with its strange emotions. The breaking of the red pickle-dish by the cat, Zeena's familiar spirit, is a stand-in for the sexual event that did not occur, Mattie's loss of virginity, and at the same time reduces Matt and Ethan to frightened children fearing the wrath of their mother at a misdeed. As in the rebellion of Humphrey and Maud in *The Sea Wolf*, the emotions of the scene suggest the Gothic inappropriate family unit, the lovers assuming the role of siblings conspiring against a dominating parent.

The dark fear of *Ethan Frome*, the narrator's fear, is that an appealing young woman ensnares a man, then transforms herself into a witch and destroys him. The final horror of the novella occurs when the narrator finally steps through the doorway of Ethan's house and beholds Mattie's 'bright witch-like stare'.[82] In *Summer*, apparently envisioned as a counterbalance to the earlier novella,[83] the fear men have of women is answered by the fear women have of men.

Summer, like *Ethan Frome*, is filled with Hawthorne-like touches, especially the familiar patterns of looking through windows and of threshold crossings.[84] Thus *Summer* begins, as do almost all of Hawthorne's narratives, with the protagonist stepping through a door. Charity Royal walks out of the red house, looks up the street, sees a handsome young stranger in city clothes, and murmurs her first words in the novella, 'How I hate everything!'[85]

This brilliantly economical beginning contains, as in an egg, the entire plot of the novel to follow, which will concern the attempts of the bitter adolescent girl to escape her galling life. She hates her life in the red house, and hates her guardian, Mr Royal. She hates her job as a librarian. Inevitably, her discontent and longing for escape from the constraints of her provincial life will lead to an affair with that handsome young stranger in city clothes we see walking down the street of her village, and the trap of her pregnancy. It leads to her flight up the Mountain in search of her degenerate relatives, a futile journey that is the nightmare inversion of 'Rip Van Winkle'. And it leads to her marriage to Mr Royal.

The ending of *Summer* has produced sharply different readings, even among feminist critics. Wharton was justly proud of Mr Royal: 'Of course *he's* the book', she exclaimed to a friend.[86] As a complex Gothic villain-hero, he is a figure of power and menace. The most painful scene of the book may be the episode at the Fourth of July picnic in which Royal, drunk and in the company of the prostitute Julia, discovers Charity with Harney and publicly denounces her as a whore. This scene reveals everything that that is hateful about Royal for Charity. He is a stereotypical dirty old man, a figure of sexual menace, exercising unjust power over her, blocking her chances for happiness and escape at every turn. Yet there is another side to Royal, which Charity begins understand at the other holiday of the summer, North Dormer's Old Home celebration. This ceremony is a time of revelation for Charity. She sees Harney seated with her rival, his fiancée from the city. Watching Royal give a speech to the admiring townspeople, she understands for the first time that he is a powerful and attractive man. Most dramatically, Charity faints and falls from her chair, an episode attributed to the heat, but which we, and Charity, understand as the first sign of her pregnancy.

At the novella's conclusion, 'all the dark spirits' that had overtaken Royal at times 'had gone out of him'.[87] He is kindly and protective of her in every way; he understands that Charity is pregnant, and is tacitly willing to accept her child. He does not impose himself on her during their wedding night. The conclusion seems like that of *Jane Eyre*, Royal, like Mr Rochester, transformed from a monster into a suitable husband. Thus one reading of *Summer* sees it as a female initiation story, in which, simply, Charity has grown up, set aside the impossible adolescent dreams represented by Harney, and accepted her adult role and responsibilities.[88]

Another reading is possible, however, one that takes account of the queasiness many will feel at this ending. Charity, one might assert, is simply crushed, passively accepting the only option remaining for her. In a telling image, an impulse to flee near the end is described as 'only the lift of a broken wing'.[89] The red house to which she returns is the trap she has failed to escape. Royal may appear kindly, and in many ways is an admirable man, but, psychologically, Charity has married her father. In this interpretation, *Summer* is not the softer Gothic of *Jane Eyre*, but as bitter a fable of defeat as *Ethan Frome*, a dark tale of how one gender wages war against and destroys the other.

Charlotte Perkins Gilman, who was a grand-niece of Harriet Beecher Stowe, also told of women silenced and broken. Her 1891 story 'The Giant Wisteria' is a miniature rewriting of Hawthorne's *The Scarlet Letter*. Gilman's Hester figure is allowed only eleven words at the beginning of the story: 'Give me my child, mother, and then I will be quiet!'[90] She is silenced without being allowed to see her baby. We learn that she has borne this child out of wedlock, and that she is to be locked in her room by her stern Puritan family until she consents to marry a cousin and be returned to England. Her unacknowledged baby must be raised as an orphan by the town. We do not even learn the name of this minimalist tragic heroine, whose only identifying mark is the carnelian cross she wears about her neck: a glancing allusion to Hester Prynne's scarlet letter.

The story then shifts to Gilman's own time. Several young couples are vacationing together in coastal New England and rent an old house that they delight in imagining to be haunted. And so it is. During their first night in the house, each dreams of a sad young woman with a red cross. The following day they find a baby in the bucket of the well in the cellar, preserved by the cold mineral water, while workman repairing the porch find a skeleton with a carnelian cross around its neck. We are left to imagine the defiance and courage of the imprisoned woman, and the possible acts that might have led to the deaths of mother and child.

Gilman's most celebrated story, 'The Yellow Wallpaper' (1892), is based on an incident of the author's life that has become a

---

touchstone of feminist history and theory. Gilman suffered from a mental illness that probably would be diagnosed today as depression. She sought treating the most famous and respected American clinical psychologist of the day, S. Weir Mitchell, who specialized in treatment of 'hysterical' disorders of prosperous desperate housewives. (Hysteria was thought to be a disease peculiar to women, as its Greek root, referring to the womb, indicates.) Mitchell was a novelist himself, but had little sympathy for the creative lives of women. He subscribed to conventional notions of the proper behaviour for women, who were to find the outlet for all their energies in the domestic duties of wife and mother. His treatment, enforced bed-rest and overeating, reduced his patients to dependency and passivity. The prescription he wrote for Charlotte Perkins Gilman has earned him the enduring contempt of thinking women everywhere: 'Live as domestic a life as possible. Have your child with you all the time . . . Lie down an hour after each meal. Have but two hours' intellectual life a day. And never touch pen, brush, or pencil as long as you live'.[91] After enduring several months of this regimen, Gilman threw over the treatment and, anticipating generations of women after her, moved to California, divorced her husband and began anew.

'The Yellow Wallpaper' (1892), Gilman's most reprinted story, is based on the author's experience as a mental patient. The story is justly celebrated, for it extends the mad-narrator experiments of John Neal and Poe, while anticipating such twentieth-century women's narratives about mental illness as Sylvia Plath's *The Bell Jar* (1963), Joan Didion's *Play It as It Lays* (1970), and *To The Is-land* (1982), by New Zealand author Janet Frame. Gilman's nameless first-person narrator[92] is both the wife and sister of clinical psychologists who follow the system of S. Weir Mitchell. With this story, the clinical psychologist replaces earlier versions of the evil doctor, and joins the schoolteacher and the judge as guardians of authority and patriarchy, the sinister destroyers of freedom and creativity.

Gilman's narrator tells a haunted house story. She is taken to a long-abandoned country house that has something 'queer'[93] about it, and that has 'hedges and walls and gates that lock'.[94] There she is expected to recover from hysteria. Her sickroom has a bed bolted to the floor, barred windows and rings fastened to the wall. These details are explained by the room's past duty as children's quarters and as an exercise room, but could as easily signify its function as a place of torture, for so it will be for the narrator. The tortures are boredom, her husband's smug incomprehension, and the ugliness of the room's patterned yellow wallpaper. (The narrator's fixation on irritating details of her surroundings will be psychologically credible to anyone who has spent time in a sickroom.) As her personality shatters into fragments, she becomes convinced that another woman is 'shaking' the barred pattern of the wallpaper and trying to escape. By the story's end, the narrator has become that other woman. Her madness, like her obsessive writing (another patterning on paper), is a sign of her rebellion against the mind-forged manacles that her culture has imposed upon her.

The theme of women and madness has been significant in literature in English since Mr Rochester locked his first wife, Bertha, in the upper room of his mansion, in *Jane Eyre*. Gilman takes that theme and reframes it in terms of modern psychology in a way that would seem relevant through the twentieth century and beyond.

3

American Gothic and Modernism

ॐ

Modernism, the dominant aesthetic of the middle twentieth century, began as an avant-garde movement in the years before the First World War. It produced its major defining works in the 1920s, and had hardened into orthodoxy by the 1950s.

These were turbulent decades for the United States, which escaped the worst devastation of the 'Great War' and entered a period of exuberance and prosperity (though unevenly distributed), before the bleak disillusionment of the Great Depression. The cataclysm of the Second World War changed the United States profoundly. By the 1950s the nation was the most prosperous and powerful country in the world, though its confidence was shadowed by the threat of new enemies, and paranoia about spies and citizens who might harbour 'un-American' beliefs.

While the division of history into eras is always arbitrary, we may see the 1960s as ending the post-war period and beginning something loosely defined as a post-Modern age. Certainly, most Americans who lived through the Sixties saw the decade as one of major upheaval. The markers of change were the assassinations of John F. Kennedy and his brother Robert, and of Martin Luther King Jr., the interminable war in Vietnam, the emergence of new ideas in music and film and in popular culture generally, and the growing influence of the 'Boomers', the generation born between 1946 and 1964. Chapter 4 will discuss the period from the Sixties to the present.

The Gothic, adaptive as always, provided some of its most innovative works in the Age of Modernism, both in literature and in the new medium of film. As before, it offered a counter-reading to the American narrative.

As might be expected in an increasingly secular age, there was little of the supernatural in most works of Gothic modernism. Few educated people in the twentieth century, or now, would admit to a belief in ghosts. Psychoanalysis had located the source of most of our fears in our own subconscious, and indeed some regard the major writings of Sigmund Freud as among the great Gothic works of the century. There are few literal spectres in the novels and stories of William Faulkner, for example, though his old Southern mansions are nonetheless haunted, and their inhabitants nonetheless cursed.

Ghosts, witches and vampires do not disappear entirely in the period of modernism, however. Ellen Glasgow (1873–1945), for example, who began her long career in the nineteenth century, continued the tradition of James and Wharton of writing ghost stories as a minor but significant part of a diverse shelf of work. Her story 'The Shadowy Third' (1923) is a psychologically complex story involving the ghost of a murdered child. Glasgow also wrote Southern Gothic without supernatural elements, such as her story 'Jordan's End', about an isolated rural family cursed with a genetic strain of madness.

The supernatural also flourished in the work of marginalized writers, as well as in mass-market products such as B-grade movies and comic books. H. P. Lovecraft continued the tradition of the weird tale he inherited from Chambers, Bierce and Poe. Lovecraft's stories, recently elevated in critical esteem, anticipate a revival of the occult in literature and film that began in the 1960s and 1970s. Movies about Frankenstein and Dracula, made in the 1930s and 1940s, reappeared on the new televisions of the 1950s, and were watched by a generation of post-war children who were also, often without the knowledge of their parents, reading horror comic books. These exuberant if trashy products of popular culture would shape the sensibilities of many artists of the late twentieth century and the next, and their audiences.

Southern Gothic and Modernism

The American South, with its legacy of profound social and economic problems, became a major focus and source of American literature in the twentieth century, and the principal region of American Gothic. The South had a great burden of history and myth, and a treasury of stories to tell, many of them twisted and tragic. Among the writers who shaped these stories to Gothic effect were William Faulkner (1897–1962), Eudora Welty (1909–2001), Flannery O'Connor (1915–64) and Carson McCullers (1917–67).

No American writer has excelled William Faulkner in his evocation of Southern Gothic. Faulkner invented his mythical kingdom of Yoknapatawpha County and peopled it with intermingling lines of Chickasaw, black and white families, up and down the social scale, and portraying its evolution from the time of the earliest white settlement to the 1950s. His Compsons, Sutpens, Sartorises, Griersons and McCaslins, the failed dynasties of the old ascendancy, were all unwitting builders of haunted houses.

Faulkner's story 'A Rose for Emily' (1930) centres on the old Grierson house in Jefferson, the county seat, and what was found there after the death of Miss Emily, the last of her line. Told in the first-person plural voice, the story begins with the death of the elderly Miss Emily as it was apprehended by the townspeople. Thus, 'we' recall the details of Emily's long life: her difficult relationship with her father, her refusal to accept his death, her courtship by the outsider Homer Barron and his disappearance, her difficulties with the town elders about her taxes and over a bad smell around her house, and her long and lonely passage into old age.

At the story's end, after Emily's funeral, a group of townspeople force the door to an upstairs bedroom of the Grierson house. The point of view, representing the collective vision of the group, acts like a movie camera panning over the details of the room, ending at last as 'we' gaze at the bed. In true horror-movie fashion, a disgusting image seems to end the narrative, but it is followed by yet another shock, equally revolting in its implications.

'A Rose for Emily' shows Faulkner's fusion of Southern Gothic themes and modernist narrative techniques. The reclusive Emily is a convincing case of psychological pathology.[1] Her mental illness, manifesting itself in a stubborn refusal to acknowledge change, time or loss, is understandable in terms of her life and her relationship with her father. It is also linked to her social class, which had lost wealth and land with the defeat of the Confederacy, and saw its power pass to rising and often unscrupulous entrepreneurs, represented elsewhere in the Yoknapatawpha saga by the Snopes family. Like Miss Emily, many Southerners clung to memories of the past, and to faded symbols of the dead. She is an extreme example of a common theme, in a culture that was collectively haunted.

The narrative technique of 'A Rose for Emily' seems casual and conversational, but is calculated to release key bits of information that come together with a snap and a shock at the conclusion. The story, in fact, is a good example of the modernist devices of which Faulkner was a master.

During the period of realism, the most significant technical experiments in fiction concerned narrative technique, especially the use of unreliable narrators. As we have seen (with James's *The Turn of the Screw*, for example), Gothic narratives afford memorable instances of this innovation. In the period of modernism, innovation in narrative voice was joined to experiments with chronology. The assumption that a story must begin at the beginning and move straight ahead to its conclusion was set aside, as such early modernists as Joseph Conrad and Ford Madox Ford broke time into fragments and reordered their narratives according to other principles. As in 'A Rose for Emily', this technique can simulate the natural flow of talk and memory ('stream of consciousness'), with one event or image suggesting another. It thus makes possible striking or ironic juxtapositions rendered in the way that we naturally think and remember, rather than in the rigid movement of clocks and calendars.

Faulkner's novels often combine multiple points of view with fragmented chronology. The reader is asked to reconstruct complex family histories that display in miniature the burden of Southern history, and often the difficult relationship of black and white Southerners. In *The Sound and the Fury* (1929) Faulkner presents the story of the Compsons, a family, like many of the old ascendancy, now living in the kind of decaying plantation house that was a feature of the Southern landscape and principal site of the Southern Gothic. In the novel's present, the 1920s, the Compson plantation has been sold away in parcels, the last being sacrificed in 1910 so that the most promising son, Quentin, might attend Harvard. The last of the Compsons live attended by a few servants, who are the descendants of the family's slaves.

The narrative of the last thirty years of the Compsons' decline is presented in four sections, one objective, three filtered through the minds of the Compson sons, Benjamin, Jason and Quentin (on the last day of his life in 1910). Since Benjamin is mentally retarded, has no sense of past or present, and cannot organize his memories, the Benjy section is pure stream of consciousness, fragments of memory linked by association, and is one of the remarkable achievements of American prose. Though he is an idiot, Benjamin's swirling memories, like torn fragments of a photo album, are trustworthy, not distorted by passion or bias, as are those of the brilliant but disturbed Quentin, or the amoral, malicious, yet often sardonically funny Jason.

But the central character of *The Sound and The Fury* is the sister, Candace (Caddy), who has no section of her own. Seen only in the memories of her brothers, she is both victim and perpetuator of the Compson family decline. A Gothic heroine, Caddy escapes her haunted mansion at a terrible price. Her promiscuity torments Quentin and leads to his suicide at Harvard. The daughter she leaves behind, also named Quentin, is a mean-spirited and vacuous creature compounded of all the worst traits of the degenerating Compsons.

Absalom, Absalom! (1936) is the story of another failed Yoknapatawpha dynasty, that of Thomas Sutpen, and is indeed one of the finest of Gothic novels, without qualification. It is linked to *The Sound and the Fury*, since its principal narrator is Quentin Compson (the male Quentin, not his niece), and some crucial information about Sutpen comes from Compson family lore. If we know of Quentin's obsession with his sister Caddy's honour, we understand his fascination with the story of Henry and Judith Sutpen. However, *Absalom, Absalom!* is a free standing novel, not a sequel, and can be read and appreciated without knowledge of the earlier work.

Like Caddy Compson, the complex villain-hero Thomas Sutpen is seen at a distance, in the memories of others. Sutpen died before Quentin's birth, but Quentin has heard, all his life, stories of the master of Sutpen's Hundred. When Quentin's Canadian room-mate Shreve challenges him to tell a story that would explain the South, it the story of the House of Sutpen that he tells. The story that he begins is not yet complete in his own mind. As the story moves forward, Quentin and Shreve are like two players assembling a difficult jigsaw puzzle, and their interchanges are a process of discovery for both, and for the reader. Again and again we circle the career of Thomas Sutpen, and revise our judgement as new bits of information are brought to light.

A child of poor mountain people who migrated to the Tidewater, the boy Sutpen was once sent to a plantation house on an errand by his father, but was turned away from the front door by the liveried servant. Thus, going off into the woods to think about it (as Huck Finn might have done), Sutpen conceived his 'design' of founding a rich dynasty himself, of being the entitled man in the mansion, not the child turned away. In pursuit of his destiny, Sutpen journeys as a young man to Haiti and marries into a wealthy French planter family. However, he 'sets aside' this first marriage when he learns that his wife has a drop of African heritage, and that consequently their infant son is not suitable for the design cast in the social model of the American South.

To a contemporary such as his sister-in-law Miss Rosa (who survives in the novel's present), Sutpen was simply a demon, a destructive force whose motives – in forbidding his daughter's wedding, for example – are unfathomable. Quentin's reading of the flawed patriarch is more informed and nuanced. In a startling insight, he suggests that Sutpen's problem was 'innocence'.[2] We have seen before (as in Charles Brockden Brown's *Arthur Mervyn*) that the innocent hero is a distinctly American character-type and that his apparent moral purity can be destructive. Sutpen is a saint or hero of a flawed cause. He naively accepts a tainted version of the American Dream, and pursues it with limitless dedication. (In this he resembles Fitzgerald's Jay Gatsby.) The dream is flawed because it is based on an uncritical acceptance of slavery and the racial dogmas underlying it. In pursuit of his design, he is willing to sacrifice anything, and in his determined course he leaves a swath of wreckage behind him.

Thus Thomas Sutpen, who was once the boy turned away from the door of the mansion, refuses to recognize the son of his Haitian marriage, Charles Bon, when Henry brings him back with him from college. Sutpen surely understands that Charles courts his half-sister Judith simply to force his father to acknowledge him. Instead, as Quentin surmises, Sutpen reveals to Henry, on separate occasions, the two taboos that Charles threatens to break, incest and miscegenation. (Quentin imagines that Henry could accept the first, but not the second.) Henry kills Charles at the gate of Sutpen's Hundred, setting in motion events that bring down Sutpen's dynasty, though four decades must pass until the final act of the tragedy is played out. Sutpen dies, cut down by a scythe, symbol of time, which the ageing man battles as he tries to restart his design. When the rotting mansion burns in December 1910, it destroys the last of Sutpen's children, Clytemnestra (child of a slave) and Henry, the fugitive who has returned as an old man to die. A final Sutpen heir, a retarded black man named Jim Bond (Charles Bon's grandson), runs crying into the night, never to be seen again.

The title of *Absalom, Absalom!* contains a reference that would have been recognizable to Faulkner's audience in a Bible-reading era. Like the House of Sutpen, the House of King David witnessed incest (the rape of Tamar) and the rebellion of a son, Absalom, against his father. Yet David's lament (II Samuel 18) on hearing of Prince Absalom's death in battle – 'O my son Absalom, my son, my son Absalom!' – is never echoed by Sutpen. Slave-owning, to which Sutpen was committed by his design, requires the denial of humanity to others, a thick callus over the soul. There is no evidence that Sutpen ever mourns the death of his son Charles. Thus, Sutpen, for all his courage and personal magnetism, remains a Gothic monster, a manifestation of the monstrous moral system he embraced.

Other Faulkner works of the racial Gothic include *Light in August* (1932), which is in part the story of Joe Christmas, a mixed-race murderer who is another example of the 'tragic mulatto' theme; *The Bear* (1942), the story of the McCaslin clan, in which a story of slavery, miscegenation and incest is joined to a lament for the passing of the wilderness; and the stories 'A Justice' (1931), 'Red Leaves' (1931) and 'Was' (1942), depicting the last of the Chickasaw culture of Yoknapatawpha. *Sanctuary* (1931) is a Gothic of a different sort, in which the heroine, Temple Drake, finds herself in the power of a feral killer called Popeye. *As I Lay Dying* (1930), another novel with multiple points of view, depicts the bizarre journey of the poor white Bundren family to bury the decaying body of its matriarch, and mixes black humour, the grotesque and the Gothic.

Southern Gothic and the grotesque

Eudora Welty, Flannery O'Connor and Carson McCullers often present characters whose appearance or behaviour are grotesque. As noted in the Introduction, grotesqueness, which involves distortion to the point of the monstrous, is a quality that overlaps with the Gothic, but neither is necessary or sufficient for the other. The grotesque may evoke horror and the uncanny, but it may also produce sadness, compassion or humour. For example, the characters in Sherwood Anderson's *Winesburg, Ohio* (1919) are described as 'grotesques', but we are led to view them with a mixture of tolerance, sympathy and perhaps nostalgia, as figures of a passing and simpler era. Thus *Winesburg, Ohio* is not a Gothic work, I would assert, though small towns are certainly potential Gothic sites. Even the antics of Jeeter Lester and his family in Erskine Caldwell's *Tobacco Road* (1932), while certainly grotesque, generate more dark comedy and pathos than horror.

Some works by Welty, O'Connor and McCullers, important writers all, may be described as Gothic, others not, though the distinction is sometimes difficult. Consider, for example, 'Keela, The Outcast Indian Maiden' (1940), whose title-character has performed in a 'geek show', eating live chickens before a carnival audience.

The audience at a sideshow pays for the voyeuristic enjoyment of the grotesque, a complex and morally compromised position depending on rubes, or bumpkins in the audience enjoying awe or revulsion whilst believing in their own safe superiority or normalcy. Indeed, the relation of rube gawking at freak mimics, in many ways, the relationship of the audience and the Gothic text or horror movie. But this relationship depends on the smug sense of otherness: whatever we are, we are not like *that*. This distance collapses in 'Keela, The Outcast Indian Maiden' when a compassionate stranger approaches the performer, stretches out his hand and says 'Come here'.[3] The 'Indian Maiden' is revealed to be an African American man named Little Lee Roy who had been kidnapped, put in a dress and forced to perform in the geek show. His real identity was not known even to Steve, the barker for the spectacle.

As we read Welty's story, however, the identity of the title-character is never in doubt, since the narrative present is two years after Lee Roy's rescue. We observe the occasion when the barker, Steve, appears at Lee Roy's home, bringing with him another white man, and, recalling the curious episode of the carnival, tries to justify his failure to see the truth about 'Keela'. At the end of the story the two white men have left, and, at dinner, Little Lee Roy begins to tell the younger members of the family about the two visitors who came and spoke about the time 'when I use to be with de circus—'. He is, however, told to 'Hush up'.[4]

'Keela, The Outcast Indian Maiden' is freighted with the ambiguity and excess of meaning that we expect in the Gothic. However, the response of the reader is less likely to be horror or dread than a thoughtful and sympathetic consideration of the story's implications. We see a demonstration of the way that received narratives (that is, the script about Keela) can shape and distort the reality in front of us. We see also an allegorical history of slavery in America in this account of a black man kidnapped and forced to play a degrading role. We do not hear the former slave's own story, since the white man Steve is interested only in justifying himself, not in conversing with Lee Roy. The younger black generation apparently is too embarrassed or bored to hear about its heritage.

The compassion Welty evokes toward her characters typically qualifies her stories' Gothic effects. This observation holds true even for a work like 'Clytie' (1942), which uses the familiar materials of Southern Gothic: a family with a history of madness, alcoholism and suicide living in a decaying mansion. The title-character, Clytie Farr, wanders the streets of the town, literally too crazed to come in out of the rain. But we see Clytie both from without, as the townspeople see her, and within. We are not led to fear her, like the barber who comes to shave Clytie's paralysed father and who runs screaming from the Farr house when she impulsively touches his face. Rather, from our glimpses into her disordered mind, we understand that her fascination with faces comes from an attempt to recover her lost identity. When Clytie drowns after glimpsing her own face in a barrel of rainwater and plunging herself into it, most readers will feel sadness and pity. While we would call the story Gothic, horror and uncanny blend with other responses, doubtless varying with the reader, and boundaries are elusive.

Flannery O'Connor's sternly Catholic vision presents a fallen world of deeply flawed people. Her vision has much in common with the dark Romantics of a century before, but her voice is her own, and instantly recognizable. Characters bicker and whine as we all do in our worst moments, but continuously edit out of our memories. O'Connor intends readers to discover themselves in her fables. Though she seldom preaches (and first-time readers often miss her religious implications), the implicit message of her fiction is that people are not capable of achieving grace and salvation by their own efforts.

O'Connor's narratives are always grotesque, sometimes Gothic. She describes middle-class, working-class and poor white characters who have in common their misunderstanding of their selves and their worlds. They try to solve their domestic problems with blundering and destructive consequences. They attempt to slake their religious cravings through the distorted and undisciplined forms of Southern backwoods fundamentalism. Inevitably, their situations slip from their control, and lead to moments of horrifying enlightenment. The grandmother in O'Connor's frequently anthologized story 'A Good Man is Hard to Find' (1955) is vain and flighty, and her decision to hide her cat in the car when leaving on a family vacation results in an accident, her capture by a killer called 'The Misfit' and his gang, and her death, as well as those of her son, daughter-in-law and grandchildren. In the moment before she is shot, the grandmother has a strange insight that seems mad but is intended by O'Connor to represent a moment of grace. Touching the murderer on the shoulder, she says 'Why you're one of my babies. You're one of my own children!'[5] The ending is typical of the author, horrifying, uncanny, yet suggesting the possibility of redemption.

Thomas, the central character of 'The Comforts of Home' (1960), is similarly deluded. A historian living with his mother, he believes himself sane and practical. When his mother takes into their home a young woman who is a promiscuous drunken thief, he tries to demonstrate that this object of charity is unworthy. As in 'A Good Man is Hard to Find', events move swiftly from banal to ghastly. Thomas's increasingly frustrated attempts to expel the interloper result, finally, in his shooting his mother to death as she throws herself between him and the young woman. The tableau is complex, as we view it from differing perspectives. The sheriff arrives just in time to witness the killing, and believes that it is the climax of a murder plot: 'He saw the facts as if they were already in print: the fellow had intended all along to kill his mother and pin it on the girl.' [6]

The sheriff's interpretation is not entirely wrong. O'Connor, employing a narration like Henry James's 'reflector' technique, lets us into the mind of Thomas. As he tries to assert himself, he begins to hear the voice of his dead father, a blunt and crude local politician. Thomas is clearly becoming deranged while believing himself the voice of sanity. He shoots his mother in response to his father's order to fire. The deadly tableau seems the last act of a repressed Oedipal drama, or the revenge of an angry spirit. Ironically titled, 'The Comforts of Home' is a perfect example of the Gothic uncanny, the snug refuge revealing itself as a place of crazy horror.

Carson McCullers, like Flannery O'Connor, was a Georgian whose life was shortened by catastrophic disease. Some of McCullers's fiction (like all of O'Connor's) is grotesque, shading into Gothic.

The Ballad of the Sad Café (1943) is the story of a derelict building and the woman whose face is seen in its window: 'It is a face like the terrible dim faces known in dreams—sexless and white, with two gray crossed eyes which are turned inward so sharply that they seem to be exchanging with each other one long and secret gaze of grief.'[7] McCullers's novella will tell how the once-thriving café and the powerful Amazon, Miss Amelia, came to ruin.

Here, as in most of her work, the author presents a tale of strange longing among mismatched, sexually ambiguous characters. Love, subject of a meditation at the centre of the novella, is unaccountable and both elevating and destructive. The lover creates 'a whole inward world—a world intense and strange', and the lover and the beloved always 'come from different countries.'[8] Thus, the local stud and petty criminal Marvin, who has ruined many a village girl, attempts a respectable life when he unaccountably falls in love with the asexual Amelia. When she (again unaccountably) marries him and then throws him out, the marriage unconsummated, he reverts to violent crime and is sent to prison. Miss Amelia, rich and proficient in many things (shopkeeping, bootlegging, molasses-making, carpentry, doctoring, boxing and wrestling), falls in love with the hunchback Lymon, who reaches only to her waist, and claims to be her cousin. During the few years of Lymon's life with Miss Amelia, her already formidable powers blossom, she becomes less misanthropic, and she turns her store into a café, which becomes a social centre and source of pride to the poor and remote Georgia mill-town.

The grotesque hunchback Lymon, with his old-fashioned pantaloons, long stockings and shawl, seems a character from 'Rip Van Winkle'. When he, in turn, falls in love with Marvin, who has been paroled from prison, the narrative reaches a weird symmetry. Lymon's astounding leap on to Amelia's back, after she has battled Marvin to the ground, is an act of betrayal that destroys her. Marvin and Lymon leave together after wrecking the café, and Amelia, like the building, slides rapidly into decay.

The Ballad of the Sad Café is, in a sense, the legend of a haunted house. The story evokes the Gothic in its overarching strangeness, and there are touches of the supernatural in the portents (strange weather, poisonous meat) that accompany Marvin's return. Certainly the story has the excess of meaning characteristic of the Gothic. It teases us with hints of private symbolism. The strange triangle of characters may echo the author's troubled life and ambiguous sexuality, and Miss Amelia's wasting body and distorted face recall McCullers's partial paralysis after a series of devastating strokes.

For many readers, however, the dominant effect of the story will be less horror than the powerful melancholy signalled by the title. With Miss Amelia's defeat, and the closing of the café, the creative energy drains from the community, and it is left a dreary wasteland.

Other Southern Gothic in the modern age

The term 'Southern Gothic', first used by Ellen Glasgow, became so common in the modern period that each word came to evoke the other. From the long list of writers in this category, we may mention especially such Gothic-shaded plays of Tennessee Williams as *Cat on a Hot Tin Roof* (1955), *Orpheus Descending* (1957) and *Suddenly Last Summer* (1958).

Richard Wright's urban Gothic

Clearly, the enduring tragedy of American racial relations pervades the Gothic of the American South. The South in the early twentieth century witnessed hundreds of lynchings of black American men, often in response to alleged sexual transgressions against white women. Such an event is the horrifying denouement of Faulkner's *Light in August*, in which Joe Christmas is castrated and killed. The mixed-race writer Jean Toomer (1894–1967) makes a lynching the climax of the Gothic story 'Blood-Burning Moon' in his story cycle *Cane* (1923).

Racial conflict, of course, did not end at the borders of the old Confederacy, nor do populations in America remain static. An important demographic shift of this period was the migration of rural Southern black families into Northern cities. The life and career of Mississippi-born Richard Wright (1908–60) reflects this migration. His fiction, as well his autobiography, *Black Boy* (1945), describes life in the rural South as well as the Northern slums in which country-born migrants found themselves. Wright's *Native Son* (1940) is one of the most powerful works in the tradition of American racial Gothicism, and is still controversial and divisive.

Native Son combines Gothicism and naturalism, an easy alliance that we saw before in Norris's *Vandover and the Brute*. The work's naturalism is apparent in its violence and animal imagery (the first action of the book has Bigger killing a rat with an iron skillet), and in powerful social and environmental forces that overwhelm the individual. As in most naturalistic novels, the plot turns on an unintended event, here Bigger's accidental suffocation of Mary. We see the Gothicism of *Native Son* in such nightmarish, Poe-like scenes as Bigger's frantic efforts to dispose of Mary's body (cutting off her head before stuffing the corpse in the basement furnace) and the subsequent discovery of her bones by newspaper reporters while Bigger rakes the ashes. Throughout the novel, or rather for its first two-thirds, before it turns into a political tract, Wright produces a nearly overwhelming atmosphere of fear and disgust.

The novel has been criticized for its potentially destructive use of racial stereotypes. The response is inevitable, since those very stereotypes are a fact of American life that Wright wished to explore. His villain-hero Bigger, accidental killer of white Mary, deliberate killer of black Bessie, is an embodiment of America's racial nightmares. He is the monster that American racism has begotten.

Other hauntings: the north-east

After the South, New England is the most evoked site of American Gothic. Like the South, New England, aside from a few metropolitan centres, endured a long decline, and writers from the time of Jewett and Freeman saw Gothic potential in its isolated villages and abandoned farms, places with long histories and many secrets. The legacy of the Salem witchcraft trials continued to fascinate. Yet Americans also idealized the New England small town as a locus of traditional democratic virtues and simple honest living. This idealization can be reversed to Gothic effect, the apparent simplicity, so appealing to busy urbanites, concealing the uncanny secret or threat.

The best-known twentieth-century Gothic story of village life is probably Shirley Jackson's 'The Lottery' (1948), remembered as the most controversial story ever published in the *New Yorker*. In this tightly constructed account of a festival in a New England town square on a bright day in June, the first-time reader comes to understand with horror only late in the narrative that the civic event being described is the choosing of a sacrificial victim who will be stoned to death. Jackson's poisonous little tale is both a classic account of scapegoat behaviour and an open-ended fable about the ways that illogical and destructive acts can be sanctified by tradition.

135

The story draws on the paranoia of early Cold War politics, especially the Red-hunting scares of that era, as does Arthur Miller's play *The Crucible* (1952), which was set in 1692 Salem. Clearly, both works refer by analogy to contemporary events.

New England's haunted houses

Shirley Jackson was also the author of two elegant haunted-house novels, *The Haunting of Hill House* (1959) and *We Have Always Lived in the Castle* (1962). The first, unlike most works by serious authors of this period, openly evokes the supernatural. A worthy successor to James's *The Turn of the Screw*, *The Haunting of Hill House* has provoked much critical discussion and has been filmed twice.

Jackson reverses a common pattern of the haunted-house story, in which an apparently welcoming home eventually reveals its concealed horror. Hill House, in contrast, is repellent at the outset, constructed with odd disorienting angles and filled with unpleasant surprises, like zones of unnatural cold. Yet Hill House intends to seduce its intended victim, Eleanor Vance, not to frighten her away.

Eleanor Vance arrives as a part of a group recruited to experience psychic phenomena in a reputedly haunted house. She is at first alarmed by its poltergeist knockings and by the ambiguous messages that suddenly appear chalked on the wall: 'help Eleanor come home Eleanor'. By the novel's end Eleanor has been rejected by the group, with which she tried to form an ersatz family. She is claimed instead by the house, its formerly *unheimlich* qualities inverted for her so that it has become her long-desired home. But one can only 'come home' to a haunted house through death.

The psychology of *The Haunting of Hill House* is remarkably complex, especially in the interaction of Eleanor with the other occupants such as her room-mate, the apparently lesbian Theodora, and in the ambiguity of Eleanor's motives and self-awareness. Jackson creates a similarly rich psychology in *We Have Always Lived in the Castle*, which some readers consider her finest work.

The haunted house of Jackson's last novel is not a sentient force, but (as in *Absalom, Absalom!*) the site of crimes and secrets. Six years before the novel's opening, several members of the Blackwood family died of poison. The only survivors are a brain-damaged old man and his nieces Constance and Mary Catherine (Merricat). The people of the New England village believe that Constance murdered her family, though there was insufficient evidence to convict her. The villagers shun Constance, so that only Merricat, who is barely tolerated, dares to venture out from the family mansion for supplies.

We Have Always Lived in the Castle is told by Merricat, and is a notable demonstration of unreliable first-person narration. We understand Merricat's strangeness from the first paragraph, in which she wishes she had been born a vampire, and expresses her love for Richard Plantagenet and death-cap mushrooms. She is in fact quite mad, and most readers will suspect, long before it is revealed, that Merricat, not Constance, murdered the Blackstones. Constance is not the death angel imagined by the villagers, but is the saintly protector of her crazy sister. She is the captive maiden of Gothic tradition, and will never escape from the castle. At the novel's end, the mansion looted and burned, Constance and Merricat survive in the still-standing kitchen, where they are apparently doomed to linger out the rest of their lives.

A play by America's finest playwright, Eugene O'Neill (1888–1953), provides a final example of a New England haunted house. *Long Day's Journey into Night* (1956) spans, from the time of its setting to the date of its first performance, almost the entire modern period. The events of the drama occur in 1912, but the play, completed in the early 1940s, was not published and performed until 1956, after the author's death.

Long Day's Journey into Night is the story of the 'four haunted Tyrones', as O'Neill called his characters on the dedication page. The play reveals the secrets of the four – mother, father and two adult sons – including the drug addiction of the mother, Mary Tyrone.

The play, exhibiting a tight and nearly claustrophobic unity of place, is set entirely in the Tyrone's summerhouse in a New England coastal town (based on Providence, Rhode Island). It is not a sentient, actively hostile force, but, like the Blackstone mansion or Sutpen's Hundred, it is a repository of the secrets and crimes of the family that has inhabited it. Like all haunted houses, the Tyrone house has failed to be the nurturing space its inhabitants need.

Especially Mary Tyrone senses this failure: 'I've never felt it was my home. It was wrong from the start.'[9]

In the first scene, with the family at breakfast, we seem to be in a happy and successful household. But as the day progresses, as tensions emerge and secrets are revealed, the mood becomes ominous and recognizably Gothic. The fear shared by Tyrone and his sons, at first only hinted at, then expressed, is that Mary has resumed taking morphine. She has. By night, Tyrone says, she will become 'a mad ghost'.[10] Her final, zombie-like appearance, dragging her wedding dress behind her and prattling about her girlhood in a convent school, is one of the heartbreaking moments of American theatre.[11]

Indeed, in some sense each of the residents has become a ghost. Mary knows that because of her addiction she has lost her 'true self forever'.[12] But so has Tyrone. Once one of the most promising Shakespearean actors of his generation, he bought a popular play about the Count of Monte Cristo and, as its title-character, became its slave, as surely as Mary became the slave of morphine. Jamie too is trapped by a pattern of nihilistic self-destruction and alcoholism. Even Edmund, the youngest son, speaks of dying inside and living like a ghost.[13] Yet Edmund, who has just been diagnosed with tuberculosis and is to be sent to a sanatorium (to die, his father apparently believes), will be the only one of the Tyrones to escape the haunted house.

Weird tales

The pre-eminent theorist and practitioner of the supernatural tale in America during the modern period was H. P. Lovecraft (1890–1937). Much of Lovecraft's fiction was published originally in pulp magazines such as *Weird Tales*, and was read only by fans of horror fiction. After his death a publishing house, Arkham Press, was created to keep his work in print. The publication of a collection of his tales by the Library of America in 2005, edited by the contemporary horror writer Peter Straub, indicates the higher critical esteem in which his work is now held.

A native of Providence, Rhode Island, Lovecraft may be considered a writer of New England Gothic. The tradition he

builds upon comes from Poe through Ambrose Bierce and
R. L. Chambers, with admixtures of the British writers Lord
Dunsany and Arthur Machen, but he evokes Hawthorne's Matter of
Salem repeatedly. Lovecraft's fictional landscape is a re-imagined
New England, dominated by the town of Arkham (based on
Providence) and its Miskatonic University. Behind the visible world
are the Great Old Ones of Lovecraft's Cthulhu Mythos, who are
described in the dangerous book of lore called the *Necronomicon*.
(This imaginary book recalls the play *The King in Yellow* of
Chambers's stories.) The Old Ones are malicious, and past outbreaks
of horrifying events, such as Salem witchcraft, are imperfectly
understood manifestations of their power. Moreover, there are
monsters in the world, and they can interbreed with humans, so
that normal-appearing people may embody a monstrous heritage,
unknown to themselves.

Lovecraft's 'The Dreams in the Witch House' (1933) shows his
blending of New England materials with the Cthulhu Mythos. The
story in fact is a reworking of Hawthorne's 'Young Goodman
Brown'. Lovecraft's protagonist, Walter Gilman, is a student at
Miskatonic University who explores, as Lovecraft's characters often
do, dangerous texts including the *Necronomicon*. He becomes
convinced that occult powers can be explained by modern physics,
and that the Salem witches had mastered the art of multidimensional
travel. Trying to recover this power, Gilman moves into the witch
house, an Arkham dwelling where an escapee from Salem gaol,
Keziah Mason, had once lived. Once under Keziah's roof, he soon
begins to see her in dreams, along with her rat-like familiar spirit,
Brown Jenkin, and, of course, a black man with cloven hoofs, who
invites Gilman to attend a coven and to sign his name in a book.
When Gilman resists, Brown Jenkin gnaws out his heart.

'The Shadow Over Innsmouth' (1936) is a story about monsters
and the monstrous in one's self. Lovecraft's narrator survives a
terrifying expedition to the coastal town of Innsmouth, where he
discovers that the inhabitants have been interbreeding with sea
monsters. The young man is stranded in the town overnight and
makes a hairbreadth escape from the seedy hotel in which the
aroused inhabitants surround him. His story seems to arrive at a
successful conclusion, when he reaches safety and persuades the

authorities to attack Innsmouth and destroy the monsters. He returns to the bland normalcy of Ohio, and even graduates from the bastion of Emersonian liberalism, Oberlin College. However, at the story's end he discovers that he, too, shares a sea-monster lineage – a revelation that has been subtly anticipated by hints throughout the story. Inevitably, he will mutate into the loathsome Other and return to the ocean to join his immortal ancestors.

Lovecraft's fiction has had an immense impact on writers of supernatural horror in the post-modern period, including Stephen King, Peter Staub and Thomas Ligotti.

The return of vampires

The literature of vampires, a very small part of American Gothic at the beginning of the twentieth century, has grown tremendously in recent decades. We will discuss contemporary vampire fiction and cinema in chapter 4.

The British vampire tradition develops rapidly through the nineteenth century, from John Polidori to Joseph Sheridan Le Fanu to Bram Stoker. Stoker's *Dracula* (1897), of course, is the great defining novel of the tradition. A quality of *Dracula*, like all Gothic, is that it generates an excess of meaning, being a highly ambiguous text that can be read in many ways. As Ken Gelder summarizes in *Reading the Vampire* (1994), Stoker's novel has been, and continues to be, the source of interpretations from many ideological positions. After all, Dracula himself is shape-shifting and many faceted.

In spite of the rich potential of the vampire tradition as defined by Stoker, American vampire stories in the early twentieth century reveal little influence of British models; rather, like Freeman's 'Luella Miller' and Wharton's 'Bewitched', they draw on regional traditions.[14] However, the influence of Stoker on movies in the early twentieth century was immense. The many film versions of *Dracula*, like those of *Frankenstein*, overlay the original texts and energize recent literature. These days even vampires, it would seem, watch vampire movies.

Richard Matheson's *I am Legend* (1954), which seems to draw its emotional energy from the paranoia of the Cold War, stands at the beginning of a redefined American convention that links vampires to apocalyptic themes from science fiction. In Matheson's revision of the vampire story, Stoker is represented as having used European superstitions and cultural memories about an actual bacterial disease that has appeared at intervals in human history. In his near future (the novel's narrative frame is 1976–8, with flashbacks to catastrophes in 1975), a barely mentioned nuclear war has changed the climate, hastening the spread of a resurgent vampire sickness. Once infected, a victim progresses from a still-living creature thirsting for blood to a living corpse animated by the bacteria. However, at least one man (in a plot device recalling *The Scarlet Plague*) is immune. The protagonist, Robert Neville, fights vampires while attempting to understand the disease scientifically. Ultimately, however, he is captured by a group of infected survivors who have learned to control the disease's progress. Before committing suicide, Neville realizes that in this new society, he, the vampire slayer, is the freak or monster.

Matheson's novel forms a new set of conventions that would be explored with every possible variation in novels and films of subsequent decades. *I Am Legend* itself has been filmed three times. In 1964 Vincent Price, that stalwart of vampire movies, starred in *The Last Man on Earth*. More recent adaptations of *I Am Legend* take us into the post modern period. In *The Omega Man* (1971) Robert Neville, as played by Charlton Heston, becomes a Christ figure, and, in a final scene over-stuffed with Christian imagery, the dying Neville, in a bloody fountain, his side pierced with a spear, offers a vial of his blood, which will be used to make the vaccine that will save humanity. A 2007 film with the novel's original title, starring Will Smith, changes the setting from Los Angeles to New York, but retains the idea of Neville sacrificing himself to save a few uninfected survivors.

The Gothic poetry of Sylvia Plath and Anne Sexton

Vampire, witches and other Gothic motifs have flourished in late twentieth-century poetry, as illustrated particularly by that of New Englanders Sylvia Plath (1932–63) and Anne Sexton (1928–74).

In her last great poems, written in the weeks before her death in London, Sylvia Plath's imagination took her deep into the realm of the Gothic. 'The Moon and the Yew Tree', for example, is placed in a country churchyard. The setting, we assume, was from the village in the west of England where Plath lived with her children and husband, the British poet Ted Hughes, before the couple's separation and her removal to London. The elements of the poem, the church and moonlit cemetery, take this American poet back to the favourite setting of the English 'graveyard school' and the major early Romantics. Yet this is not a calm or melancholy meditation, such as might have been written by Gray or Wordsworth, but is suffused with the agony that has taken her to – using the title of another poem of this period – the 'Edge'. There is no consolation to be found in this churchyard. The moon is 'White as a knuckle and terribly upset'. The 'message of the yew tree', which another poet might have seen as pointing toward heaven, 'is blackness—blackness and silence'.[15]

In other late poems Plath evokes vampire imagery from *Dracula*. In 'Daddy', probably her most famous poem, she taunts her 'man in black', a composite of her father, Hitler, Dracula and Ted Hughes: 'There's a stake in your fat black heart /And the villagers never liked you.'[16] The bloodsucker has been humiliated and destroyed. On the other hand, in one of her last poems, 'Lady Lazarus', she seems to identify not only with the biblical Lazarus, but with *Dracula*'s Lucy revenant as the 'Bloofer Lady'. This poem is explicitly a suicide note, and one cannot encounter it today without the knowledge that the threat was genuine. Reading Plath's last poems places the reader in the horrified position of watching a tragedy unfold while being powerless to intervene.

Sylvia Plath's contemporary and rival Anne Sexton evokes the figure of the witch, reinterpreted as a feminist symbol of dark power and resistance. In her 1960 poem 'Her Kind', she envisions herself having 'gone out, a possessed witch /haunting the black air, braver at night'. This was Sexton's signature poem, with which she began her public readings, and was usually printed first in anthologized selections of her verse. Like many of Plath's works, Sexton's poem is death-haunted, a forecast of her suicide: 'A woman like that is not ashamed to die. / I have been her kind.'[17]

California Noir

Crime fiction and the Gothic are inherently similar and have developed within overlapping traditions. Both reveal secrets and transgressions, exploring the borderland that detective Philip Marlowe, created by Raymond Chandler (1888–1959), called the 'shadow line', dividing everyday life from the deviant and criminal.[18] The detective solves the crime using his powers of 'ratiocination', in Poe's term, dispelling mystery and restoring order. However, in Gothic crime fiction, of which the noir is the dominant American tradition, the shadows are never completely illuminated. While a criminal may be identified and arrested, the the reader is left with a sense that the past continues to haunt the present, and justice is imperfectly achieved. In essence, the noir combines Poe's Gothic and Detective traditions.

Noir has its roots in American popular culture. The tradition first appeared in pulp magazines like *Black Mask*, which published early work by Chandler and Dashiell Hammett (1894–1961), and in the black-and-white crime movies that often were shown second (the 'B' position) in the popular double features of the 1930s and '40s. These films often featured stories of cynical, world weary characters, and employed a dark, shadowy cinematography and dizzy angles influenced by German expressionist movies. The film style came to be called *noir*, and the body of corresponding fiction shares the name. Noir film and fiction continued to interact with each other and with comic books and their later evolution, the graphic novel.

While his British counterpart, from Holmes to Wimsey, is a gentleman and an amateur (in the style of Poe's Dupin), the American noir detective has rougher edges. He is of working-class background, a professional detective (usually a private investigator) with a keen sense of justice but careless about the law, and willing to break rules, or a few heads, to obtain the truth. Usually he narrates his own story in a vernacular speech peppered with slang and vivid imagery. Contemporary noir film, like the recent graphic-novel-styled *Sin City* (2006), often uses voice-over narration that recalls the first-person narrators of classic noir crime fiction.

Because of its film connections and the setting of many of its most famous novels, the noir tradition is especially associated with

California in the early and middle twentieth century. (Contemporary noir often revisits this period of classic noir.) Typical of Gothic oppositional history, noir undercuts the self-promoting image of the Golden State as a sun-drenched paradise.[19]

Dashiell Hammett and Raymond Chandler defined the classic phase of noir crime fiction with their novels about Sam Spade and Philip Marlowe. Chandler's literary heir was Ross Macdonald (the pen-name of Kenneth Millar, 1915–83), who wrote a series of eighteen novels about Lew Archer, a southern California detective who often works cases around Santa Barbara (called Santa Teresa). The Archer novels represent the pinnacle of the first or classic phase of California noir detective fiction.

Archer's investigations often lead to successive layers of discovery that will take him through three generations of buried crimes and secrets. Thus, in *The Blue Hammer* (1976), the last of the Archer novels, an investigation into a missing painting segues into a case with two murders in the present. Soon Archer is in Arizona, looking into a crime that occurred during the Second World War, an apparent Jacob-and-Esau murder of a man by the half-brother (as it was believed) who had stolen his birthright. The case involves a house in Santa Teresa that seems haunted in some sense, and another that yields a body buried under its greenhouse. Archer uncovers crimes and deceptions leading back fifty years, a suppressed genealogy, a sequence of switched identities, a threat of incest, as well as the three murders. Near the end Archer says, 'I felt the weight of the past like an extra atmosphere constricting my breathing'.[20] This sense of history as a curse is typically Gothic.

The noir continues in the post modern period and, as we will see, often blends with other Gothic traditions.

4

Gothic in a Post-American World

෨

Gothic literature continues to provide an alternative reading of American culture in the volatile decades from the 1960s to the present. As new voices from minority groups have emerged, they have often expressed themselves though the Gothic, while changing and enriching the Gothic tradition. Gothic writers still explore the American past, its wilderness legacy, the anxieties of its cities and its emerging suburban culture, and push their speculations into the imagined, often terrifying, future.

As political realities shifted near the end of the twentieth century, and the dominance of the United States began to erode, so too did the powerful complex of ideas known as modernism. While the emerging sensibility is still defining itself, one clear feature of a post-modern sensibility is the collapse of the firewall between high culture and popular culture. The Gothic tradition, which has roots in the corner news-stand and the cinema as well as the university library, has been further energized by infusions from the comic book, its successor the graphic novel, and television.

Monsters, ghosts and vampires, banished to the fringe during the Modernist period, have returned to haunt and menace us in the present. The 1960s, and especially the 1970s, began a resurgence of the supernatural Gothic, with best-sellers by writers including Ira Levin (1928–2007), Anne Rice (b. 1941), Peter Straub (b. 1943) and Stephen King (b. 1947). These writers, and others, brought

Gothic themes to a broad audience in works that skilfully kept readers turning pages with a blend of tight plotting, universal fears and contemporary anxieties. Many of these novels became the bases of horror movies, in a period when restrictive Hollywood codes were loosening and screens were generously splashed with gore.

The dispossessed write back

American writers of colour in this era resemble writers of former European colonies in their creation of counter-narratives, stories in which their voices and experiences, long distorted or excluded, are finally heard. Like Salman Rushdie and other 'post-colonial' British writers, such Americans as Toni Morrison, Louise Erdrich and Maxine Hong Kingston turned to the Gothic to help shape their stories.

If *Absalom, Absalom!* was the premier American Gothic novel of the first half of the twentieth century, *Beloved* (1987), by fellow Nobel laureate Toni Morrison, is perhaps the greatest of the second half. Like Faulkner's tale, *Beloved* is a family saga of Southern life in the era of slavery, the Civil War years and their aftermath. Like Faulkner's, it is a novel about a haunted house, in which terrible past events are revealed through a fragmented, tormented narration. Each work explores the theme of the returning child, and in each there is a horrifying scene when a child's throat is cut.

Morrison's novel focuses resolutely on the black experience, following the unanswerable logic that the essential stories about slavery are found in the lives of the slaves and their descendants. The haunted house of *Beloved* is not the mansion of the master, but the seemingly ordinary home at 124 Bluestone Road, Cincinnati, Ohio, where former slaves reside. The house is haunted by the ghost of a black child who died there. There is no point in moving, as the child's grandmother says, because 'Not a house in the country ain't packed to its rafters with some dead Negro's grief.'[1]

Yet there is a plantation in the novel, as in most narratives about escaped slaves, and it is called Sweet Home. All the inhabitants of 124 Bluestone once lived there – all except the girl, Denver, born during the escape of her mother, Sethe. The name Sweet Home is obviously packed with irony; clearly, a part of Morrison's programme is to deconstruct sentimental stereotypes about the ante-bellum South. The name Sweet Home recalls Stephen Foster's 1853 song 'My Old Kentucky Home', just as Sethe's escape across the Ohio River is meant to evoke that of Eliza in *Uncle Tom's Cabin* (1852).

The slave-driver at Sweet Home plantation, 'schoolteacher',[2] joins Stowe's Simon Legree as a great villain in the literature of slavery. An evolved version of the schoolmaster or judge figure we have seen before, he is indeed one of the profound monsters of American literature. Like Hawthorne's Chillingsworth, schoolteacher perverts reason in the service of an evil ideology. His racial beliefs are those of his society and time, even among Americans opposed to slavery; that is, he is convinced that Africans are subhuman. Studying his slaves, he makes notes about their behaviour, instructing his sons to make parallel lists of Sethe's human and animal characteristics. Without anger, without raising his voice, he enforces a regime that breaks Sethe's husband Halle and kills their friend Sixo. Schoolteacher even extends slavery's tentacles northward across the Ohio River in search of his runaway property. He is responsible for the death of Sethe's baby, initiating the time of the Misery (as Stamp Paid calls it) that drives Baby Suggs to a despairing death. Schoolteacher's arrival, as one of the 'four horsemen',[3] turns 124 Bluestone into a haunted house.

Beloved is an intricate book and, like *Absalom, Absalom!*, it employs complex shifts in time and narrative point of view. Key moments of the story are circled and revisited, and shocking revelations (such as the killing of Sethe's baby) are delayed. But at its simplest, *Beloved* is the story of a haunted house trying to capture and destroy its occupants. Paul D arrives one day in 1873 and immediately exorcises the house's poltergeist; the house counter-attacks, trying to drive out the intruder and reassert its control over Sethe and Denver. The counter-attack begins on the day of carnival, when Beloved appears among various signs and portents. Denver believes immediately what comes to Sethe only later as a revelation: Beloved is the lost child, whom Sethe killed rather than allowing it to be enslaved by schoolteacher.

Like all Gothic, *Beloved* projects contradictions and alternatives. There is compelling evidence that Beloved indeed is the ghost of

Sethe's third child, returned to claim her love and fill her with guilt. Other evidence suggests that Beloved is a different person altogether, that she was a survivor of the 'middle passage' from Africa as a small child, was kept in sexual bondage by a white man after the end of slavery, and eventually murdered him to escape. Beloved's interior monologue, a haunting and uncanny sequence, can be read either way.[4] In the end it hardly matters, since the source of ultimate evil in the novel, slavery, is the same in either case.

Bruja and *Curandera*

Writers of American Indian and Hispanic heritage were long underrepresented in the national conversation.[5] Writers of both groups, emerging in the 1960s and 1970s, enriched American Gothic with indigenous traditions of shamanism and witchcraft.

For example, *Bless Me, Ultima* (1972) by Rudolfo Anaya (b. 1937) is a boy's initiation novel, and, while often sentimental and nostalgic, the plot includes Gothic elements drawn from the *mestizo* culture of New Mexico, which has developed in its remoteness from the political centres of, successively, Spain, Mexico and the United States. In the world of the boy, Antonio, there are *curanderas*, women who use herbs and magic to heal the sick and combat evil, as well as *brujas*, witches who conduct black masses and place curses on their victims. In *Bless Me, Ultima*, Antonio's mentor, Ultima, is a *curandera* who defends the boy's family against the three evil Trementina sisters and their father Tenorio. By the novel's end the witches are all dead, but Ultima herself is dying. As the title predicts, Antonio survives, carrying the blessing and protection of Ultima.

Tracks (1988), by Louise Erdrich (b. 1954), illustrates the use of traditional magic, or 'medicine', in Gothic fiction by American Indian authors. Elements of shamanism or witchcraft have characterized American Indian fiction since the pioneering *House Made of Dawn* (1968) by N. Scott Momaday (b. 1934). They continue in the work of Leslie Silko (b. 1948), the late James Welch (1940–2003) and Erdrich. These writers are of different tribal backgrounds, and sometimes have engaged in public disagreement. All, however, have drawn on indigenous medicine, often contrasting it to the 'witchery' of Anglo culture. Incidents in dreams or visions are often presented as equivalent to everyday reality, in the manner of Latin American 'magic realism'. Elements of tribal tradition or magic are often left unexplained (as, for example, the lake monster in Erdrich's *Tracks*), so that the non-Indian reader becomes the disadvantaged outsider, a reversal of the frequent situation of the Indian in mainstream American society.

Louise Erdrich has created a continuing saga, spanning over one hundred years, out of the lives of interrelated white and Ojibway families in North Dakota and Minnesota. Her achievement is comparable to Faulkner's in his Yoknapatawpha cycle. Readers meet Pillagers, Moresseys, Lazarres and Kashpaws, among others, at different points in their histories, and must struggle to untangle one of the most challenging genealogical puzzles in American literature. Often new information forces us to reconsider what we had learned in an earlier text, as when, in *Tracks*, we discover that the mad nun Leopolda was the mother of Marie Morrissey, information withheld when we first met them in *Love Medicine* (1984).

Tracks is set in the period from 1912 to 1922, a time when both disease and government policy are threatening the Ojibway nation. Lands are passing from tribal to private ownership, and some families are declining while others rise. Against this background we learn of the rivalry of two women of great power, Fleur Pillager and Pauline Puyat. Like *Bless Me, Ultima*, Erdrich's novel can be read as the struggle between a *curandera* and a *bruja*, though these terms would not be used in Ojibway culture. The witch war is viewed through the double lens of two narrators: Pauline herself, and the tribal elder Nanapush. Pauline is an insane narrator, who tells the story to explain and justify her crazed and destructive actions. We trust Nanapush more, but we are often reminded that he is a prankster, a trickster.

The mystery that surrounds Fleur is heightened by this narrative distancing. In a technique earlier used by Faulkner, the story of the central character is told by others. As a child Fleur had already acquired the reputation as a witch, someone into old 'half-forgotten medicine',[6] that she would carry through her life. Fleur has some connection with the monster at the bottom of Lake Matchimanito, a figure from Ojibway mythology. She has nearly drowned in the lake twice, and the men who rescued her have both subsequently died. When she is raped by the white men in Argus whom she has beaten in a poker game, she sends a tornado to destroy the town. Unfortunately Fleur's magic has limited power against the forces of change and modern money-based society. She and her husband Eli are cheated of their land. Her daughter, Lulu, product of the rape, is sent away to an Indian boarding school, an act the girl sees as betrayal and never forgives. But Fleur remains a powerful shaman who will reappear on the fringes of Ojibway and white society in other parts of the *Love Medicine* cycle. So too will the death-angel Pauline, who becomes the sadistic teaching nun Sister Leopolda, another schoolhouse Gothic figure. As usual in literature by American Indian authors, such as Silko's *Ceremony* (1977), the traditional tribal magic is associated with life and healing, while death and sterility accompany the forces of white progress. Not surprisingly, Leopolda conceals her Ojibway heritage, and identifies herself as white.

Maxine Hong Kingston and ghosts

Maxine Hong Kingston's *The Woman Warrior* (1976) stands in relation to Chinese American literature as Momaday's *House Made of Dawn* does to that of American Indians: it is a pioneering work with immense influence on subsequent writers.

The Woman Warrior, one of the most taught literary texts in American universities, is not usually considered Gothic, and indeed, not always a novel; yet this postmodernist narrative is filled with Gothic elements, beginning with its subtitle, *Memoirs of a Girlhood Among Ghosts*. There are many ghosts: the ghost of Maxine's aunt, a suicide, whose name must never be spoken; ghosts in traditional Chinese stories told by Maxine's father and mother; the ghost successfully fought by her mother when she was a medical student in China. The word ghost is also marvellously problematized as the translation of the Chinese term for a white person: the mail was delivered to the Hong home by the mail ghost, garbage collected by the garbage ghost (who presumably took it away and ate it), and young Maxine attended a school taught by ghosts, among ghost children. She recalls a childhood spent in the cellars of houses and in exploring a labyrinth of storage rooms and underground passages beneath her parents' laundry in Stockton, California.

In one uncanny episode, young Maxine bullies a Chinese girl at school who is unable to speak. The girl is clearly a double, an alter ego, vaguely recalling Poe's William Wilson. Maxine, also, is unable to speak above a whisper in the ghost school. In punishing the other girl she is trying to expel a part of herself that seems to be sliding toward permanent silence. She fears that silence and madness may await her, since her own neighbourhood hides many madwomen – people, she believes, who were simply unable to articulate their stories. This fate befalls Maxine's own aunt, Moon Orchid, who descends to madness and is sent to an asylum.

The Woman Warrior describes a haunted, Gothic childhood, in which an artist struggles to save her sanity and find the voice that will ultimately produce the work we are reading.

Errand into the wilderness

As we saw in chapter 1, the foundational narratives of European Americans were voyages and journeys: discovering, exploring and conquering the new land. (This is a narrative, of course, that minority writers always have disputed.) Perched on the Atlantic seaboard, the colonies and the early nation engaged in seafaring and the exploration of the western frontier. In our own time, some American writers continue to revisit the earlier period of wilderness and frontier. Alternatively, they situate stories in pockets of present-day surviving wilderness.

Gothic stories typically vex received narratives, whether these are sponsored by ruling institutions or are the products of popular culture. Popular accounts of pioneers and cowboys, the stuff of nineteenth-century dime novels, have created a mythology that survives in the present, spread by print, film and television. As we would expect, the Gothic Western complicates the conventional story of the cowboy hero or lawman who brings order to the wild land and dispenses justice. As always, Gothic tales are morally ambiguous, challenging a world of simple opposites, of black hats and white hats.

Cormac McCarthy's *Blood Meridian, Or the Evening Redness in the West* (1985) is perhaps the most celebrated of revisionist Westerns. McCarthy's novel follows the life of a nameless character called 'the kid' from his birth in 1833 until his death in 1878, and thus encompasses most of the classic period of the opening of the West and development of its cowboy culture. Much of the action occurs in 1849 and 1850, during the Gold Rush, when the kid is in his teens.

Blood Meridian is in some respects an initiation story, tracing the development of the kid from a brawler with a 'taste for mindless violence'[7] to a seasoned veteran of the trail. Nonetheless, *Blood Meridian* is not an ordinary coming-of-age story, and no one would mistake it for a conventional Western. Though based on an historical account of the Glanton gang, a band of renegade scalp-hunters that the fictional kid joins, *Blood Meridian* is an encyclopedic epic and metaphysical discourse that asserts some kinship with *Moby-Dick*. It is also one of the most disturbing and violent among major American novels. As readers have seen since its publication, it is intended to debunk cultural myths about cowboys and the West.[8]

Foremost among the Glanton posse is 'the judge', an enigmatic and mythic figure, and a villain to place alongside Morrison's schoolteacher. But while schoolteacher perverts reason to the service of slavery, the judge uses knowledge in a project of universal dominance and destruction. As schoolteacher kept notebooks about the habits of his slaves, Judge Holden records his observations of the human and material world in a black ledger. A kind of mad scientist, the judge proposes to capture all knowledge in this way. He destroys Anasazi glyphs and pottery after sketching them in his book. He wishes that all birds were kept in zoos. He believes that war is God. He dances naked in apparent celebration and joy after killing (and probably raping) a small captive child. The judge's great erudition is in the service of slaughter and chaos.

This strange creature is the kid's mentor, antagonist and, ultimately, killer. He cannot forgive the kid for harbouring some small reservation or reluctance about the tutorial in savagery he has received. This reluctance allows us to retain some respect for the kid as a protagonist, but it is the reason the naked judge rises from the primitive toilet in the last chapter to enfold the now middle-aged protagonist in his murderous arms. At the novel's action ends, the judge dances, as he had danced earlier after killing the helpless child. McCarthy says, and repeats twice as a kind of refrain, that the judge believes he will live forever. The lust for dominance and violence he represents endures in nature, and in human nature.

Et in Arcadia Ego

Engraved on the stock of the judge's rifle are the Latin words 'Et in Arcadia Ego'. The words are from one of Virgil's Eclogues, where shepherds see them carved on a tomb. Usually they are translated thus: 'I (Death) am present even in Arcadia'. The most obvious reference here is to the rifle as an instrument for killing. But the line also suggests something about the nostalgic, Arcadian view of the old West as a time of freedom and heroic deeds: the savagery represented by the judge was always present, even there.

The anti-Arcadian, revisionist and often Gothic view of the frontier and the West can be seen in a number of movies since Sam Peckinpah's *The Wild Bunch* (1969) and the Italian director Sergio Leone's series of Westerns starring Clint Eastwood. The 1992 film *Unforgiven*, directed by Eastwood, is a further example of the revisionist Western. But the most Gothic of cinematic treatments of the Old West is the Home Box Office series *Deadwood* (2004–6), created by David Milch (b. 1945). The Hobbesian brutality of the world of *Deadwood* is signalled by the sequence that plays behind the opening credits, which includes a view of blood running down the side of a rude butcher's block. The emerging town of Deadwood is an abattoir. People are killed in every episode, their bodies often thrown into a pen to fatten hogs. The apparently clear distinction between villains (pre-eminently Al Swearengen, the owner of a brothel) and the noble lawman, Seth Bullock, grows more problematical with each episode. Swearengen, played by British actor Ian McShane, is foul-mouthed, brutal, charismatic and funny – a Gothic villain-hero recalling George Lippard's Devil Bug.

Unsettling settlements

Deadwood is a Gothic reprise of the settlement story, a literary tradition developed in the nineteenth century by James Fenimore Cooper and continued in the early twentieth by Willa Cather, Mari Sandoz and O. E. Rolvaag, among others. While the novel of settlement often depicts pioneers in heroic or elegiac terms, the narrative is often shadowed by violence and by loneliness and even madness, especially among isolated women.

Gothic revisions, as we have seen repeatedly, qualify and challenge received myths and foundational narratives. As pioneers carved out new homes in the wilderness, there was always the *unheimlich* possibility that the savage wilderness would not be defeated, that it would return or be found in one's self, and that the new residence would never be homelike.

One such Gothic revision of the novel of settlement is *Killing Mister Watson* (1990), by Peter Matthiessen (b. 1927), the first volume of a trilogy comprising also *Lost Man's River* (1997) and *Bone by Bone* (1999).[9] The novel is based on an actual event, the 1910 murder of Edgar J. Watson, a pioneer of the Ten Thousand Island region of south-western Florida, by a posse of neighbours. In a manner typical of modernist Gothic fiction, the story emerges from several contradictory points of view. Watson is both a heroic and visionary developer of this region, and a murderous thug who may have killed the outlaw queen Belle Starr before fleeing into the Florida wilderness. While developing the ambiguous life of this complex villain-hero, Matthiessen portrays a regional community with interwoven, sometimes obscure, European, Indian and African bloodlines.

Country of nine-fingered men

Edith Wharton's novella *Summer* evoked the belief that remote pockets of the country, especially mountain hollows, harbour menacing degenerates, the uneducated and inbred descendants of original settlers. This vision is the obverse of 'hillbillies' as represented comically by the old *Li'l Abner* comic strip of Al Capp,

the television series *Hee-Haw,* or *The Dukes of Hazzard* (TV series
and recent film). Residents of Appalachia and other rural regions
bitterly resent both versions of the stereotype. Nonetheless, the
degenerate hillbilly – a literary figure going back at least as far as
the eighteenth-century writings of William Byrd (1674–1744)
– remains a potent figure for the writer or film-maker today. Such
characters may be used to refute the belief in progress or the
Emersonian vision of a life close to nature, or just to provoke terror.
City folk are repeatedly stranded on country roads or go on
doomed camping trips, to find themselves menaced by the bumpkin
with bad teeth and a shotgun or a snarling chainsaw.

A benchmark work in this tradition is the novel *Deliverance* (1970)
by James Dickey (1923–97), which was followed by a movie
adaptation in 1972 by the English director John Boorman.

The four Atlanta businessmen who set out on a canoe expedition
into a Southern wilderness area ignore repeated warnings, and
inevitably they find themselves deep in redneck Gothic. Their
leader, Lewis, a muscular survivalist and bow-hunter, has promised
them a challenging wilderness experience, and two days into the
expedition only three men survive, huddled at nightfall at the base
of a cliff alongside the river rapids. One of the group, Bobby, has
been sodomized at gunpoint, another killed by a sniper as they
attempt to run the rapids. Lewis's leg is broken and he is
incapacitated, though he had earlier managed to kill one of the pair
who had brutalized Bobby. Thus it falls upon the narrator, Ed, to
scale the cliff, locate the remaining attacker, and kill him with a
bow and arrow.

The cliff scaling and the encounter with the sniper are the
imaginative core of this novel. To succeed, Ed must merge his mind,
somehow, first with the landscape itself, then with his opponent.
The ascent of the cliff face is a mystical experience recalling, and
probably based on, John Muir's famous account of climbing Mount
Ritter in *The Mountains of California* (1904). Ed is able to extend his
awareness so that, in the moonlight, fissures seem to appear in the
solid rock, and he climbs the bluff in apparent union with the
landscape. While this sequence seems an affirmation of an
Emersonian view of nature (as in Muir's account), the encounter
with his other, the feral sniper, is darker. Ed's attempt to think

himself into the mind of his opponent, necessary to find the sniper's nest, is so successful that, after killing his man with a well-placed arrow, Ed lifts the sniper's rifle and lines up its sights on Bobby, passing below in the canoe. He comes within a finger-twitch of completing the sniper's mission.

An even more unsettling novel in the tradition of redneck Gothic is Cormac McCarthy's *Child of God* (1974), where we are continuously in the presence of a monster. The protagonist, Lester Ballard, is a rural Tennessee serial-killer who takes up residence in a limestone cavern with the corpses of his victims. McCarthy's third-person narrator describes Ballard's actions dispassionately. The reader finishes the novel chilled by a vision of a grotesque, morally blighted world, as in Flannery O'Connor's fiction, where grace is achingly needed but withheld.

Shipwrecks

The canoe excursion in Dickey's *Deliverance* reminds us of the continuing vitality of the trip or voyage as a Gothic pattern. The Gothic sea-voyage, brought to eminence by Poe and Melville and extended by Jack London, continues as a minor tradition to the present. Inevitably, such narratives describe a doomed passage, in which disturbing encounters (at sea or in port) evoke revelations about the voyagers and their quest.

Peter Matthiessen's *Far Tortuga* (1975) describes a turtle-fishing excursion in the Caribbean. Its central figure, a Cayman Islander named Raib Evers, is a true 'sailin mon, and used to de old-time way'.[10] Though a skilled seaman, Captain Raib's reputation is shadowed by stories of cruelty, smuggling and arson; in other words, he is the novel's Gothic villain-hero. He carries on a feud with another captain, Desmond Eden, who is, though Raib will not acknowledge it, his half-brother. The recurring similarity or identity of names of people and ships in the novel (for example Desmond Eden and the *Lillias Eden*, Raib's ship) suggests a Gothic tangle of suppressed genealogy that only the alert reader can begin to unsnarl.

Despite clear parallels with *Moby-Dick* and *The Sea Wolf* (the latter with its rival brothers Wolf and Death Larsen), *Far Tortuga* is an original work, grounded in the natural history of the Caribbean and its maritime culture, as well as the island folk magic called 'Obeah'. The book is written with Zen minimalism, and largely in the Cayman Islands dialect. The reader learns to interpret the book's unique graphic symbols as part of the narrative, with variously shaded circles representing the weather, time of day, or even the death of characters.

A more recent contribution to the sea Gothic is *The Voyage* (1999) by Philip Caputo (b. 1941), whose main narrative is a disastrous cruise in 1901 by three boys in their father's yacht, accompanied by a college-age friend. Starting in Maine, they sail down the Atlantic coast, stopping in New York and in South Carolina, and eventually wrecking off Cuba. The itinerary thus links the three great Gothic locales of North America: New England, the southern United States and the Caribbean. The tale is told by the granddaughter of one of the boys, the appropriately named Sybil Braithwaite, who attempts to solve the voyage's mysteries, which are mysteries of her family's history. Why would the boys' father have sent them on such a dangerous voyage? Why did the boys' older half-brother Lockwood commit suicide? This sea Gothic becomes a tale about the secrets of houses – Southern houses and Northern houses – and brings into play the classic elements of incest and miscegenation.

The protagonist of *Outerbridge Reach* (1992) by Robert Stone (b. 1937), Owen Browne, competes in a round-the-world race of yachts with single-man crews. While the novel does not seem Gothic at first, as Browne prepares for the race, later chapters at sea portray the sailor's crossing into madness. Like *Far Tortuga* and *The Voyage*, *Outerbridge Reach* reveals the influence of Melville, whose writing Browne quotes in the logs found in his abandoned boat. As in several other works of contemporary Gothic fiction (for example Stone's own 1986 novel *Children of Light*), the novel describes a movie that is a parallel and competing narrative. Browne's antagonist Strickland, who becomes a kind of double, attempts to create a documentary film about Browne and his voyage. This project becomes a destructive folly like the race itself.

The South in the postmodern era

The South continues as a major locus of American Gothic in our time, though no single writer now dominates the terrain as William Faulkner once did. While much of the South now resembles the rest of the country, and the American racial drama is no longer seen as a regional issue, Gothic material is still to be found in its pockets of poverty and backwardness (exploited by Dickey in *Deliverance*), and in the atmosphere of its older cities, especially Savannah and New Orleans. Old, often decaying mansions continue to appear, though such symbols of the old South are often perfunctory gestures in an age with its own issues, such as the legacy of the civil rights movement, new immigrant groups, and drugs such as methamphetamine.

The past is evoked in many ways in contemporary southern Gothic. In *Lancelot* (1977) by Walker Percy (1916–90), the past has been turned into a commodity. The pre-Civil War mansion Belle Isle is open for paid tours, and it is now being used as a set for a Hollywood movie. Though of an old Louisiana family, Lancelot Andrewes Lamar, the owner of Belle Isle, is most concerned with the immediate past and the repugnant present.

Lancelot employs many themes of Southern Gothic: the mansion that will be destroyed, a declining family, a genealogical secret, revenge and murder. A transitional work, the obvious use of grail-quest allusions, with the names Lancelot, Percival and Merlin, points back to the mythological interests of Modernists like T. S. Eliot. The novel seems more contemporary in its fairly explicit sexuality, its references to the civil rights movement, and its use of cinema: both the movie being shot at Belle Isle, which resembles Williams's *Orpheus Descending* and counterpoints the novel's action, and the surveillance videos that reveal the sexual transgressions of Lancelot's wife and daughter.

Louisiana Power and Light (1994) by John Dufresne (b. 1948) is a kind of half-parody Gothic, with outrageous black humour and grotesqueness in the tradition of Erskine Caldwell. It is the story of the last of the Fontana family, who have 'bad water in the gene pool'.[11] Presented alongside the Gothic apparatus and bizarre Fontana family history, the story of present-day Billy Wayne Fontana is a series of stupid relationship choices, the common stuff of country and western music (his ex-wife, in fact, writes such music). Billy Wayne's death, however, in a nest of poisonous water moccasins, has real uncanny impact.

The South's rich variety of poisonous snakes is also used to Gothic effect by Donna Tartt (b. 1963) in *The Little Friend* (2002). Snakes boil up in an unfortunate suburb built near a swamp. Snakes escape from crates in the room of a minister of a snake-handling Pentecostal cult. An imported cobra is dropped from an overpass into a moving open-topped car.

The Little Friend has many of the classic elements of the Southern Gothic, including the lost mansion, symbol of the aristocratic claims of the family of the twelve-year-old protagonist, Harriet Dufresne.[12] But it is not the distant past that haunts the family of the twelve-year-old Harriet. It is, rather, the unsolved murder of her older brother Robin when she was a baby. Harriet sets out to find the killer and avenge her brother.

The story fails to end as Harriet envisions. As in the scene in which she rips the wing off a trapped bird while trying to free it, Harriet's actions spread pain and destruction. She persecutes a troubled young man, who in fact is innocent of Robin's death – a crime that remains unsolved. Rather than triumphant detection and revenge, Harriet creates a narrative of uncanny doubling and ambiguity. 'She had almost been a hero', she muses at the end. 'But now, she feared, she was something else entirely'.[13] Thus, Harriet echoes a basic pattern of American Gothic we have seen as far back as Crèvecoeur: we are not the people we thought we were.

Midnight in the Garden of Good and Evil (1994) by John Berendt (b. 1939) is a best-selling book based on an actual murder case in Savannah, Georgia. In a hybrid form recalling Truman Capote's 'non-fiction novel' *In Cold Blood*, the reportage is mixed with invented dialogue and local Voodoo lore and shaped into a Gothic novel. Savannah, with its old houses built around a series of stately shadowed squares, is almost a character in the book (and in fact Berendt's work has resulted in a tourist boom). The book was turned into a film of the same title, directed by Clint Eastwood, released in 1994.

Contemporary Noir

The distinction between noir and other non-supernatural Gothic seems increasingly blurred in recent cinema and film, and even supernatural Gothic often shows influence of the noir. It is curious, incidentally, how often characters in recent Gothic works show a fondness for classic noir. For example, the narrators of Percy's novel *Lancelot* and Tartt's *The Secret History* (1992) are both admirers of Raymond Chandler.

Recent California noir, a large body of material that can only be sampled here, often reaches back to the classic period of the 1930s, 40s and 50s. Roman Polanski's 1974 film *Chinatown*, scripted by Robert Towne, is a summation and updating of the California noir tradition. The background of the case investigated by detective Jake Gittes (played by Jack Nicholson) is an only slightly abridged version of an actual, and successful, conspiracy by Los Angeles oligarchs to use funds collected from Los Angeles taxpayers to bring water to the San Fernando Valley, and thus inflate the value of their real-estate holdings there.[14] California noir is sceptical of progress, as is Gothic generally, and so it is the movie's villain, Noah Cross (John Houston) who speaks glowingly of the 'future' that he is creating. It is the past, however, that haunts Gittes's investigation. Besides the murder of Cross's former partner and son-in-law, Hollis Mulwray, Gittes learns of another of Cross's crimes: his rape of his own daughter, Evelyn Cross Mulwray (Faye Dunaway). In attempting to aid Evelyn and her daughter / sister Katherine, Gittes is drawn into one of those doublings or repetitions that evoke the Gothic uncanny. Long ago he had left the police department after his attempt to aid a citizen had unwittingly brought about her death in Chinatown. Now, in the present, he sets in motion a sequence of events that, to his horror, produce the same result, and in the same place.

Two noir novels are based on the notorious 1947 murder and mutilation of Elizabeth Short, who came to be known as the Black Dahlia: *True Confessions* (1977) by John Gregory Dunne (1932–2003) and *The Black Dahlia* (1987) by James Ellroy (b. 1948). Both novels have been made into movies. Other notable recent Los Angeles noir films are *Pulp Fiction* (1994) and *LA Confidential* (1997, from a novel by Ellroy) whose titles pay homage to the popular-culture roots of LA noir.

Ridley Scott's 1982 movie *Blade Runner*, adapted from a novel by Philip K. Dick (1928–82) extends the LA noir tradition into the science-fiction future, though the costumes, hairstyles, dark palette and incessant smoking of the characters are all intended to evoke the noir style of the 1930s and 40s.

Noir crime fiction and film is not confined to California, of course. David Fincher's 1999 film *Seven* (often typographically represented as *Se7en*) is set in a nameless big city where it rains perpetually, and the homicides of a psychopath are intended to represent the seven deadly sins. The even more metaphysical 1987 movie *Angel Heart*, directed by Alan Parker, is set in New York, New Orleans and Hell – or at least that is the apparent destination of the elevator in the final scene. The antagonist of the detective is not just satanic, like Noah Cross, but is Lucifer himself.

John Sayles's remarkable 1996 movie *Lone Star* is set on the border of Texas and Mexico. Here, as in much literature of the south-west, the international border is a natural symbol for other boundaries of race and culture. The movie questions how narratives are constructed from the past, and who has the authority to tell these stories. The unearthing of the skeleton of a former sheriff leads to escalating revelations about Rio County's history, and finally the current sheriff, Sam Deeds, must confront the discovery that he and his lover Pilar are brother and sister.

Rural community and small town

The rural community and the small town, so long idealized in American culture, remain subjects of Gothic counter-narrative in the contemporary period.

In Cold Blood (1966) by Truman Capote (1924–84) describes the actual murder of the four members of the Clutter family, wheat farmers in western Kansas, and the murderers' trial and execution by hanging. In this work Capote claimed to have invented a genre of 'non-fiction novel', though the work draws on the traditions of naturalism and the Gothic, a familiar American hybrid. The Clutters are represented as a decent, if flawed, family, in many ways embodying heartland American values of hard work and a simple rural life. They are brought into collision with the ex-convicts Dick Hickock and Perry Smith, who invade their home in a futile search for a non-existent safe full of money, and slaughter father, mother and two children.

Capote's work, controversial from the beginning, affronts conventional moral expectations in its description of the criminals. Smith and Hickock, in Capote's treatment, become American archetypes, drifters and outsiders like Huck and Tom gone wrong, or a sinister version of Jack Kerouac and Neal Cassady. Perry Smith killed the Clutters, at least some of them, but he is shown as sensitive and artistic, tormented by physical pain and a blighted childhood.[15] He is a monster toward whom Capote clearly feels fascination, if not love.

Other contemporary authors have returned to the small town, often the New England village, that classic American locus of community virtues and nightmares, with a rich Gothic tradition running back though Shirley Jackson and H. P. Lovecraft to Nathaniel Hawthorne.

Ira Levin's *The Stepford Wives* (1972) and Thomas Tryon's *Harvest Home* (1973), for example, draw on the anxieties about marriage and gender roles in a time of rapid sociological change. Both novels begin with a family moving from New York to small-town Connecticut in search of simplicity and renewal. In each case the family discovers a picturesque and welcoming community, which in fact is ruled by a secret cabal imposing the dominance of one gender over its citizens. In *The Stepford Wives*, the protagonist Joanna finds friends among a few other new residents, creative, messy, independent, feminist women like herself, but observes that most wives in Stepford are impossibly beautiful, compliant and uninterested in life outside their homes. When one of Joanna's new friends is suddenly changed into a typical Stepford wife, she begins to suspect that the town's men's association, housed in an old mansion, is responsible for these transformations. As in Levin's earlier best-selling *Rosemary's Baby*, the heroine's husband proves an opportunist and spineless betrayer; Joanna, like Rosemary, is delivered to the power of an evil cabal.

The 1975 movie adaptation directed by Brian Forbes included an uncanny encounter, not in the novel, between Joanna and her robot double. The movie's final scene has the perfectly dressed and coiffed Joanna replicant greeting another Stepford wife in a supermarket, a scene of apparent elegance and graciousness that we view with horror.

Harvest Home is an elaboration of the idea of Shirley Jackson's 'The Lottery': an apparently ordinary New England town practising pagan blood rituals. In Cornwall Combe, the centre of authority is the Widow Fortune, who seems, like Jewett's Mrs Todd, a purveyor of herbal remedies and folk wisdom. We learn, as the narrative unfolds, that she is a priestess of an ancient cult of Earth Mother worship, complete with woodland orgies and human sacrifice. Ned Constantine, the novel's protagonist and narrator, attempts to investigate the secrets of the town, and discovers the great cost of challenging the power of this matriarchal culture.

John Updike (b. 1932) sets *The Witches of Eastwick* (1984) in an imagined Rhode Island town, and lightly evokes the most celebrated of Rhode Island Gothicists, H. P. Lovecraft. Deep in the novel we find this spot-on homage to, or parody of, a Lovecraft opening: 'for years after the events gropingly and even reluctantly related here, the rumor of witchcraft stained this corner of Rhode Island, so that a prickliness of embarrassment and unease entered the atmosphere with the most innocent mention of Eastwick.' [16] As Updike continues his playful allusions, we discover that one of the families in Eastwick is named Lovecraft. [17] However, the novel is not in the tradition of Lovecraft's Gothic; it is a performance in Updike's speciality, the melodrama of small town and suburban adultery. Updike's coven of witches, Sukie, Alexandra and Jane, engage in orgies with their demon lover, Van Horne, but ultimately they use their magic to summon ordinary husbands, abandoning witchcraft for conventional lives. Most of their spells are mischievous pranks. Nonetheless, the scene in which the witches place a deadly hex on their rival, Jenny, is truly uncanny. Elements of the curse – chants, a wax figure and the victim's body hair – are counter pointed with the banal details and brand names (Formica, Scot Towel, Reynolds Wrap) of a suburban kitchen.

Another version of small-town Gothic is the television series *Twin Peaks,* created by David Lynch and Mark Frost, which ran for two seasons in 1990 and 1991. As we might expect, the investigation into the death of a high-school beauty queen, Laura Palmer, exposes the unsavoury secrets of the victim and her apparently idyllic Washington-state town. But the investigation does not move toward a conventional unmasking of one of the citizens as the murderer. Rather, the narrative enters the supernatural Gothic through the dreams and visions of FBI Special Agent Dale Cooper, where we encounter ghosts, giants and dancing dwarves. At the end of the second season, Cooper pursues his antagonist, a demon named Bob, into a mysterious 'black lodge'. Apparently, as revealed in the last scene, he is captured by Bob and exchanges identities with him. This turn of events was too weird for most viewers, as well as the network, which cancelled the series. The movie *Twin Peaks: Fire Walk with Me* (1992), directed by Lynch, returned to the town and its mysteries.

Gothic suburbs

The geography of James Dickey's *Deliverance* places the wilderness, land of the nine-fingered men, at one extreme, and his Atlanta suburbs, where the novel ends, at the other. Historically, suburbs are the end point of the process of exploration and settlement that has been the heroic narrative of American experience. When nature has been tamed, suburbs ultimately replace it. By the 1950s, suburban life was supplanting the traditional small town as a cultural norm, the embodiment of what was supposedly good and wholesome in American life.

Yet, while early television series like *The Adventures of Ozzie and Harriet* (1952–66) and *Leave it to Beaver* (1957–63) celebrated the American home in the suburbs, writers quickly understood their Gothic potential, the easy inversion of the suburban hominess to the uncanny. The very names of streets and housing developments are often ghostly, evoking what is no longer there, what has been destroyed to make suburbia: Cherokee Lane, Old Mill Road, King Farm. The detached homes, set back on lawns and eerily quiet, with no living soul in sight, often strike observers from cities or other countries as sinister.

The 1982 movie *Poltergeist* (written and co-produced by Steven Spielberg) is based on the premise that the suburbs are a fragile covering over previous life that refuses to stay buried. A suburb has been built over an old cemetery, and the disturbed, vengeful spirits of the dead trouble the homes sitting above them. The television set, which has replaced the hearth as the centre of American family life, proves a conduit through which the family's younger daughter is dragged into another plane of existence. The sequel, *Poltergeist II: The Other Side* (1986), takes the logic of the film further (and deeper), imagining that below the cemetery are the remains of a nineteenth-century millennial cult. The suburb, so apparently fresh and new, is only a layer in a historical palimpsest; the earlier script keeps bleeding through.

The Gothic writer most associated with the suburban uncanny is Joyce Carol Oates (b. 1938). A writer of great erudition and ferocious energy, Oates has explored the Gothic potential of most aspects of American life. Her novel *Bellefleur* (1980), a multi-generational saga in a fantastic north-eastern state, is at the same time a half-parodic history of the Gothic novel. *Beasts* (2002), set in a women's college, continues the tradition of schoolhouse Gothic. The suburbs, however, remain a favourite setting for Oates. In a seminal work, her 1969 short story 'How I Contemplated the World from the Detroit House of Corrections, and Began My Life Again', a high-school girl flees the boredom of her exclusive Detroit suburb for the life of drugs and prostitution on the streets of the city.[18] In another early work, *Expensive People* (1968), the upper-middle-class suburbs are so indistinguishable that even the parents of her child-protagonist, Richard Everett, find them disorienting. Richard, the villain-hero, is a confessional madman in the manner of Poe's. In the first line of the novel, he speaks of his career as a 'child-murderer', and, as the narrative unfolds, the ambiguous term gradually reveals its full meaning. At the end, Richard is living alone, his confessions not believed by the police, and, fulfilling his social role as an American consumer, he is attempting to kill himself by overeating.

Gothic city

American writers have exploited the Gothic possibilities of big cities since colonial times, as we saw in Charles Brockden Brown's *Arthur Mervyn* and George Lippard's *The Quaker City*, both set in Philadelphia, then the largest urban settlement in the United States. For many Americans still, the city remains the opposite of the Jeffersonian dream of a society of farms and villages: a place, rather, of corruption, crime and disease, the legacy of the Old World that immigrants to America were trying to escape. Popular literature and film retain this dark image of the big city, as can be seen, for example, in the series of graphic novels by writer and artist Frank Miller, whose Sin City (that is, Basin City) is a western metropolis somewhat resembling Los Angeles. The Batman franchise, comic books and comic strips, graphic novels (to which Miller contributed) and films, is set in Gotham, which of course is a long-standing nickname for New York – though in *The Dark Knight* (2008) Gotham City is recognizably Chicago. The entire noir tradition, in fact, though it can be adapted to any setting, is most often found in the mean streets of a metropolis.

Some city Gothic imports the uncanny from the forest or village into a new setting. Thus, in Ira Levin's *Rosemary's Baby*, we find a coven of witches, not in a New England town like Salem, but in an apartment building in New York, where they continue to recruit new participants for the black mass.

In a pattern set by Wright's *Native Son*, the big city has become the primary setting in which American racial conflict is enacted. The supernatural thriller movie *Candyman* (1992, directed by Bernard Rose), for example, draws on the history of racial oppression reaching from slavery to the slums of contemporary Chicago. A modern housing project, shown in gritty naturalism, was built over the site where a black man was long ago burned to death by a white mob; the Candyman is his avenging ghost. A white graduate student, played by Virginia Madsen, unwittingly summons the ghost while studying this 'urban legend', and ultimately becomes an avenging demon herself.

The HBO series *The Wire* (2002–8), one of the most critically celebrated programmes ever shown on American television, explored the urban and racial landscape of Baltimore, Maryland. Like its frontier counterpart, *Deadwood*, *The Wire* can be considered a Gothic-naturalism hybrid, a bleak and angry view of a crumbling, corrupt city. The combination of Gothic and civic exposé goes back, ultimately, to Lippard's *The Quaker City*. Much of the series concerns drug gangs in the city's housing projects and a special police squad trying to identify and arrest its leaders. As we would expect, the moral lines between gangsters and police often blur, and sometimes there is complicity between the higher levels of each. Gang lords such as Stringer Bell follow a kind of code of honour, and sometimes, at least briefly, earn the audience's respect. The betrayal and assassination of Stringer Bell evoke powerful and conflicting emotions in the viewer. Yet the most harrowing passages in the series track the lives of the black slum children who aspire to careers in the drug trade, having been offered no other model of successful adulthood. Boys must repress every sign of innocence or compassion, since the least hint of weakness may be punishable by death.[19]

What we fear now

Contemporary Gothic continues to explore the range of fears that the tradition has always invoked. The fear of the other, which is also the fear of what we may become, is embodied in tales of monsters, freaks and aliens. And horror may still be found, as Freud described, in the home we believed safe and comfortable: the haunted house continues to haunt in contemporary Gothic. Demons and other supernatural antagonists continue to erupt from our uneasy dreams.

Monsters, freaks and aliens

The monster always has been one of the central figures, and sources of fear, in the Gothic tradition. While in literature and film (or on an amusement park ride) a scary-looking figure may jump up and frighten us, this is a shallow and transient fear. Real Gothic fear of the monster occurs when some unexpected relationship is felt, or when we discover that the creature is within us, or us within it. The ideas of the normal and the monstrous are reciprocally linked, each defining the other, as in R. L. Stevenson's brilliant fable *The Strange Case of Dr Jekyll and Mr Hyde* (1886). Thus, in 'The Last Feast of Harlequin' by Thomas Ligotti (b. 1953), a story dedicated to the memory of H. P. Lovecraft, the narrator visits a small New England town to witness a local midwinter carnival. He finds himself in an underground chamber in which the masqueraders metamorphose into hideous worm-like creatures. This transformation is harrowing enough, and yet the real moment of horror is yet to come. As the narrator runs away, the master of revels calls out to his followers not to harm him, since 'He is one of us . . . He has *always* been one of us.'[20]

Serial killers

Unlike the ordinary murderer who kills out of anger, passion or greed, the familiar temptations, the serial killer occupies another category of crime. He or she is a monster who wears normalcy as a mask, killing for pleasure and the satisfaction of private rituals. We have seen such a creature in McCarthy's *Child of God*.

In noir crime fiction, the detective who hunts serial killers succeeds by thinking as the criminal does, thus crossing the frontier between the normal mind and the sociopath, and often discovering a kinship that was always there. FBI agent Will Graham, in *Red Dragon* (1981) by Thomas Harris (b. 1940) is able to capture the serial killer and cannibal Hannibal Lecter because, as Lecter later tells him, 'we're *just alike*'.[21] This ambiguous zone where the monster and the guardian of the law exchange identities, as do Agent Cooper and Bob in *Twin Peaks*, is the realm of the Gothic.

Throughout the quartet of Hannibal Lecter books, Harris obscures the distinction between the serial killers and the detectives who hunt them. Nowhere is this blurred boundary crossing more apparent than at the conclusion of *Hannibal* (1999), where Dr Lecter and Clarice Starling, heroine of *The Silence of the Lambs* (1988, film adaptation 1991) share a cannibal feast of the brains of Starling's still-living former boss.

But readers, not just FBI agents, are invited to cross this border. Lecter is a serial killer and a cannibal, but he is also charismatic and seductive. Like Dracula, with whom he has much in common, Lecter is a European nobleman and a scholar. He is witty and stylish. We find it easy to take his side against such boors as the pretentious bureaucrat who is his jailor in Baltimore. Similarly, the reader may sometimes identify even with Francis Dollarhyde, the serial killer sought by agents in *Red Dragon*. Dollarhyde, a kind of apprentice to Lecter, known as the 'Tooth Fairy' for the bites he leaves on his victims, may seem irredeemable. Yet we are taken into his mind for several chapters, and may find ourselves thrilling to his sinister power, as in the episode when he defends the blind girl Reba McClane against the attentions of a leering gas-station attendant.

Readers make odd transitions and passages, and participate in strange deeds. Indeed, we may see the 'Atlájala', the creature of the story 'The Circular Valley' by Paul Bowles (1910–99) as a trope for the reader: a transparent creature who can enter the mind and body of any living thing and experience and enjoy its sensations.[22] Such transgressions lie at the core of reading fiction, and the Gothic author exploits their uncanny potential. We are reminded, in such moments, of the Puritans' suspicions about fiction.

In a particularly disturbing version of the serial-killer narrative, the detective disappears and, in an evolution of Poe's technique, we meet the sociopath telling his own story, drawing us into his world. Such an imaginative experience can be harrowing. Brett Easton Ellis's *American Psycho* (1991) was fiercely debated even during its journey to publication, and one publisher withdrew from his commitment. Ellis's protagonist, Patrick Bateman, is a successful and fashionable stockbroker, one who pursues a hidden life as a savage murderer of young women.

Bateman can be seen as a satirical embodiment of the ego, narcissism and sense of entitlement of successful members of his 'yuppie' generation. In contrast, the serial killer and narrator of Joyce Carol Oates's novella *Zombie* (1995) is a drop-out and loser, whose only job is as the manager of an apartment house owned by his grandmother. Most of Quentin's murders are the accidental consequences of his failures to produce zombie sex-slaves through ice-pick lobotomies. Quentin is himself a zombie of sorts, devoid of remorse or compassion, perpetually stoned or drunk. He has been convicted of sexual assault on a fifteen-year-old boy, but his parents, grandmother, therapist and parole officer persist in seeing him as only misguided and redeemable. He continues to plot, murder and dismember, wrapped in layers of protective banality afforded him by family and society. As usual in the Gothic, *Zombie* critiques the conventional and normal: we see the apparently safe world of the suburb as compromised and complicit in the monstrous. Quentin's father, a respected professor of biology, studied under an honoured scientist who won the Nobel Prize. But we learn that the great man, in the 1950s, had conducted dangerous radiation experiments on children. The extremes of society, serial killer and Nobel laureate, are linked by concealed crimes against helpless victims.

Zombie, like McCarthy's *Child of God*, was based on an actual case, as were the films *Badlands* (1973, directed by Terrence Malick), *Summer of Sam* (1999, Spike Lee) and *Zodiac* (2007, David Fincher). American popular culture is endlessly fascinated and haunted by the serial killer.

Freak shows

Another category of otherness includes people whose appearance or behaviour evokes instinctive fear, revulsion or outrage in those whom society defines as normal: the disfigured (like Crane's Henry Johnson) or deformed, or the performer of bizarre acts, like the carnival geek who bites the heads off live chickens (as in Welty's 'Keela, The Outcast Indian Maiden'). At a carnival sideshow, ordinary townsfolk pay to gaze upon freaks and watch the performance of geeks. As noted in the previous chapter, the transaction of the sideshow is complex. What do the rubes, or spectators get for their money? The list would include fear, loathing and disgust transformed into voyeuristic pleasure, confirmation of their own status and good fortune, and, lurking within these emotions, envy of the carnival world and the escape from normalcy it represents.[23]

The relationship between freaks and 'norms' is at the centre of two remarkable novels separated by a decade, *Geek Love* (1989) by

Katherine Dunn (b. 1945) and *Invisible Monsters* (1999) by Chuck Palahniuk (b. 1962).

Dunn's *Geek Love* describes the Binewski family and its source of livelihood, the Carnival Fabulon. In the second generation of the show, the couple who own and manage it, Al and Lil (a former geek) decide to produce their own family of freaks by having Lil ingest poisons during her pregnancies. Of Crystal Lil's many monstrous births, some die and are preserved in glass jars as sideshow attractions, while others survive: a bald albino dwarf girl, a boy with flippers instead of arms and legs, conjoined twin girls, and a boy almost abandoned as a mere 'norm', until his parents discover that he has marvellous telekinetic powers.

The saga of the Binewski family, covering several decades, is narrated by Olympia, the albino dwarf, who in the present of the narrative is the only surviving child. In her nostalgic vision, her childhood, spent on the road with the carnival, was perfect. The Binewskis were a loving family, and the children never doubted that they were beautiful and superior to the gawking norms. The fall from this Eden followed the developing sexual maturity of the twins and the ambitions of Arturo, the boy with flippers, who became the centre of a strange cult whose followers voluntarily have limbs amputated in tribute to him. In the diminished present, the Fabulon is gone, and her siblings are dead. Olympia is willing to murder to prevent her horse-tailed daughter, product of a telekinetic incestuous union with Arturo, from being surgically turned into a mere norm.

Invisible Monsters, by Chuck Palahniuk, author of the hugely popular *Fight Club* (1996), is a grotesque and often funny book about mutilation, and, like *Geek Love*, it is contemptuous of the 'norms'. The narrator, Evie, a former fashion model who has had her jaw shot off, tells of her relationship with Brandy Alexander, a transvestite who is awaiting sexual reassignment surgery. Much of the action takes place during the drug-fuelled odyssey of Evie, Brandy and Manus, a bisexual who has been the boyfriend of both. But this is a trickster narrative, and the real identities as well as the names of the characters shift as we learn, or think we learn, more and more about their past identities and relationships. The point of the action is the violation of bourgeois taboos, and

Brandy's slogan is the book's motto: 'Find out what you're afraid of most and go live there.'[24]

Clones and evil twins

The double, one of the enduring figures of the Gothic, sometimes appears in contemporary literature as the natural twin or its genetically engineered equivalent, the clone.

Gothic portrayals of identical twins, which are surprisingly few, often involve speculation about the psychological relationship of the pair. The 'evil twin' pattern assumes that the two, like Dr Jekyll and Mr Hyde, are moral opposites. Thomas Tryon's *The Other* (1971) presents twin boys, Niles and Holland, who live on an idyllic New England farm. The evil twin is a serial killer who eliminates most members of his extended family in the course of the narrative. But Tryon introduces a number of twists and turns into the story, which is narrated by the familiar Gothic madman in an asylum. We assume that the voice belongs to one of the twins, but for much of the novel are not sure which. Perhaps, in a sense, it is both.[25]

Gothic stories about twins and doubles threaten the cherished belief that we are unique and individually significant. This is an especially powerful myth in the United States. Human cloning, now technologically feasible, or at least imaginable, gives rise to ideas that may be exhilarating ('I can be physically immortal') or disillusioning ('I can be replaced and never missed'). Among several manifestations of the cloning idea in recent films, Michael Bay's *The Island* (2005) envisions an evil corporation that clones doubles for wealthy patrons, who use the clones as a source for replacement organs or (in the case of women) as surrogate mothers. The movie features an uncanny encounter between a clone and his original, both played by Ewan McGregor (with alternating American and Scottish accents).

Demons

The attack upon the innocent by evil spirits, or perhaps Satan himself, is an American nightmare that runs back to colonial times.

The old adversary, as described by Cotton Mather, continues to vex characters in American literature and film, as do other evil beings not part of Christian symbolism. Demonic possession is a variant of the doubling, twinning and infection themes found throughout the Gothic.

The eruption of demons into contemporary popular culture began with Ira Levin's *Rosemary's Baby* in 1967, followed by the film adaptation directed by Roman Polanski and released the next year. Rosemary's baby was the Antichrist, produced by satanic rape. The subsequent career of the child is described in *Son of Rosemary* (1997).

Another demon, awakened in Iraq, somehow makes its way to America and infects young Regan McNeill in the Georgetown section of Washington, DC, as described in William Peter Blatty's novel *The Exorcist* (1971). Regan's possession recalls that of the Salem girls recorded by Cotton Mather. Readers, and viewers of William Friedkin's film adaptation (1973), have the naughty thrill of seeing the innocent Megan spew obscenities and various bodily fluids until the demon is exorcised though the ministrations of Fathers Lankester Merrin and Damien Karras, although both priests perish in the effort. Another appearance of the Antichrist child is recorded in *The Omen*, a 1976 novel by David Selzer, with a film version directed by Richard Donner. The film has been remade once, and has spawned various sequels.

Satan's return in the 1960s and 1970s may be just a literary and movie fad, but may also imply a reaction against the dominant secularism of the modern period. Certainly, Blatty suggests that the existence of demons proves the obverse, the existence of a Christian God. On the other hand, creeds other than Christianity have their own kinds of possession, and may still be evoked by artists today. In Donna Tartt's *The Secret History*, the group of classics majors in a small elite college summon Dionysus in a woodland ceremony, and apparently are in a god-crazed ecstasy when they run through the forest and murder a farmer they encounter.

Peter Straub imagines ancient demons, enemies of humanity, in *Ghost Story* (1979). Straub, like Joyce Carol Oates, possesses a deep scholarly knowledge of American literature and popular culture, to both of which he pays sly homage throughout the novel. Thus we encounter characters named Mather, Maule, Hawthorne and James. The name of an evil possessed creature is Gregory Bate, which lightly chimes with the Norman Bates of Alfred Hitchcock's *Psycho* (1960), and a climactic battle between the possessed and their human hunters occurs in a theatre where George A. Romero's film *Night of the Living Dead* (1968) plays continuously.

In a key episode, the lawyer Sears James tells a ghost story to a group of friends who style themselves the Chowder Society. Thus, Straub recreates the classic narrative frame of nineteenth-century ghostly tales. James tells of going to a remote village in rural New York State as a young schoolmaster, early in the twentieth century. He tries to shield two of his students, a boy and a girl, from some evil, which he identifies first as their sexually abusive older brother, then, seeing the grave of Gregory Bate, as the brother's ghost. The story, in fact, is Straub's retelling of *The Turn of the Screw*, with admixtures of Irving's 'The Legend of Sleepy Hollow'. This story, in turn, opens up into a plot spanning several decades. As demonic attacks kill several Chowder Society men, the dwindling band is augmented by the novel's protagonist, nephew of an original member and a writer of Gothic fiction. The characters encounter, with growing comprehension, the oft-reappearing Gregory Bate and other possessed souls, and their master, a female shape-shifting demon. Like Lovecraft, Straub has invented his own mythology, in which his demons and their servants stand behind all other accounts of werewolves, vampires, manitous and so on, that are but imperfect representations of the enemies the Chowder Society survivors must hunt and destroy.

Bug-eyed monsters

Like other forms of the Gothic, science fiction in the Gothic mode also explores the relationship of the human and the monstrous, or alien. Consider, for example, the *Alien* movie quadrillogy: *Alien* (1979), *Aliens* (1986), *Alien³* (1992) and *Alien: Resurrection* (1997). The threat of penetration by the monstrous is soon apparent, as Executive Officer Kane in effect gives birth to the alien who then hunts down and kills the remaining crew of the spaceship *Nostromo*.

Though Science Officer Ripley escapes, and seems to escape again in the sequel *Aliens*, we learn in *Alien³* that she now carries an alien embryo. After Ripley immolates herself in a furnace to destroy the alien within her, the 'Company' recreates her (in the final film) from a blood sample. But the cloned Ripley now carries alien genetic material and is used by Company scientists to create new monsters. The same premise – the human mixed with non-human life – is used to great effect in David Cronenberg's magnificently creepy 1986 remake of the 1958 movie, *The Fly*.

Ripley's impregnation by the monster could be described as an infection, since any infection is, by definition, an invasion by an alien life-form. One way to think about the *Alien* movies is as an extended metaphor about disease, and in fact the popularity of these films may owe something to cultural anxiety about HIV and AIDS, an epidemic that emerged in this period. As we have seen from *Arthur Mervyn* to *The Scarlet Plague*, the diseased body has always been one of the interests of the Gothic.

Humans and alien creatures interbreed in many novels and stories by Octavia E. Butler (1947–2006), most notably in her Xenogenesis trilogy, *Dawn* (1987), *Adulthood Rites* (1988) and *Imago* (1989). In Butler's unconventional vision, which always has valued change and hybridization, the mixing of human and alien strains is viewed not with horror, but as a necessary step for the evolution of the flawed human species.

Aliens have invaded earth repeatedly, in the pattern set by H. G. Wells's *The War of the Worlds* (1898). The direct assault of Martians or other space creatures is a staple of modern movies, as in Stephen Spielberg's recent re-filming of Wells's classic (2005), and M. Night Shyamalan's *Signs* (2002). But perhaps aliens have visited, or are among us, and we have discovered this, *and no one will listen*. This belief, or paranoid delusion, is shared by many Americans, and is surely Gothic material. Shyamalan uses it at the beginning of *Signs*, and it is the basis of the long-running television series, *The X-Files* (1993–2002), created by Chris Carter (b. 1956). FBI agents Scully and Mulder investigate the possibility of alien contact, which is also the possibility of a government conspiracy to conceal it. Within this large story-arc, individual episodes explore free-standing cases of strange events or paranormal phenomena.

The Gothic ambiguity of the series is enforced by the divergent responses of the two agents: Fox Mulder's intuitive openness, and Dana Scully's scientific scepticism.

Androids and cyberspace

Cyberpunk, a Gothic style of visionary fiction and film, was popularized and defined by Ridley Scott's movie *Blade Runner* (1982) and William Gibson's novel *Neuromancer* (1984). Influenced by Fritz Lang's *Metropolis* and noir detective fiction and film, Cyberpunk inhabits a world where the boundaries between human body and its synthesized or mechanical equivalent are blurred, as are those between the human mind and artificial intelligence. The confrontation between the android (or 'replicant') warrior Roy and his creator, the scientist and industrialist Tyrell, recalls encounters between Dr Frankenstein and his creature, reminding us of just how long the Gothic has been exploring the borderlands of humanity.

Blade Runner has the plot of a prison-break movie, but the fugitives hunted by the bounty hunter (or 'blade runner') Deckard are Roy and his band of replicants, who have escaped from an off-Earth colony. At first Deckard accepts his assignment to hunt down and 'retire' the replicants (two men and two women), but his values are complicated when he falls in love with the experimental replicant Rachel, who believes that she is human. As the movie ends, Deckard and Rachel flee together. An insoluble argument among viewers and critics, like that concerning the governess's sanity in *The Turn of the Screw*, concerns the status of Deckard himself. Is he also an unknowing replicant? The boundaries of humanity have become so blurred that it is impossible to tell.

The future world of *Neuromancer* by William Gibson (b. 1948) is also recognizably Gothic, with the satellite mansion or fortress Villa Straylight substituting for the haunted castle, while its masters, the Tessier-Ashpool clan, who reproduce by cloning, stand in for the decadent, inbred aristocrats of older Gothic. Instead of a labyrinth, Gibson's protagonist, Case, must hack through layers of cybernetic encryption. Humans gain not supernatural powers, but artificially enhanced senses and bodies, like the warrior-girl Molly with her retractable razor claws. Brooding over the plot are not gods or demons, but the powerful artificial intelligences Wintermute and Neuromancer. Rather than as ghosts, human personality survives as electrons in cyberspace.

The Cyberpunk conventions established by these two works of the 1980s greatly influenced subsequent speculative fiction and film. For example, they are evident in such Japanese *anime* as *Ghost in the Shell* (1995) and in the two Stephen Spielberg movies *AI: Artificial Intelligence* (2001) and *Minority Report* (2002), which, like *Blade Runner*, was based on a story by Philip K. Dick.

More haunted houses

Haunted houses, so central to the very definition of Gothic, continue as a standard setting for Gothic literature to the present. We have seen already the haunted house, 124 Bluestone, in *Beloved*, Toni Morrison's reclaiming of the Southern Gothic tradition.

One pattern of haunting is enacted by the evil parent, an enduring figure of Gothic literature. A vicious father or mother accomplishes the Gothic inversion of turning the refuge of the home into a place of menace. Stephen King's *The Shining* (1977) is such a story of a threatened child in a haunted house. The house in this case, the Overlook Hotel in Colorado, clearly suggests many of the features of a medieval castle. King repeatedly makes reference to Poe's 'The Masque of the Red Death', and the evil ghosts of the Overlook gather in midnight masquerade balls.

The little boy of the novel, Danny, has telepathic and precognitive abilities. The haunted hotel tries to capture the family in order to absorb the child's powers, and to this end the evil spirits first capture the family's most compromised member, the father, Jack Torrence, a failed writer and prep-school teacher. Jack's murderous attacks on his wife and son, now as an avatar of the Overlook, only amplify the abusive behaviour he has shown before, in breaking his boy's arm and in attacking one of his students. Jack is himself the son of an abusive father. The psychological truth underlying this facet of King's novel is that a cruel parent can indeed, in a literal sense, haunt a family for generations.

Stanley Kubrik's 1980 film adaptation of *The Shining*, with Jack Nicholson as Jack Torrence, is true in most ways to the mood of King's original. In the novel's ending, an exploding boiler destroys the hotel; in Kubrick's the set is spared, and Jack freezes to death in the hedge maze outside. The maze or labyrinth is an appropriate counterpart of the haunted castle, an uncanny inversion of the safe, familiar and cosy, all associated with the normal home.

House of Leaves (2000), by Mark Z. Danielewski (b. 1966), is a novel about a haunted house that is also a labyrinth. The novel itself is labyrinth-like, and a bravura display of postmodernist technique. The book calls attention to itself as an artefact through the complex story of its own publication and its unusual graphic design. It was issued first on the Internet, and the word 'house', in the title and throughout the text, is printed in blue, simulating an Internet link. The main text is in varying fonts and layouts, with (for example) few words sited among much white space in some sequences, passages reversed as in a mirror, and so on. There is also a largely parodic use of footnotes and appendices. All of these elements provide great fun and conform to the postmodern aesthetic of the self-referencing literary text, which is mainly about itself. But at its core, *House of Leaves* is a tale about a sentient haunted house. Like Morrison's 124 Bluestone, Jackson's Hill House, and the Overlook Hotel, the House of Leaves attempts to capture or kill its inhabitants: Will Navidson, his family and the band of allies he assembles to explore this shape-shifting horror. While the main text describes this struggle, its footnotes chronicle the slide of the book's fictional editor, Johnny Truant, into poverty, violence, alcoholism and drug abuse. Thus, house and manuscript are parallel structures (like Lippard's Monk Hall), and both radiate evil force.

Carpenter's Gothic (1985) by William Gaddis (1922–98) is a brilliant and eccentric work, difficult to classify, but one that clearly draws on Gothic conventions. The nineteenth-century wooden house in the Carpenter's Gothic style is even referred to as a haunted house,[26] and much of the action takes place on or around Hallowe'en. Many of the events within the house will strike readers as not uncanny, however, but darkly comic, recalling the plays of David Mamet (b. 1947). The interior is a dustbin of paper scraps, overflowing ashtrays, dirty dishes, a ringing telephone and a

frequently referenced sack of onions. Paul and his brother-in-law
Bobby argue endlessly and pursue murky financial schemes. Yet
Liz, the heroine, has many of the qualities of a confined Gothic
heroine; and the Orson Welles version of *Jane Eyre*, playing on the
television, suggests parallels between her and both Jane and Bertha
in that novel. The house does have its secrets, and its secret room,
where McCandless, the owner, keeps his documents and treasure
maps. When McCandless fails to be the needed rescuing knight,
Liz is murdered.

The vampire renaissance of the 1970s

Stephen King, Chelsea Quinn Yarbro and Anne Rice published their
first vampire novels within three years in the 1970s. It may not be
coincidence that this was the period when the public became aware
of the AIDS epidemic, in spite of the long and notorious silence of
the Reagan administration. Vampire stories carry a subtext of
infection, as did the movie *Alien*. The Gothic in the 1970s and early
1980s, as in the Victorian period, offered indirect expression of an
issue that was suppressed in public discourse.

Stephen King acknowledges Richard Matheson as a major
inspiration for his career. However, King's *'Salem's Lot* (1975) is a
homage to *Dracula*, rather than to *I Am Legend*. His first vampire
novel is an adaptation of Stoker's novel, naturalized to the
contemporary town of Jerusalem's Lot, an apparently typical New
England community. Its name, however, colloquially shortened to
'Salem's Lot, evokes the old site of witchcraft.

About a third of the novel passes before the first clear evidence
of vampire crime appears. There is then the predictable gathering
of a resistance band, recalling the Band of Light, as the evidence of
supernatural terror overwhelms their scepticism. They try to
remember what they know about vampires from Stoker's novel and
old movies. Eventually the vampire, Straker, and his familiar and
front-man, Barlow, are destroyed, but so are most of the vampire
hunters. Remaining are one man, Matt Burke, and a boy, Mark
Petrie. The novel begins with a narrative frame in which we see
Matt and Mark living together as father and son in a Mexican

coastal town. As the novel closes, Matt and Mark are returning to Maine to hunt down the vampire progeny left by Straker.

King suggests that the dissolving social bonds of the small town make possible 'the relative ease with which a vampire colony could be founded'.[27] The vaunted cohesion of the American small town is, King suggests, little more than a comfortable legend.

Both Chelsea Quinn Yarbro (b. 1942) and Anne Rice (b. 1941) attended San Francisco State College in the 1960s (though Rice is a native of New Orleans), and both take the radical step of making vampires the heroes of their novels. However, their individual visions of the vampire could not be more different.

While King's vampire Straker is arguably even more evil than Dracula himself, Yarbro's Count Saint-Germain, hero of some two dozen novels, is simply and unambiguously good. True, like Dracula, he must travel with boxes of his native soil, and must drink human blood to live, but he feeds without killing, and never kills without reason. He is an accomplished lover (though impotent), and his values are humane, scientific and benevolent. Yarbro's Saint-Germain novels, I would argue, are not Gothic at all, but well researched and elegantly crafted historical romances that make use of the hero's immortality to place him in a series of interesting places and times. As Saint-Germain makes rational and moral choices, he appeals to the educated reader's most reassuring self-image.

Rice's vampires, in sharp contrast, are perverse, bisexual, morally ambivalent and preeningly stylish. They evoke a different response altogether. In *Interview with the Vampire* (1976), for example, Louis takes the girl vampire Claudia to a performance of the Théâtre des Vampires in Paris. The theatre is operated by a colony of vampires who stage 'vampire shows' for Parisians, who imagine that they are watching simulations by human actors. In the climax of the evening's performance, Louis and Claudia watch as the vampire actors drag a terrified young woman on stage. Her clothing is stripped away, as Rice describes in voluptuous detail. (We are reminded here that Rice, under other pen-names, is also an author of erotic fiction.) Then the vampires kill her and drink her blood.

What response does Rice ask of the reader in this scene? Clearly, we are not to identify with the audience of Parisians, who are mere rubes, no wiser than bumpkins at a carnival sideshow. Rice has manoeuvred the reader into viewing the performance through the sophisticated vampire eyes of Louis and Claudia, and we are invited to watch a murder being stylishly performed, and to enjoy it. This is indeed Gothicism at its most transgressive and disturbing, in the tradition of D. A. F. De Sade and Aphra Behn.

Vampires now

In a later novel of Rice's *Vampire Chronicles*, Lestat, who had transformed Louis into a vampire in *Interview with the Vampire*, develops a new career as a rock star. Rice thus makes explicit the connection between vampire film and fiction and the music-addled Goth subculture of disaffected adolescents.[28] This subculture is the subject of the vampire fiction of Poppy Z. Brite (b. 1967), in whose novels most vampires are rock musicians, and vice versa. Brite, like Rice born in New Orleans, pushes to extremes the sadism and perversity of Rice's cycle, mixed with the junkie sensibility of William F. Burroughs.

Brite's vampires, though primarily queer, are capable of interbreeding with humans. In *Lost Souls* (1992) a young man who takes the name Nothing discovers that he is half vampire, and leaves his suburban home in quest of his vampire father. The plot captures the essential fantasy of the Goth teenager, who tries to invent a new identity through a confrontational style of dress and music that will validate his rebellion against boring suburban or small-town life. In Nothing's road trip, he discovers hard drugs and rough trade, and eventually meets his vampire father and becomes his lover.

In *Fledgling* (2005), Octavia E. Butler follows Yarbro and Rice in creating a first-person vampire narrator. Possibly intended as the initial novel of a vampire cycle, *Fledgling* was the author's last novel before her death in early 2006. She came to vampire fiction from her science-fiction background, and, like Matheson, Butler eliminates the supernatural. Her vampires are a separate species, possibly of extra-terrestrial origin, which has existed in symbiotic relationship with humans for thousands of years.

Fledgling is a murder mystery, in which the heroine, Shori, awakens in great pain, blind, and with amnesia from traumatic wounds, the only survivor of her murdered vampire family. We learn about vampires, and about Shori, as she does. She regains sight and some memory, and thereafter we follow her in her quest for justice against the vampire faction that has massacred her family.

While Shori is logical and ethical, like Yarbro's Saint-Germain, Butler does pose some difficult, and Gothic, challenges for the reader. Shori's first act of the novel is to kill and eat a man. (She needs meat to heal, and acts out of literal blind instinct.) Her first live blood-feeding and sexual relationship in the narrative is with a husky young construction worker. Shori is actually fifty-three years old (as she learns later), and is sexually mature enough for human sexuality, though not old enough to marry a vampire male. However, since she appears to be a ten-year-old black girl, the pairing with Wright, the construction worker, suggests paedophilia. Also disturbing is the physical addiction of human symbionts to their vampires. Vampires are, in essence, a drug.

The Historian (2005) by Elizabeth Kostova (b. 1964), the author's debut novel, is another variation on Stoker's *Dracula*. Like Stoker's book, which is mentioned several times as an authoritative but limited source, the novel is set partially in England. It describes a group of vampire hunters who travel to Transylvania in an attempt to destroy the vampire king. This is a complicated book, with several layers of time, major sections occurring in the 1930s, the 1950s, the 1980s and 2008. The novel is in part a travelogue, with realistic scenes in Istanbul, Budapest, rural Bulgaria and elsewhere that balance the fantastic elements. Dracula retains many of the characteristics of the medieval king and warrior he once was, Vlad the Impaler, a role only briefly recalled in Stoker's novel. At the novel's end we are given a view of the medieval Vlad at the height of his powers, standing on the parapet of an abbey he has endowed. To the abbot who watches him, it seems as if the lordly Vlad has 'all the world before him', a phrase that echoes the closing of Milton's *Paradise Lost*; but it is not Adam and Eve being described, but the satanic Dracula. The world at his disposal is our own.

Our vampire chronicles would not be complete without mentioning the witty television program *Buffy the Vampire Slayer* (1997–2003), created by Josh Whedon (b. 1964). The show's eponymous heroine tries to balance her role as the destined champion of the war against vampires with her life as an otherwise normal California high-school student. The challenges of each seem about equal. The mean popular girls in the cafeteria prove nearly as formidable as the monsters pouring out of the rift that opens to the underworld. There is a considerable feminist slant to the show, with the petite blonde Buffy serving as the warrior leader of a small band that includes two other students and Giles, the school librarian, who speaks in the plummy tones of the British upper classes. Much of the programme's humour comes from slight tweaks to familiar patterns of adolescence. In one first-season episode several students are enslaved by the spirits of demonic hyenas, and begin, consequently, to mimic the behaviour of a hyena pack. The joke, of course, is that there is essentially no difference.

The end of everything

The end of the world has been a favourite theme of modern and postmodern literature, and is hardly confined to America. Among many recent films, *Last Night* (1998) portrayed apocalypse in Canada, *28 Weeks Later* (2007) in Britain. Monsters have devoured downtown Tokyo repeatedly. But apocalypse has had a special meaning for Americans. In the *Course of Empire* paintings by Thomas Cole (1801–48) the last of the five panels, titled *Desolation*, portrays the ruins of the great city we saw invaded and burning in the fourth painting, *The Destruction of Empire*. Cole's series stands as a warning, a possible counter-narrative to the American gospel of endless opportunity and progress.

Similarly, the contemporary Gothic apocalypse imagines civilization stripped away, 'The frailty of everything revealed at last', as Cormac McCarthy succinctly puts it.[29] In the post-apocalypse world most survivors turn into brutes, while a few try to salvage scraps of morality, or what was once called humanity. Meanwhile, actual humanity has been exposed as something else.

It is fitting that so many novels and films of apocalypse are set in California, the terminus of western migration, the place where the American dream (in its European version, at least) must be realized, or not at all. Thus, as we have seen, the modern novel of apocalypse was invented by Jack London in *The Scarlet Plague* (1912), whose Berkeley professor James Howard Smith was among the few survivors of the devastating disease. Nearly four decades later, novelist and Berkeley professor George Stewart (1895–1980) provided an updated version in *Earth Abides* (1949).

Incurable disease continues to be a reliable means for exterminating all or most of humanity, but nuclear attack (the nightmare of the Cold War), alien invasion and sudden climate change are also effective. California continues to be a favoured, though not inevitable, target. Matheson's *I am Legend*, of course, was set in Los Angeles, though the most recent film adaptation is placed in New York. *Golden Days* (1987) by Carolyn See (b. 1934) depicts a band of survivors in the hills above Los Angeles following a nuclear exchange.[30]

Stephen King turns his active imagination repeatedly to apocalypse, as in *The Stand* (1978) and *The Tommyknockers* (1987). His 2006 novel *Cell* imagines most of humanity turned into zombies by their cell phones.

Two remarkable novels of apocalypse conclude our study. Octavia Butler's *Parable of the Sower* (1993) and Cormac McCarthy's *The Road* (2006) both portray desperate attempts to escape from a world destroyed by fire. In that way they are retellings of ancient tales, like that of Aeneas leading his band of survivors from burning Troy. But they are also freighted with nightmare images of our own time, taken from old and current newsreels: burned and gutted cities, refugees on the roads of Eastern Europe or the Balkans, civil wars in Africa, terrorist bombings.

Butler envisions a future – again, located in Los Angeles – where social order has failed and even ordinary people live in walled communities. When the community of Butler's heroine, Lauren Olamina, is attacked and burned, and most of her family killed, she takes to the road with one fellow survivor. Hoping to find refuge somewhere in the north of the state, she forms a small band of followers on the way.

In giving the name Donner to the President of the United States in this time, Butler evokes one of the horrors of California's past: the harrowing journey of the Donner party of emigrants who were trapped by snow in the Sierras, and degenerated into cannibalism

(1846–7). This echo becomes real in some of the horrifying scenes Lauren and her followers witness. Cannibalism is the final stage of civilization in collapse.

The fires that burn through the novel also capture a universal human fear that is heightened in southern California. Los Angeles, though a coastal city, backs on to a desert, and is subject both to earthquakes and to the fire-fanning Santa Ana wind (the 'red wind' that gives a title to a story by Raymond Chandler). As Joan Didion observed, 'The city burning is Los Angeles' deepest image of itself.'[31] Yet, for a black resident of Los Angeles like Butler, fire may suggest social upheaval and racial conflict. The Watts Riots of August 1965 and the uprising that followed the acquittal of the policemen who beat Rodney King in 1992 vividly enforce this connection. Lauren leading her followers northward also recalls epochal moments of African American history, such as Harriet Tubman leading escaped slaves to freedom.

Menaced by fire and earthquake, fighting off attacks by drug-crazed outlaws, Lauren at last reaches a tentative and provisional refuge in the wooded North. She has been preaching a new religion, called Earthseed. She accumulates, of course, twelve followers. Readers of this novel will need to read its sequel, *Parable of the Talents* (1998), to learn if one of her disciples will prove a Judas. A planned third novel was never written, Butler's attention having turned to the vampires of *Fledgling*.

McCarthy's recent Pulitzer Prize-winning *The Road* (2007) is the bleakest, most minimal, of post-apocalypse stories. As the novel opens, a man and his son (neither are named) push a shopping cart filled with their few possessions down a road through a grey, ashen landscape. The supermarket shopping-cart is an evocative American image, since homeless persons can be seen pushing their few miserable possessions in such carts in any large American city. Now this wretchedness is the best life available.

The ashes painfully recall the grey clouds that settled over Manhattan following the terrorist attacks of 11 September, 2001. In this novel they are the result of a barely mentioned nuclear holocaust. All plant life is dead, and all animal life too, except a few humans. Since no food can be grown, the few survivors eke out a kind of life by eating what is available: the diminishing remnants of salvaged preserved food, and each other.

The novel chronicles the journey of the man and his son through the bleak wasteland (apparently in Tennessee and the Carolinas), moving south away from the cold, foraging for supplies, and trying to avoid cannibals. They witness terrible scenes, which may be among the most disturbing ever written: a group of men and women prisoners held as food and eaten a limb at a time by their captors; two men and a woman cooking her newborn infant. Throughout his struggle the man's goal is not just to keep himself and his son from being killed, or starving or freezing, but to preserve the boy from the despair that overwhelmed his mother and led to her suicide. He tells the boy 'old stories of courage and justice'.[32] Like Professor Smith in *The Scarlet Plague*, he describes a world that is forever gone, in words that are losing their meaning. As the man must kill and act ruthlessly to survive, it is harder and harder to maintain that they are different from the 'bad guys'. As usual in the Gothic, moral distinctions blur.

The vaguely religious final paragraphs – a description of trout in wilderness streams – is an elegy for all that has been lost, all that humanity has destroyed. Unlike most earlier apocalypse stories, there is no Eden here to be repopulated. Earth does not abide. This ultimate Gothic counter-narrative to progress records the triumph of Nothing.

Conclusion

೪

American author Joan Didion once observed that 'we tell ourselves stories in order to live'.[1] Americans often have told themselves Gothic stories. If the dominant American narrative has been of success, progress, innovation and opportunity, Gothic has provided a counter-narrative in which skepticism, bitterness and nightmare are acknowledged. It is remarkable how soon this counter-narrative appears. In Crèvecoeur's *Letters from an American Farmer*, we see both emerge virtually simultaneously. At present, when the confidence America felt after the Second World War has faded, and its future role is uncertain, Gothic seems to have become the dominant mode of American imagination.

And yet, as was suggested in the Introduction, a reading of the Gothic as an expression of the national psyche has its uses, but also its limits. By seeing in one way, we prevent ourselves from seeing in others. If nations today still have immense power over individual lives and imaginations, so too do great corporations, economic zones of influence, religions, music and the tides of popular culture. People, including artists, travel, and sometimes change nationality. Ideas travel electronically, at the click of a key or a mouse.

The Gothic now is everywhere. It has been 'globalized', along with much else in our lives. Now no longer an expression of a single country, American Gothic may be seen as one part of an emerging world culture in a troubled age.

A Note on Gothic Criticism

❦

The meaning of the term 'Gothic' continues to evolve, as do the boundaries of the body of literature described by it. This brief overview will stress the importance of the 1960s in establishing the agenda for subsequent discussion, but it is useful to review relevant criticism before the transitions of that critical decade.

In addition to academic scholarship, we should recall that authors themselves, past and present, are often the best source for insights into their motives and the intellectual currents that shape their work. Anyone interested in American Gothic should read Hawthorne's prefaces to his four major narratives, including the brilliant 'Custom-House' introduction to *The Scarlet Letter*. Edgar Allan Poe's essays are also essential, especially his 'The Philosophy of Composition'. Herman Melville's 'Hawthorne and His Mosses' is the single best contemporary summary of the 'Dark Romantic' sensibility that we now recognize as Gothic. At the end of the nineteenth century, Frank Norris's essay 'A Plea for Romantic Fiction' is in essence a manifesto for the hybrid Gothic-naturalism of his work.

In the 1930s H. P. Lovecraft wrote of *Supernatural Horror in Literature*, and more recently Stephen King's *Danse Macabre* (1983) offers a glimpse into the imagination of the current maestro of the popular Gothic. Toni Morrison's collection of Yale Lectures, *Playing in the Dark* (1992), is a meditation on race in American culture, always one of the key concerns of American Gothic.

Contemporary academic criticism of the Gothic assumes an understanding of the term 'uncanny', as defined by Sigmund Freud, and for that reason his essay '*Das Unheimliche*' ('The Uncanny') is essential background. It should be read with E. T. A. Hoffmann's story 'The Sandman', which Freud uses as a literary illustration.

In the first decades of the twentieth century American scholars were attempting to define a core syllabus of American literature and to justify the field as distinct from English literature. Melville was rediscovered only in the 1920s, and Emily Dickinson was imperfectly understood in texts that had been vandalized by nineteenth-century editors. The 1940s and 1950s were a classic period in the study of American literature, as scholars, believing that the canon had been established – a belief soon to be challenged – began to explore the issues of the new field. Some of the studies of this period, without using the term 'Gothic', anticipate later concerns of Gothic studies. Harry Levin, in *The Power of Blackness* (1958), adapting a term from Melville, mapped connections among the Dark Romantics. Richard Chase, in *The American Novel and Its Tradition* (1957), found a key concept in Hawthorne's prefaces and used it to define a romance tradition distinct from that of realistic fiction.

Leslie Fiedler's *Love and Death in the American Novel* (1960) is a founding text in the scholarship of American Gothic. Fiedler used the term 'Gothic' as it is used today, drawing under this umbrella term previous discussion of American Dark Romanticism and the 'romance tradition' by Levin, Chase and others. After Fiedler, Gothic is used to describe a broad tradition of transgressive, oppositional literature running from colonial days to the present. Fiedler attacked the text-centred New Criticism then widely practised in American universities, and stressed the importance of gender and race literary studies. He saw important texts as frequently in opposition to the cultural narrative provided by governments and dominant institutions, and intelligent reading as a subversive activity.

Love and Death in the American Novel anticipated the decades to follow in Gothic studies, in which racial and gender issues have been in the foreground. As critical approaches changed, neglected authors like Charles Chesnutt, Kate Chopin and Charlotte Perkins Gilman were rediscovered. Scholars from Juliann Fleenor to Terry Castle, among many others, traced a partially suppressed tradition of female Gothic in both British and American literature. The issue of race is central to Teresa A. Goddu's important *Gothic America: Narrative, History, and Nation* (1997), a work that has influenced the approach of this study.

The legacy of Fiedler's belief in the subversive power of the Gothic is continued in the recent collection *American Gothic: New Interventions in a National Narrative*, edited by Robert K. Martin and Eric Savoy. The frontier experience, long a centrepiece of American Studies, has been re-envisioned through a Gothic eye in *Frontier Gothic: Terror and Wonder at the Frontier in American Literature* a collection of literary texts edited by David Mogen, Scott P. Sanders and Joanne B. Karpinski (1993).

The Gothic is a literature of boundaries and frontiers of all sorts. Donna J. Haraway's *Simians, Cyborgs, and Women: The Reinvention of Nature* (1991) is a splendid companion for journeys into territories such as cyberspace. Judith Halberstam's *Skin Shows: Gothic Horror and the Technology of Monsters* (1995), which traces monsters from Frankenstein's creature to contemporary vampire and monster narratives, theorizes the boundaries of the human and the non-human.

A growing community of scholars in Gothic studies led to the formation of the International Gothic Association, organized by Alan Lloyd-Smith in 1991. Its journal, *Gothic Studies*, edited from its inception by William Hughes, has served as a forum of scholarship on British, American and, increasingly, other Gothic traditions.

In part due to IGA influence, recent scholarship often compares British and American Gothic texts. Notable works are Fred Botting's *Gothic* (1996); David Punter's *Gothic Horror* (1998) and his two-volume *Literature of Terror* (1980 and 1996), his edited *Companion to the Gothic*, and Punter and Glennis Byron's *The Gothic* (2004); Victor Sage's *The Gothic Novel* (1990); and Andrew Smith's recent *Gothic Literature* (2007). All of these works, as well as the University of Wales Press series of which this book is a part, testify to the growing interest in the Gothic in university studies.

Another trend in Gothic studies, evident in many of these recent books, is an openness to popular culture and new media. The cinema, Fred Botting observes, sustains Gothic in the twentieth century.[1] We find many recent studies of Gothic cinema, or comparisons of literary texts with movies, television programmes, and graphic novels. This direction is apparent in *Fictions of Unease: The Gothic from Otranto to the X-Files*, edited by Andrew Smith, Diane Mason and William Hughes (2002), and in Jack Morgan's *The Biology of Horror: Literature and Film* (2002).

While the Gothic was once considered a narrow area of literary studies, we now understand that Gothic describes a significant and growing area of cultural production. Gothic literature, movies, and other forms of art now can be seen everywhere. Through Gothic studies we comprehend an essential component of an anxious age.

Notes

Introduction

1   See David Mogen, Scott P. Sanders and Joanne B. Karpinski, *Frontier Gothic: Terror and Wonder at the Frontier in America* (Rutherford, N J : Farleigh Dickinson University Press, 1993).

2   See William Veeder, 'The nurture of the Gothic, or how can a text be both popular and subversive?', in Robert K. Martin and Eric Savoy, *American Gothic: New Interventions in a National Narrative* (Iowa City: University of Iowa Press, 1998), p. 28.

3   In England, Romanticism took a more conservative turn after the French Revolution gave way to the Terror under Robespierre.

4   See Sherry R. Truffin, *Schoolhouse Gothic: Haunted Hallways and Predatory Pedagogues in Late Twentieth-Century American Literature and Scholarship* (Newcastle upon Tyne: Cambridge Scholars, 2008).

5   *New Literary History*, 7 (1975), pp. 525–48.

6   Joyce Carol Oates, 'The Doll', *Haunted: Tales of the Grotesque* (New York: Dutton, 1994), p. 48.

7   Sylvia Plath, 'Black Rook in Rainy Weather', *Crossing the Water: Transitional Poems* (New York: Harper & Row, 1971), p. 42.

8   *The Complete Novels and Selected Tales of Nathaniel Hawthorne* (New York: Modern Library, 1937), p. 590.

9   In the prefaces to his book-length narratives, Hawthorne was at pains to call them 'romances', which he saw as more imaginatively free than the more realistic 'novel'. There is a long critical discussion, given impetus by Richard Chase's *The American Novel and Its Tradition* (1957), about this distinction. However, in this study we consider Hawthorne's romances as a subset of the term 'Gothic novel'.

10   Nathaniel Hawthorne, 'Alice Doan's Appeal', *Nathaniel Hawthorne: Tales and Sketches* (New York: Library of America, 1982), p. 215.

[11] Chadwick Hansen, *Witchcraft at Salem* (New York: New American Library, 1969), p. 191.

[12] *Tales and Sketches*, p. 216.

[13] Ibid.

[14] Ibid.

[15] See Judith Halberstam, *Skin Shows*, p. 2, and William Veeder in Martin and Savoy, *American Gothic: New Interventions*, p. 29.

[16] See Anne Williams, *The Art of Darkness: A Poetics of Gothic* (Chicago: University of Chicago Press), p. 22.

[17] The terms America and Americans are used to signify the United States and the colonies and territories from which it was formed, and its inhabitants. There are reasonable objections to the words, but no others are satisfactory. These are the terms by which the citizens of the country define themselves, and they did so even before the colonies separated from Britain.

1 *American Gothic to the Civil War*

[1] *Of Plymouth Plantation* was written between 1630 and 1651, and was known in manuscript by later New England historians like Cotton Mather, but it was not published until 1856.

[2] *Of Plymouth Plantation 1620–1647*, ed. Samuel Eliot Morison (New York: Alfred A. Knopf, 1953), p. 62.

[3] Ibid., p. 316.

[4] Cotton Mather, *On Witchcraft* (Mineola, NY: Dover, 2005), p. 14.

[5] Ibid., p. 15.

[6] *Letters from an American Farmer*, ed. Susan Manning (Oxford and New York: Oxford University Press, 1997), p. 41.

[7] Ibid., p. 44.

[8] Ibid., p. 159.

[9] Ibid.

[10] Ibid., p. 164.

[11] *Three Gothic Novels: Wieland, Arthur Mervyn, Edgar Huntly*, ed. Sydney J. Krause (New York: Library of America, 1998), p. 641.

[12] Ibid., p. 522.

[13] The type is defined in R.W.B. Lewis, *The American Adam: Innocence, Tragedy, and Tradition in the Nineteenth Century* (Chicago and London: University of Chicago Press, 1955).

[14] Introduction by David S. Reynolds, *The Quaker City; Or, The Monks of Monk Hall* (Amhurst: University of Massachusetts Press, 1995), p. xxiii.

[15] See Judith Fetterley, *The Resisting Reader: A Feminist Approach to American Fiction* (Blooming, Indiana University Press, 1978), pp. 1–11.

[16] The unfortunate major was the subject of a play, *André* (1789), by the popular author William Dunlap (1766–1839), that has some Gothic elements, as Benjamin F. Fisher IV has argued.

[17] *History, Tales and Sketches*, p. 1077.

18 Ibid., p. 781.
19 Ibid., p. 770.
20 *The Leatherstocking Tales*, ed. Blake Nevius, 2 vols (New York: Library of America, 1985), I, 671.
21 *Studies in Classic American Literature*, in Edmund Wilson (ed), *The Shock of Recognition* (New York: Modern Library, 1943), p. 965.
22 In Charles L. Crow (ed), *American Gothic: An Anthology 1787–1916* (Malden and Oxford: Blackwell, 1999), p. 70.
23 Herman Melville, 'Hawthorne and His Mosses', in Wilson (ed), *The Shock of Recognition*, p. 192.
24 James Russell Lowell, 'A Fable for Critics', in Wilson, *The Shock of Recognition*, p. 65.
25 Joyce Carol Oates, 'Afterword: Reflections on the Grotesque', *Haunted: Tales of the Grotesque* (New York: Dutton, 1994), p. 305.
26 Edgar Allan Poe, *Poetry and Tales*, ed. Patrick F. Quinn (New York: The Library of America, 1984), p. 64.
27 Ibid., p. 829.
28 Ibid., p. 853.
29 Ibid., p. 848.
30 Ibid., p. 841.
31 Ibid., p. 842.
32 Edgar Allan Poe, *Essays and Reviews*, ed. G. R. Thompson (New York: The Library of America, 1984), p. 19.
33 See Faye Ringel, *New England's Gothic Literature: History and Folklore of the Supernatural From the Seventeenth Through the Twentieth Centuries* (: Lewiston/Queenston/Lampeter The Edwin Mellen Press, 1995), pp. 137–56.
34 Allan Lloyd-Smith, *American Gothic Fiction: An Introduction* (New York and London: Continuum, 2004), p. 46.
35 *Poetry and Tales*, p. 1174.
36 Ibid., p. 1179.
37 Ibid., p. 204.
38 Ibid., p. 352.
39 Ibid., p. 247.
40 Ibid., pp. 570–1.
41 Ibid., p. 627.
42 Ibid., p. 628.
43 Ibid., p. 1248.
44 Ibid., p. 878.
45 *Pierre* (New York: Grove Press, 1957), p. 126.
46 Ibid., p. 424.
47 Ibid., p. 91.
48 Ibid., pp. 153–4.
49 Ibid., p. 151.
50 Ibid., p. 410.
51 Ibid., p. 489.

[52] *Billy Budd, Sailor and Other Stories* (Harmondsworth and New York: Penguin, 1970), p. 200.

[53] Ibid., p. 306.

[54] Ibid., p. 220.

[55] Dickinson's poems will be identified by the standard numbers assigned to them in the Thomas H. Johnson edition of her poems (Cambridge: Harvard / University Press, 1955).

[56] See Daneen Wardrop, *Emily Dickinson's Gothic: Goblin With a Gauge* (Iowa City: University of Iowa Press, 1966).

2 *Realism's Dark Twin*

[1] See Judith Fetterley and Marjorie Pryse (eds), *American Regional Realists 1850–1910* (New York: Norton, 1992). The editors of this important collection do not note the relationship of this tradition to the Gothic, however.

[2] Charles L. Crow (ed), *American Gothic: An Anthology 1787–1916* (Malden and Oxford: Blackwell, 1999), p. 132.

[3] Ibid.

[4] Fetterley and Pryse, *American Regional Realists* pp. 208, 211.

[5] Ibid., p. 267.

[6] Ibid., p. 272.

[7] The story was included in the Everyman's Library collection of *American Short Stories of the Nineteenth Century* (1930), but was generally forgotten until reprinted by Alfred Bendixen in *Haunted Women: The Best Supernatural Tales by American Women Writers* (1985). Recently the story has been discussed by Jeffrey Andrew Weinstock in *Scare Tactics*, forthcoming from Fordham University Press.

[8] Crow, *American Gothic: An Anthology*, p. 141.

[9] Since Alcott had reached the advanced age of thirty four when she published this work, there may be some self-deprecating irony at work here.

[10] Dan Brown's absurdly popular novel *The Da Vinci Code* shows that the Louvre still has Gothic possibilities.

[11] In *Haunted: Tales of the Grotesque* (New York: Dutton, 1994).

[12] As a writing exercise, one might attempt to complete the Governess's letter of application for her second appointment: 'Although in my first position I killed one of my students, and drove the other insane. . .'

[13] As pointed out by Jack Morgan in *The Biology of Horror: Gothic Literature and Film* (Carbondale and Edwardsville: Southern Illinois University Press, 2002), p. 173.

[14] Crow, *American Gothic: An Anthology*, p. 277.

[15] See George Santayana, *The Genteel Tradition: Nine Essays* (Cambridge: Harvard University Press, 1967).

[16] *My Year in a Log Cabin* (New York: Harper & Brothers, 1893), p. 60.

[17] Leon Edel (ed.), *The Ghostly Tales of Henry James* (New York: Grosset & Dunlap, 1963), p. 397.

18 Ibid., p. 427.
19 To which a contemporary American girl doubtless would respond, in the vernacular, 'Well, *duh!*'
20 *Shapes that Haunt the Dusk: Harper's Novelettes* (New York: Harper & Brothers, 1907), p. v.
21 *Complete Novels and Selected Tales*, p. 105.
22 'True, I Talk of Dreams', *Harper's Monthly*, 90 (May 1895), 839.
23 *The Shadow of a Dream and An Imperative Duty*, Ed. Edwin H. Cady (New Haven: College and University Press, 1962), p. 73.
24 Ibid., p. 35.
25 George Spangler, '*The Shadow of a Dream*: Howells' homosexual tragedy', *American Quarterly*, 23 (1971), 112.
26 Walter Blair (ed.), *Mark Twain's Hannibal, Huck & Tom* (Berkeley and Los Angeles: University of California Press, 1969), pp. 37–8. Italics in original.
27 The 'Raftsmen' chapter was included in *Life on the Mississippi* (1883), where it was identified as a selection from a work in progress. However, Clemens chose to delete it from the version of *Huckleberry Finn* he published in 1884. Many contemporary editions of *Huckleberry Finn* restore the chapter.
28 *Pudd'nhead Wilson* (New York: Grove Press, 1955), p. 213.
29 *The Mysterious Stranger*, ed. William M. Gibson (Berkeley and Los Angeles: University of California Press, 1970), p. 405.
30 *Frederick Douglass: The Narrative and Selected Writings*, ed. Michael Meyer (New York: Modern Library, 1984) pp. 21–2.
31 The relationship of the little white boy and Uncle Remus in Joel Chandler Harris's tales also seems to promote this idealized vision, but the fables themselves more accurately reflect the conditions of slavery.
32 The view of the romance and glamour of plantation life and the loyalty of slaves would receive its definitive statement in Margaret Mitchell's novel *Gone with the Wind* (1936) and its movie adaptation. Toni Morrison's account of the Sweet Home slaves in *Beloved* is a savage rebuttal.
33 *The Illustrated Souls of Black Folk*, ed. Eugene F. Provenzo, Jr. (Boulder and London: Paradigm Publishers, 2005), pp. 164–5.
34 For a discussion of the racial heritage of Louisiana, including the *plaçage* system, see Suzanne Disheroon-Green, 'Romanticizing a difference: regional identities in Louisiana and the Bayou country', in Crow, *A Companion to the Regional Literatures of America* (Malden, MA, and Oxford: Blackwell, 2003), pp. 306–23.
35 *George W. Cable: The Life and Times of a Southern Heretic* (New York: Pegasus, 1969), p. 96.
36 *Heath Anthology of American Literature*, 3rd-ed, vol. II, (Boston and New York: Houghton Mifflin, 1998), p. 333.
37 Ibid., p. 335.
38 Ibid., p. 408.
39 Ibid., p. 411.
40 Crow, *American Gothic: An Anthology*, p. 53.

[41] In Gail Godwin's *Violet Clay* (1978) the protagonist is a cover artist for a line of Gothic romances, and at the novel's beginning is painting such a scene, using her own face for that of the heroine.

[42] Chesnutt's novels are *The House Behind the Cedars* (1900), *The Marrow of Tradition* (1901), *The Colonel's Dream* (1905), *Mandy Oxendine* (1997), *Paul Marchand F.M.C.* (1998) and *The Quarry* (1999).

[43] In Richard Broadhead (ed.), *The Conjure Woman and Other Conjure Tales* (Durham and London: Duke University Press 1993), p. 53.

[44] *Heath*, II, p. 267.

[45] For a full reading of both Chesnutt stories, see Charles L. Crow, 'Under the upas tree: Charles Chesnutt's Gothic', in *Critical Essays on Charles Chesnutt*, ed. Joseph R. McElrath, Jr. (New York: G. K. Hall, 1999), pp. 261–70.

[46] Bierce disappeared in Mexico during the Revolution, and the date and circumstances of his death are unknown. Carlos Fuentes's novel *The Old Gringo* is a fictional account of his last days.

[47] Bierce may be referencing either the late tenth and early eleventh century astrologer Haly Abenragel, known as Hali the Arabian, or Haly Abenrudian (c.998–c.1061), an Egyptian physician and astrologer.

[48] It seems possible that Robert Frost had this passage in mind when composing one of his best-known poems, 'The Road Not Taken'.

[49] My understanding of this story was shaped by a conversation with Bierce scholar Lawrence I. Berkove.

[50] *The Complete Short Stories of Ambrose Bierce*, ed. Ernest Jerome Hopkins (Lincoln and London: University of Nebraska Press, 1970), p. 52.

[51] Published in *The King in Yellow* (London: Chatto & Windus, 1895).

[52] In modern standardized romanization, *kaidan*. Masaki Kobayashi's 1964 movie *Kwaidan*, which won the Special Jury Prize at Cannes, adapts two stories from this book and two from other Hearn collections.

[53] The classic statement of the principles of literary Naturalism is Emile Zola's *Le Roman Experimental* (1880).

[54] Collected Poems of Edwin Arlington Robinson (New York: Macmillan, 1961), p. 460.

[55] Ibid.

[56] Ibid., p. 461.

[57] Ibid., p. 74.

[58] In Joyce Carol Oates, (ed.), *American Gothic Tales* (New York: Plume, 1996), 378–97.

[59] Crow, *American Gothic: An Anthology*, p. 432.

[60] *Form and History in American Literary Naturalism* (Chapel Hill and London: University of North Carolina Press, 1985), p. 95.

[60] The original manuscript has been lost, and it is impossible to determine the extent of Charles's changes.

[60] *Frank Norris: Novels and Essays* (New York: Library of America, 1986), p. 21.

[60] Crow, *American Gothic*, p. 382.

[60] Ibid., p. 387.

65   During his brief student days at Berkeley, London would discover that he was not the son of his stepfather John London, but probably the natural son of an astrologer with whom his mother had conducted an affair before a bungled suicide attempt. London read accounts of this scandal in old newspaper files in the university library.

66   Jack London, *Novels and Stories*, ed. Donald Pizer (New York: Library of America, 1982), p.12.

67   Ibid., p. 41.

68   Among many claims of primacy that have been made for London, he may be the first American author to have attempted a serious intellectual engagement with the pioneers of psychoanalysis.

69   See *The Complete Poetical Works of Robert Browning* (New York: Macmillan, 1930), pp. 375–8.

70   *The Ghost Stories of Edith Wharton* (London: Constable, 1975), p. 275.

71   Ibid., p. 276.

72   I have argued elsewhere that Wharton's story 'The Eyes' is a critique of the tradition of clubby masculine storytelling represented by Irving. See 'The girl in the library: Edith Wharton's 'The Eyes' and American Gothic traditions', in Jeffrey Andrew Weinstock, *Spectral America: Phantoms and the National Imagination* (Madison and London: University of Wisconsin Press, 2004), pp. 157–68.

73   For tuberculosis and New England vampirism, see Faye Ringel, *New England's Gothic Literature: History and Folklore of the Supernatural From the Seventeenth Through the Twentieth Centuries* (Lewiston/Queenston/Lampeter: The Edwin Mellen Press, 1995), pp. 137–56.

74   *The Ghost Stories of Edith Wharton*, p. 158.

75   Ibid.

76   Ibid., p. 147.

77   Wharton herself noted the influence of Robert Browning's verse narrative *The Ring and the Book* and Balzac's 1842 story, 'La Grande Bretêche'; one may speculate that Wharton also was influenced in part by the similar pattern of Emily Brontë's *Wuthering Heights*.

78   *Ethan Frome* (New York: Scribners, 1911), p. 3.

79   Ibid., p. 9.

80   Ibid., pp. 67–8.

81   Ibid., p. 72.

82   Ibid., p. 174.

83   Wharton even referred to *Summer* as 'Hot Ethan'. See R. W. B. Lewis, *Edith Wharton: A Biography* (New York: Harper & Row, 1975), p. 396.

84   The names Ethan and Zenobia, of course, are names used by Hawthorne.

85   *Summer*, intro. Cynthia Griffin Wolff (New York: Harper & Row, 1979), p. 9.

86   Lewis, *Edith Wharton: A Biography*, p. 395.

87   *Summer*, p. 284.

88   This view is articulated by Cynthia Griffin Wolff in her Introduction to the 1979 reprint of *Summer*.

89   *Summer*, p. 280.
90   Crow, *American Gothic: An Anthology*, p. 434.
91   Mary A. Hill, *Charlotte Perkins Gilman: The Making of a Radical Feminist 1860–96* (Philadelphia: Temple University Press 1980), p. 149.
92   Unless 'Jane', mentioned at the end of the story as another person, is in fact the narrator herself.
93   Oates, *American Gothic Tales*, p. 87.
94   Ibid., p. 88.

3 American Gothic and Modernism

1   It is possible that Emily's name is a sly wink in the direction of Emily Dickinson.
2   *Absalom, Absalom!* (New York: Random House, 1936), p. 220.
3   Eudora Welty, *The Collected Stories of Eudora Welty* (New York and London: Harcourt Brace Jovanovich, 1980), p. 41.
4   *Collected Stories*, p. 45.
5   Flannery O'Connor, *Three by Flannery O'Connor* (New York: Signet, 1962), p. 143.
6   Flannery O'Connor, *Everything That Rises Must Converge* (New York: Farrar, Straus and Giroux, 1965), p. 141.
7   Carson McCullers, *Complete Novels of Carson McCullers*, ed. Carlos L. Dewes (New York: Library of America, 2001), p. 397.
8   Ibid., p. 417.
9   Eugene O'Neill, *A Long Day's Journey into Night* (New Haven and London: Yale University Press, 1956), p. 44.
10   Ibid., p. 123.
11   There is a splendid film version, with Katherine Hepburn playing Mary, Ralph Richardson as Tyrone, Dean Stockwell as Edmund and Jason Robards as Jamie.
12   *Long Day's Journey into Night*, p. 61.
13   Ibid., p. 131.
14   There are of course, exceptions, such as F. Marion Crawford's 1911 story 'For the Blood is the Life', clearly influenced by Le Fanu's *Carmilla*.
15   *Ariel* (London: Faber & Faber, 1965), p. 47.
16   Ibid., p. 46.
17   Anne Sexton, *To Bedlam and Part Way Back* (Boston: Houghton Mifflin, 1960), p. 21.
18   Raymond Chandler, *The Long Goodbye* (New York: Ballantine, 1971), p. 104.
19   This opposition is explored by Mike Davis in *City of Quartz: Excavating the Future in Los Angeles* (New York: Verso, 1990).
20   Ross Macdonald, *The Blue Hammer* (New York: Bantam, 1977), p. 256.

4 Gothic in a Post-American World

1   Toni Morrison, *Beloved* (New York: Knopf, 1987), p. 4.
2   Morrison spells his name with a lower-case first letter.

3   Ibid., p. 148.

4   Ibid., pp. 210–13.

5   The term 'Indian' has returned to favour over 'Native American' with many writers and critics. Obviously, there are problems with each label. There was no word in any indigenous North American language corresponding to 'Indian', as there was no such concept before the European invasion. 'Hispanic' is another troubled term, actually invented by the Bureau of Census, but it seems unavoidable.

6   Louise Erdrich, *Tracks* (New York: Henry Holt, 1988), p. 12.

7   *Blood Meridian, Or The Evening Redness in the West* (New York: Vintage, 1992), p. 3.

8   See David Rio Raigadas, 'Cutting through mythology: Cormac McCarthy's Western novels', *American Mirrors: (Self)Reflections and (Self)Distortions*, ed. Maria Felisa López Liquete, Amaia Ibarrarán Bigalondo, Federico Eguíluz Ortiz de Latierro and David Río Radigadas (Vitoria-Gasteiz: University of the Basque Country Press, 2005), pp. 267–72.

9   Matthiessen recently has revised the three volumes into a single-volume work: *Shadow Country* (New York: Random House, 2008).

10 Peter Matthiessen, *Far Tortuga* (New York: Random House, 1975), p. 126.

11 *Louisiana Power and Light* (New York: Norton, 1994), p. 10.

12 Perhaps out of mischievousness, Tartt has given her character the family name of her older contemporary, John Dufresne.

13 Donna Tartt, *The Little Friend* (New York: Alfred A. Knopf, 2002), p. 546.

14 The Los Angeles Aqueduct was completed in 1913; however, *Chinatown* is set in the 1930s.

15 *In Cold Blood* itself became part of the larger Gothic story of Capote's life. Two recent excellent films, *Capote* (2005, dir. Bennett Miller) and *Infamous* (2006, dir. Douglas McGrath), dramatize the author's research in Kansas and his relationship with Perry Smith. The latter film, especially, suggests that Capote was in love with Smith and was devastated by witnessing his execution, an event that, as much as the wealth and fame brought by the novel, threw the writer into a fatal pattern of drug and alcohol use.

16 John Updike, *The Witches of Eastwick* (New York: Alfred A. Knopf, 1984), p. 210.

17 Similarly, the name of another character, Dawn Polanski, recalls Roman Polanski, director of the 1969 Gothic film *Rosemary's Baby*.

18 Collected in *Where Are You Going, Where Have You Been?: Selected Early Stories* (Princeton: Ontario Review Press, 1963), pp. 179–95.

19 *The Wire* was created by David Simon (b. 1960). Simon and Ed Burns (b. 1946) wrote many episodes, though other talented writers participated, including Washington-based crime novelist George Pelecanos (b. 1957).

20 Thomas Ligotti, 'The Last Feast of Harlequin', in *The Shadow at the Bottom of the World* (Cold Spring Harbor, NY: Cold Spring Press, 2005), p. 52.

21 Thomas Harris, *Red Dragon* (New York: Dell, 1990), p. 86.

22 In *Collected Stories and Later Writings* (New York: Library of America, 2002), pp. 90–9.
23 One could argue that the relationship between norms and freaks is essentially the relationship between the reader and the Gothic text.
24 Chuck Palahniuk, *Invisible Monsters* (New York and London: Norton, 1999), p. 294.
25 A 1972 film adaptation was directed by Robert Mulligan.
26 William Gaddis, *Carpenter's Gothic* (New York: Viking, 1985), p. 148.
27 Stephen King, *'Salem's Lot* (New York: Doubleday, 1975), p. 278.
28 For Goth subculture, see Carol Siegel, *Goth's Dark Empire* (Bloomington: Indiana University Press, 2005).
29 Cormac McCarthy, *The Road* (New York: Alfred A. Knopf, 2006), p. 24.
30 Mike Davis devotes an entire chapter to 'The literary destruction of Los Angeles' in his *Ecology of Fear* (New York: Henry Holt, 1998).
31 *Slouching Towards Bethlehem* (New York: Dell, 1968), p. 220.
32 Ibid., p. 35.

Conclusion

1   *The White Album* (New York: Simon & Schuster, 1979), p. 11.

A Note on Gothic Critism

1   Fred Botting, *Gothic* (London: Routledge, 1996), p. 146.

Works Consulted

৵

Alcott, Louisa May 'Behind the Mask' (1866), in Charles L. Crow (ed.), *American Gothic: An Anthology 1787–1916* (Malden and Oxford: Blackwell, 1999), pp. 136–196.

American Short Stories of the Nineteenth Century, intro. John Cournos (London: J. M. Dent, 1930).

Angus, Douglas (ed.), *The Best Short Stories of the Modern Age* (New York: Fawcett, 1962).

Anaya, Rudolfo, *Bless Me, Ultima* (New York: Warner Books, 1972).

Auerbach, Nina, *Our Vampires, Ourselves* (Chicago: University of Chicago Press, 1995).

Baldick, Chris, *The Oxford Book of Gothic Tales* (Oxford and New York: Oxford University Press, 1991).

Bendixen, Alfred (ed.), *Haunted Women: The Best Supernatural Tales by American Women Writers* (New York: F. Ungar, 1985).

Berendt, John, *Midnight in the Garden of Good and Evil* (New York: Random House, 1994).

Bergon, Frank (ed.), *The Wilderness Reader* Reno: University of Nevada Press, 1994).

Bierce, Ambrose, *The Complete Short Stories of Ambrose Bierce*, ed. Ernest Jerome Hopkins (Lincoln and London: University of Nebraska Press, 1970).

Bird, Robert Montgomery, *Nick of the Woods; Or, The Jibbenainosay; A Tale of Kentucky* (1837), (New Haven: College and University Press, 1967).

Blake, William, in *The Complete Poems and Prose of William Blake*, ed. David V. Erdman (Berkeley and Los Angeles, 1982).

Blatty, William Peter, *The Exorcist* (New York: Harper & Row, 1971).

Botting, Fred, *Gothic* (London: Routledge, 1996).

Bowles, Paul, *Collected Stories and Later Writings* (New York: Library of America, 2002).

Bradford, William, *Of Plymouth Plantation 1620–1647*, ed. Samuel Eliot Morison (New York: Alfred A. Knopf, 1953).

Brite, Poppy Z., *Lost Souls* (New York: Dell, 1992).

Brown, Charles Brockden, 'Somnambulism', 1805, in Charles L. Crow (ed.), *American Gothic: An Anthology 1787–1916* (Malden and Oxford: Blackwell, 1999), pp. 17–18.

_____, *Three Gothic Novels: Wieland, Arthur Mervyn, Edgar Huntly*, ed. Sydney J. Krause (New York: Library of America, 1998).

Brown, Dan, *The Da Vinci Code* (New York: Doubleday, 2003).

Bruhm, Stephen, *Gothic Bodies: The Politics of Pain in Romantic Fiction* (Philadelphia: University of Pennsylvania Press, 1994).

Burgess, Gelett, *The Heart Line* (Indianapolis: Bobbs Merrill, 1907).

Butler, Octavia E., *Adulthood Rites* (New York; Warner, 1989).

_____, *Dawn* (New York: Warner, 1987).

_____, *Fledgling* (New York: Seven Stories, 2005).

_____, *Imago* (New York: Warner, 1989).

_____, *Parable of the Sower* (New York: Four Walls Eight Windows, 1993).

_____, *Parable of the Talents* (New York: Seven Stories, 1998).

Byrd, William, 'History of the Dividing Line', 1841, in Frank Bergon (ed.), *The Wilderness Reader* (Reno: University of Nevada Press, 1994), pp. 15–27.

Cable, George Washington, *The Grandissimes: A Story of Creole Life*, (1880) (New York: Penguin, 1988).

_____, 'Jean-ah Poquelin', in Charles L. Crow (ed.), *American Gothic: An Anthology 1787–1916* (Malden and Oxford: Blackwell, 1999), pp. 360–72.

_____, *Old Creole Days*, 1879, (Charleston: BiblioBazaar, 2007).

Caldwell, Erskine, *Tobacco Road* (New York: Scribners, 1932).

Capote, Truman. *In Cold Blood* (New York: Random House, 1966).

Caputo, Philip. *The Voyage* (New York: Alfred A. Knopf, 1999).

Carpenter, Lynette and Wendy K. Kolmar (eds), *Haunting the House of Fiction: Feminist Perspectives on Ghost Stories by American Women* (Knoxville: University of Tennessee Press, 1991).

Cary, Alice, '*The Wildermings*', 1852, in Charles L. Crow, (ed.), *American Gothic: An Anthology 1787–1916*, (Malden and Oxford: Blackwell, 1999), pp. 131–5.

Castle, Terry, *The Female Thermometer: Eighteenth-Century Culture and the Invention of the Uncanny* (Oxford: Oxford University Press, 1995).

Chambers, Robert W., *The King in Yellow and Other Horror Stories* (Mineola, NY: Dover, 1970).

Chandler, Raymond, *The Raymond Chandler Omnibus* (New York: The Modern Library, 1980).

_____, *The Long Goodbye,* 1953, (New York: Ballantine, 1971).

Chase, Richard, *The American Novel and Its Tradition* (New York: Anchor, 1957).

Chesnutt, Charles, *The Conjure Woman and Other Conjure Tales*, ed. Richard H. Broadhead, (Durham and London: Duke University Press, 1993).

Chopin, Kate, '*Désirée's Baby*' in Charles L. Crow (ed.), *American Gothic: An Anthology 1787–1916* (Malden and Oxford: Blackwell, 1999), pp. 339–42.

Cixous, Hélène, 'Fiction and its Phantoms,' *New Literary History*, 7 (1975), 525–48.

Clemens, Samuel L. (Mark Twain), *Mark Twain's Hannibal, Huck & Tom*, ed. Walter Blair (Berkeley and Los Angeles: University of California Press, 1969).

_____, *Mark Twain's The Mysterious Stranger*, ed. William M. Gibson (Berkeley and Los Angeles: University of California Press, 1970).

_____, *Mark Twain's Which Was the Dream and Other Symbolic Writings of the Later Years*, ed. John S. Tuckey (Berkeley and Los Angeles: University of California Press, 1966).

_____, *Pudd'nhead Wilson*, 1894 (New York: Grove Press, 1955).

Clery, E. J., *The Rise of Supernatural Fiction, 1762–1800* (Cambridge and New York: Cambridge University Press, 1995).

Cooper, James Fenimore, *The Leatherstocking Tales*, ed. Blake Nevius, 2 vols (New York: Library of America, 1985).

Crafts, Hannah, *The Bondwoman's Narrative*, ed. Henry Lewis Gates, Jr. (New York: Warner, 2002).

Crane, Stephen, '*The Monster*' (1899), in Charles L. Crow (ed.), *American Gothic: An Anthology 1787–1916* (Malden and Oxford: Blackwell, 1999), pp. 373–407.

Crawford, F. Marion, '*For the Blood is the Life*', 1911, in *The Penguin Book of Vampire Stories*, ed. Alan Ryan (New York: Penguin, 1987), pp. 188–202.

Crèvecoeur, J. Hector St Jean de, *Letters from an American Farmer,* 1782, (Oxford and New York: Oxford University Press, 1997).

Crow, Charles L., 'The girl in the library: Edith Wharton's "The Eyes" and American Gothic traditions', in Jeffrey Andrew Weinstock (ed.), *Spectral America: Phantoms and the National Imagination* (Madison and London: University of Wisconsin Press, 2004), pp. 157–68.

_____, 'Jack London's "Samuel" as a Gothic tale: the terrible and tragic involved with love', *Litteraria Pragensia*, 11 (2001), 81–7.

_____, 'Jack London's *The Sea Wolf* as Gothic romance', in *Gothick: Origins and Innovations*, ed. Allan Lloyd Smith and Victor Sage (Amsterdam: Rodopi, 1994), pp. 122–31.

——, *Maxine Hong Kingston* (Boise, ID, Western Writers Series, 2004).

_____, 'Under the Upas Tree: Charles Chesnutt's Gothic', in *Critical Essays on Charles Chesnutt*, ed. Joseph R. McElrath, Jr. (New York: G. K. Hall, 1999), pp. 261–70.

Crow, Charles L. (ed.), *American Gothic: An Anthology 1787–1916* (Malden and Oxford: Blackwell, 1999).

——, *A Companion to the Regional Literatures of America* (Malden, MA, and Oxford: Blackwell, 2003).

Danielewski, Mark Z., *House of Leaves* (New York: Random House, 2000).

Davis, Mike, *City of Quartz: Excavating the Future in Los Angeles* (London and New York, 1990).

_____, *Ecology of Fear* (New York: Henry Holt, 1998).

Davis, Rebecca Harding, *Life in the Iron Mills*, 1861, ed. Tillie Olsen (New York: The Feminist Press, 1972).

Dickey, James, *Deliverance* (New York: Dell, 1970).

Dickinson, Emily, *Poems*, 3 vols, ed. Thomas H. Johnson (Harvard: Harvard University Press, 1955).

Didion, Joan, *Play It As It Lays* (New York: Bantam, 1970).

_____, *Slouching Towards Bethlehem* (New York: Dell, 1968).

_____, *The White Album* (New York: Simon and Schuster, 1979).

Disheroon-Green, Suzanne, 'Romanticizing a difference: regional identities in Louisiana and the Bayou country,' in Charles L. Crow (ed.), *A Companion to the Regional Literatures of America* (Malden, MA, and Oxford: Blackwell, 2003), pp. 306–23.

Donne, John Gregory, *True Confessions* (New York: Dutton, 1977).

Douglass, Frederick, *The Narrative and Selected Writings*, ed. Michael Meyer (New York: Modern Library, 1984).

Du Bois, W. E. B., *The Souls of Black Folk*, 1903, in *The Illustrated Souls of Black Folk*, ed. Eugene F. Provenzo, Jr. (Boulder and London: Paradigm Publishers, 2005).

Dufresne, John, *Louisiana Power and Light* (New York: Norton, 1994).

Dunbar-Nelson, Alice, 'Sister Josepha', (1899), in Paul Lauter et al. (eds), *The Heath Anthology of American Literature*, 3rd edn (Boston and New York: Houghton Mifflin, 1998), vol. II, pp. 407–11.

Dunlap, William, *André* (1798) (New York: Penguin, 1997).

Dunn, Katherine, *Geek Love* (New York: Warner, 1989).

Dunne, John Gregory, *True Confessions* (New York: Dutton, 1978).

Ellis, Brett Easton, *American Psycho* (New York: Vintage, 1991).

Ellroy, James, *The Black Dahlia* (New York: Mysterious Press, 1987).

Emerson, Ralph Waldo, *Essays and Lectures* (New York: Library of America, 1983).

Erdrich, Louise, *Love Medicine* (New York: HarperCollins, 1984).

_____, *Tracks* (New York: Henry Holt, 1988).

Faulkner, William, *Absalom, Absalom!* (New York: Random House, 1936).

_____, *Go Down, Moses* (New York: Random House, 1942).

_____, *Novels 1930–1935*, ed. Joseph Blotner and Noel Polk (New York: Library of America, 1985).

_____, *The Portable Faulkner*, ed. Malcolm Cowley (New York: Viking, 1946).

_____, *The Sound and the Fury* (New York: Random House, 1929).

Fetterley, Judith, and Majorie Pryse (eds), *American Women Regionalists 1850–1910* (New York and London: Norton, 1992).

Fiedler, Leslie, *Love and Death in the American Novel*, 1960, (Champaign: Dalkey Archive Press, 1997).

Fisher, Benjamin F., IV, *The Gothic's Gothic: Study Aids to the Tradition of the Tale of Terror* (London: Garland, 1988).

_____, '*Gothic possibilities in Moby-Dick*,' in Allan Lloyd-Smith and Victor Sage (eds), *Gothick: Origins and Innovations* (Amsterdam: Rodopi, 1994 pp. 115–21).

_____, 'James Kirke Paulding's Gothicism and American Literary Nationalism.' *Gothic Studies*, 1:1 (August 1999), 31–46.

_____, 'Poe and the Gothic Tradition,' in *The Cambridge Companion to Edgar Allan Poe*, ed. Kevin J. Hayes (Cambridge: Cambridge University Press, 2002), pp. 72–91.

Fleenor, Juliann E. (ed.), *Female Gothic* (Montreal: Eden Press, 1983).

Frame, Janet, *To the Is-Land: An Autobiography* (New York: George Braziller, 1982).

Frank, Frederick S., *Gothic Fiction: A Master List of Twentieth-Century Criticism and Research* (London: Meckler, 1988).

Freeman, Mary E. Wilkins, 'Luella Miller', in Charles L. Crow (ed.), *American Gothic: An Anthology 1787–1916* (Malden and Oxford: Blackwell, 1999), pp. 267–75.

_____, 'Old Woman Magoun', in Charles L. Crow (ed.), *American Gothic: An Anthology 1787–1916* (Malden and Oxford: Blackwell, 1999), pp. 256–66.

Freud, Sigmund, *The Uncanny*, 1919, tr. David McClintock (London and New York: Penguin, 2003).

Gaddis, William, *Carpenter's Gothic* (New York: Viking, 1985).

Gelder, Ken, *Reading the Vampire* (London: Routledge, 1994).

Gibson, William, *Neuromancer* (New York: Ace, 1984).

Gilbert, Sandra M. and Susan Gubar, *The Madwoman in the Attic: The Woman Writer and the Nineteenth-Century Imagination* (New Haven and London: Yale University Press, 1984).

Gilman, Charlotte Perkins, 'The Giant Wisteria', in Charles L. Crow (ed.), *American Gothic: An Anthology 1787–1916* (Malden and Oxford: Blackwell, 1999) pp. 434–9.

_____, 'The Yellow Wallpaper', in Joyce Carol Oates (ed.) *American Gothic Tales* (New York: Plume, 1996), pp. 87–102.

Glasgow, Ellen, *The Shadowy Third and Other Stories* (New York: Doubleday, 1923).

Goddu, Teresa A., *Gothic America: Narrative, History, and Nation*, (New York: Columbia University Press, 1997).

Godwin, Gail, *Violet Clay*, (New York: Viking Penguin, 1978).

Godwin, William, *Caleb Williams*, 1794, ed. Maurice Hindle (London: Penguin Books, 1988).

Hansen, Chadwick, *Witchcraft at Salem* (New York: New American Library, 1969).

Halberstam, Judith, *Skin Shows: Gothic Horror and the Technology of Monsters* (Durham: Duke University Press, 1995).

Harraway, Donna J., *Simians, Cyborgs and Women: The Reinvention of Nature* (New York: Routledge, 1996).

Harris, Joel Chandler, *The Complete Tales of Uncle Remus* (Boston: Houghton Mifflin, 1955).

Harris, Thomas, *Hannibal* (New York: Delacorte, 1999).

_____, *Red Dragon* (1981) (New York: Dell, 1990).

_____, *The Silence of the Lambs* (New York. St. Martin's Press, 1989).

Hawthorne, Nathaniel, *Complete Novels and Selected Tales*, ed. Norman Holmes Pearson (New York: Modern Library, 1937).

_____, *Tales and Sketches*, ed. Roy Harvey Pearce (New York: Library of America, 1982).

Hearn, Lafcadio, 'The Ghostly Kiss', in Charles L. Crow (ed.), *American Gothic: An Anthology 1787–1916* (Malden and Oxford: Blackwell, 1999), pp. 452–3.

_____, *Kwaidan: Stories and Studies of Strange Things* (Tokyo, Rutland, Singapore: Tuttle, 1971).

Hill, Mary A., *Charlotte Perkins Gilman: The Making of a Radical Feminist 1860–1896* (Philadelphia: Temple University Press, 1990).

Hoffmann, E. T. A., *Tales*, ed. Victor Lange (New York: Continuum, 1982).

Hogle, Jerrold (ed.) *The Cambridge Companion to Gothic Fiction* (Cambridge: Cambridge University Press, 2002).

Howard, June, *Form and History in American Literary Naturalism* (Chapel Hill and London: University of North Carolina Press, 1985).

Howells, William Dean, *My Year in a Log Cabin* (New York: Harper & Bros., 1893).

_____, *The Shadow of a Dream and An Imperative Duty*, ed. Edwin H. Cady (New Haven: College and University Press, 1962).

_____, 'True, I Talk of Dreams', *Harper's Monthly*, 90 (May 1895), 836–45.

_____, *Years of My Youth*, (New York: Harper & Bros., 1916).

Howells, William Dean and Henry Mills Alden (eds), *Shapes that Haunt the Dusk: Harper's Novelettes* (New York: Harper & Brothers, 1907).

Hume, Robert, 'Gothic Versus Romantic: a Revaluation of the Gothic form', *PMLA,* 84 (1969), 282–90.

Ibsen, Henrik, *Four Major Plays: A Doll's House, Ghosts, Hedda Gabler, The Master Builder* (Oxford and New York: Oxford University Press, 1988).

Irving, Washington, *History, Tales and Sketches*, ed. James W. Tuttleton (New York: Library of America, 1983).

Jackson, Shirley, *The Haunting of Hill House*, 1959 (New York: Penguin, 2006).

_____, 'The Lottery', 1948, in *The Best Short Stories of the Modern Age*, ed. Douglas Angus (New York: Fawcett, 1962), pp. 308–17.

_____, *We Have Always Lived in the Castle* (New York: Viking, 1962).

James, Henry, *The American*, 1877 (New York: New American Library, 1963).

_____, *The Ghostly Tales of Henry James* ed. Leon Edel (New York: Grosset & Dunlap, 1963).

_____, *Great Short Works of Henry James* (New York: Harper, 1966).

_____, *Hawthorne* (1879), in Edmund Wilson (ed.), *The Shock of Recognition* (New York: Modern Library, 1955), pp. 427–569.

_____, *The Portrait of a Lady*, 1881 (Cambridge: Riverside, 1956).

_____, *The Turn of the Screw*, in Charles L. Crow (ed.), *American Gothic: An Anthology 1787–1916* (Malden and Oxford: Blackwell, 1999), pp. 276–338.

Jewett, Sarah Orne, 'The Foreigner', in Charles L. Crow (ed.), *American Gothic: An Anthology 1787–1916*, (Malden and Oxford: Blackwell, 1999): pp. 241–55.

Joshi, S. T., *The Modern Weird Tale* (Jefferson, NC, and London: McFarland & Co., 2001).

_____, *The Weird Tale* (Austin: University of Texas Press, 1990).

King, Grace, 'The Little Convent Girl' (1893), in Paul Lauter et al.(eds), *The Heath Anthology of American Literature*, 3rd edn. (Boston and New York: Houghton Mifflin, 1998), vol. II, pp. 330–5.

King, Stephen, *Carrie*, (New York: Doubleday, 1974).

_____, *Cell: A Novel* (New York: Scribner, 2006).

_____, *Danse Macabre* (New York: Berkley Books, 1983).

_____, *'Salem's Lot* (New York: Doubleday, 1975).

_____, 'The Reach', in Joyce Carol Oates (ed.) *American Gothic Tales* (New York: Plume, 1996), pp. 378–97.

_____, The Shining, 1977 (New York: Pocket Books, 2001).

_____, The Stand (New York: Doubleday, 1978).

_____, *The Tommyknockers* (New York: Putnam, 1987).

Kingston, Maxine Hong, *The Woman Warrior: Memoirs of a Girlhood Among Ghosts* (New York: Knopf, 1976).

Knowles, John, *A Separate Peace* (New York: Macmillan, 1959).

Kostova, Elizabeth, *The Historian* (New York: Little, Brown, 2005).

Lauter, Paul et al. (eds), *The Heath Anthology of American Literature*, 3rd edn (Boston and New York: Houghton Mifflin, 1998).

Le Fanu, Joseph Sheridan, *Carmilla*, in Alan Ryan (ed.) *The Penguin Book of Vampire Stories* (New York: Penguin, 1987), pp. 71–137.

Le Guin, Ursula K., *A Wizard of Earthsea* (New York: Bantam, 1968).

Levin, Harry, *The Power of Blackness* (New York: Vintage, 1958).

Levin, Ira, *Rosemary's Baby* (New York: Random House, 1967).

_____, *The Boys from Brazil* (Boston: G. K. Hall, 1976).

_____, *Son of Rosemary* (New York: Dutton, 1997).

_____, *The Stepford Wives* (New York: Random House, 1972).

Lewis, Matthew, *The Monk,* 1796, ed. Howard Anderson, introduction and notes by Emma McEvoy (Oxford and New York: Oxford University Press, 2008).

Lewis, R. W. B., *Edith Wharton: A Biography* (New York: Harper & Row, 1975).

Ligotti, Thomas, *The Shadow at the Bottom of the World* (Cold Spring Harbor, NY: Cold Spring Press, 2005).

Lippard, George, *The Quaker City; Or, the Monks of Monk Hall,* ed. David S. Reynolds (Amherst: University of Massachusetts Press, 1995).

Lloyd-Smith, Allan, *American Gothic Fiction: An Introduction* (New York and London: Continuum, 2004).

———, *Uncanny American Fiction: Medusa's Face* (Basingstoke: Macmillan, 1989).

Lloyd-Smith, Allan, and Victor Sage (eds), *Gothick: Origins and Innovations* (Amsterdam: Rodopi, 1994).

London, Jack, *The Complete Short Stories of Jack London,* ed. Earle Labor, Robert C. Leitz, III, and I. Milo Shepherd (Stanford: Stanford University Press, 1993).

———, *Novels and Stories,* ed. Donald Pizer (New York: Library of America, 1982).

López Liquete, Maria Felisa, Amaia Ibarrarán Bigalondo, Federico Eguíluz Ortiz de Latierro and David Río Radigadas (eds), *American Mirrors: (Self)Reflections and (Self)Distortions* (Vitoria-Gasteiz: University of the Basque Country Press, 2005).

Lovecraft, H. P., *Supernatural Horror in Literature* (New York: Dover, 1973).

———, *Tales,* ed. Peter Straub (New York: Library of America, 2005).

Lowell, James Russell, 'A Fable for Critics', 1848, in Edmund Wilson (ed.), *The Shock of Recognition* (New York: Modern Library, 1955), pp. 23–78.

McCarthy, Cormac, *Blood Meridian, Or the Evening Redness in the West* (New York: Vintage, 1992).

———, *Child of God* (New York: Vintage, 1974).

———, *The Road* (New York: Knopf, 2006).

McCullers, Carson, *Complete Novels of Carson McCullers,* ed. Carlos L. Dewes (New York: Library of America, 2001).

Macdonald, Ross, *The Blue Hammer* (New York, Bantam, 1976).

McElrath, Joseph R., Jr. (ed.), *Critical Essays on Charles Chesnutt* (New York: G. K. Hall, 1999).

Mamet, David, *Oleanna* (New York: Pantheon, 1992).

Martin, Robert K. and Eric Savoy (eds), *American Gothic: New Interventions in a National Narrative* (Iowa City: University of Iowa Press, 1998).

Mather, Cotton, *Wonders of the Invisible World* (1692) repr. as *On Witchcraft* (Mineola, NY: Dover, 2005).

Matheson, Richard, *I Am Legend*, 1954 (New York: Tom Doherty Associates, 1997).

Matthiessen, Peter, *Far Tortuga* (New York: Random House, 1975).

_____, *Killing Mr. Watson* (New York: Random House, 1990).

Melville, Herman, *Billy Budd, Sailor & Other Stories* (Harmondsworth: Penguin, 1970).

_____, 'Hawthorne and His Mosses' (1850), in Edmund Wilson (ed.), *The Shock of Recognition* (New York: Modern Library, 1955), pp. 187–204.

_____, *Moby-Dick*, 1851, in *Redburn, White-Jacket, Moby-Dick*, ed. G. Thomas Tanselle (New York: Library of America, 1983), pp. 771–1408.

_____, *Pierre* (1852) (New York: Grove, 1957).

Miller, Arthur, *The Portable Arthur Miller* (New York: Penguin, 1971).

Miller, Frank, *Sin City. Vol. 1: The Hard Goodbye* (Milwaukie, Oregon: Dark Horse, 1991).

Mogen, David, Scott P. Sanders and Joanne B. Karpinski (eds), *Frontier Gothic: Terror and Wonder at the Frontier in American Literature* (London and Toronto: Associated University Presses, 1993).

Momaday, N. Scott, *House Made of Dawn* (New York: Harper & Row, 1968).

Morgan, Jack, *The Biology of Horror: Gothic Literature and Film* (Carbondale and Edwardsville: Southern Illinois University Press, 2002).

Morrison, Toni, *Beloved* (New York: Knopf, 1987).

_____, *Playing in the Dark: Whiteness and the Literary Imagination* (New York: Vintage Books, 1992).

Muir, John, *Nature Writings*, ed. William Cronon (New York: Library of America, 1997).

Neal, John, 'Idiosyncrasies', in Charles L. Crow (ed.), *American Gothic: An Anthology 1787–1916* (Malden and Oxford: Blackwell, 1999), pp. 30–47.

_____, *Logan, the Mingo Chief* (London: J. Cunningham, 1840).

Norris, Frank, 'Lauth', 1893, in Charles L. Crow (ed.), *American Gothic: An Anthology 1787–1916* (Malden and Oxford: Blackwell, 1999), pp. 418–33.

_____, *Novels and Essays*, ed. Donald Pizer (New York: Library of America, 1985).

Oates, Joyce Carol, *Beasts* (New York: Carol & Graf, 2002).

_____, *Bellefleur* (New York: Dutton, 1980).

_____, *Expensive People* (New York: Vanguard, 1968).

_____, *Haunted: Tales of the Grotesque* (New York: Dutton, 1994).

_____, 'How I Contemplated the World from the Detroit House of Corrections, and Began My Life Again', *in High Lonesome: New and Selected Stories* (New York: HarperCollins, 2007), pp. 267–83.

_____, *Zombie* (New York: Dutton, 1995).

Oates, Joyce Carol (ed.), *American Gothic Tales* (New York: Plume, 1996).

O'Brien, Fitz-James, 'The Diamond Lens', in *American Short Stories of the Nineteenth Century*, intro. John Cournos (London: J. M. Dent, 1930), pp. 102–29.

O'Connor, Flannery, *Everything That Rises Must Converge* (New York: Farrar, Straus and Giroux, 1965).

_____, 'The Comforts of Home', in *Everything That Rises Must Converge* (New York: Farrar, Straus, and Giroux, 1965), pp. 115–42.

_____, *Three by Flannery O'Connor* (New York: Signet, 1962).

O'Neill, Eugene, *A Long Day's Journey Into Night* (New Haven and London: Yale University Press, 1956).

Page, Thomas Nelson, 'Marse Chan', 1884, in *Nineteenth-Century American Fiction*, ed. William Holmes and Edward Mitchell (Glenview, Illinois: Scott, Foresman, 1970).

Palahniuk, Chuck, *Invisible Monsters* (New York and London: Norton, 1999).

Paulding, James Kirk, *Westward Ho!* (New York: Harper, 1832).

Percy, Walker, *Lancelot* (New York: Farr, Strauss & Giroux, 1977).

Plath, Sylvia, *Ariel* (London: Faber & Faber, 1965).

_____, *Crossing the Water: Transitional Poems* (New York: Harper & Row, 1971).

_____, *The Bell Jar*, 1963 (London: Faber & Faber, 1966).

Poe, Edgar Allan, *Essays and Reviews*, ed. G. R. Thompson (New York: Library of America, 1984).

_____, *The Narrative of Arthur Gordon Pym*, 1838 (New York: Hill & Wang, 1960).

_____, *Poetry and Tales*, ed. Patrick F. Quinn (New York: Library of America, 1984).

Polidori, John, 'The Vampyre', 1819 in Alan Ryan (ed.), *The Penguin Book of Vampire Stories* (New York: Penguin, 1987), pp. 7–24.

Punter, David, *Gothic Horror: A Reader's Guide from Poe to King and Beyond* (New York: St Martin's, 1998).

_____, *The Literature of Terror: A History of Gothic Fictions from 1765 to the Present Day*, vol. 1 (London: Longman, 1980); vol. 2 (London: Longman, 1996).

Punter, David (ed.), *A Companion to the Gothic* (Oxford and Malden: Blackwell, 2000).

Punter, David, and Glennis Byron, *The Gothic* (Oxford: Blackwell, 2004).

Radcliffe, Ann, *The Mysteries of Udolpho*, 1794, Bonamy Dobrée (ed.) and Terry Castle (introduction and notes) (Oxford and New York: Oxford University Press, 2008).

Rampo, Edogawa, *Japanese Tales of Mystery and Imagination* (Boston, Ruthland and Tokyo: Tuttle Publishing, 1956).

Reuben, Louis, *George W. Cable: The Life and Times of a Southern Heretic* (New York: Pegasus, 1969).

Rice, Anne, *Interview with the Vampire* (New York: Knopf, 1976).

_____, *The Vampire Lestat* (New York: Knopf, 1985).

Ringe, Donald, *American Gothic: Imagination & Reason in Nineteenth-Century Fiction* (Lexington: University of Kentucky Press, 1982).

Ringel, Faye, *New England's Gothic Literature: History and Folklore of the Supernatural From the Seventeenth Through the Twentieth Centuries* (Lewiston/Queenston/Lampeter: The Edwin Mellen Press, 1995).

Rio Raigadas, David, 'Cutting Through Mythology: Cormac McCarthy's Western novels', in Maria Felisa López Liquete Amaia Ibarrarán Bigalondo, Federico Eguíluz Ortiz de Latierro and David Río Radigadas (eds), *American Mirrors: (Self)Reflections and (Self)Distortions* (Vitoria-Gasteiz: University of the Basque Country Press, 2005), pp. 267–72.

Robinson, Edwin Arlington, *Collected Poems of Edwin Arlington Robinson* (New York: Macmillan, 1961).

Rowlandson, Mary, *A True History of the Captivity and Restoration of Mrs Mary Rowlandson*, 1682. (London and New York: Arnold, 1997).

Rubin, Louis, *George W. Cable: The Life and Times of a Southern Heretic* (New York: Pegasus, 1969).

Ryan, Alan (ed.), *The Penguin Book of Vampire Stories* (New York: Penguin, 1987).

Sage, Victor (ed.), *The Gothic Novel: A Casebook* (London: Macmillan, 1990).

Santayana, George, *The Genteel Tradition: Nine Essays* (Cambridge: Harvard University Press, 1967).

Scarborough, Dorothy, *The Supernatural in Modern Fiction* (New York: Putnam, 1917).

See, Carolyn, *Golden Days* (New York: McGraw-Hill, 1987).

Sexton, Anne, *To Bedlam and Part Way Back* (Boston: Houghton Mifflin, 1960).

Shelley, Mary, *Frankenstein*, 1818, ed. Maurice Hindle (London and New York: Penguin, 2003).

Showalter, Elaine, 'Syphilis, Sexuality, and the Fiction of the Fin de Siècle', in Ruth Bernard Yeazell (ed.), *Sex, Politics, and Science in the Nineteenth-Century Novel* (Baltimore: Johns Hopkins University Press, 1986).

Siegel, Carol, *Goth's Dark Empire* (Bloomington: Indiana University Press, 2005).

Smith, Andrew, *Gothic Literature* (Edinburgh: Edinbrugh University Press, 2007).

Smith, Andrew, Diane Mason and William Hughes (eds.), *Fictions of Unease: The Gothic from Otranto to the X-Files* (Bath: Sulis Press, 2002).

Spangler, George, '*The Shadow of a Dream*: Howells' Homosexual Tragedy', *American Quarterly*, 23 (1971), 110–19.

Stevenson, Robert Lewis, *The Strange Case of Dr Jekyll and Mr Hyde: And Other Tales of Horror* (London and New York: Penguin, 2002).

Stewart, George R., *Earth Abides* (New York: Random House, 1949).

Stoker, Bram, *Dracula*, 1897 (London and New York: Penguin, 2003).

Stone, Robert, *Children of Light* (New York: Alfred A. Knopf, 1986).

_____, *Outerbridge Reach* (New York: Houghton Mifflin, 1992).

Straub, Peter, *Ghost Story* (New York: Coward, McCann and Geoghegan, 1979).

Sundquist, Eric, *To Wake the Nations: Race and the Making of American Literature* (Cambridge and London: Harvard University Press, 1993).

Tartt, Donna, *The Little Friend* (New York: Alfred A. Knopf, 2002).

_____. The Secret History. New York: Alfred A. Knopf, 1992.

Thompson, G. R., *Poe's Fiction: Romantic Irony in the Gothic Tales* (Madison: University of Wisconsin Press, 1973).

Toomer, Jean, *Cane* (New York: Boni & Liveright, 1923).

Truffin, Sherry, *Schoolhouse Gothic: Haunted Hallways and Predatory Pedagogues in Late Twentieth-Century American Literature and Scholarship* (Newcastle upon Tyne: Cambridge Scholars, 2008).

Tryon, Thomas, *Harvest Home* (New York: Knopf, 1973).

_____, *The Other* (New York: Knopf, 1971).

Tudorov, Tzvetan, *The Fantastic* (Ithaca: Cornell University Press, 1975).

Updike, John, *The Witches of Eastwick* (New York: Alfred A. Knopf, 1984).

Veeder, William, 'The Nurture of the Gothic, or How Can a Text Be Both Popular and Subversive?', in Robert K. Martin and Eric Savoy, *American Gothic: New Interventions in a National Narrative* (Iowa City: University of Iowa Press, 1998), pp. 20–39.

Wardrop, Daneen, *Emily Dickinson's Gothic: Goblin With a Gauge* (Iowa City: University of Iowa Press, 1996).

Weinstock, Jeffrey Andrew, *Scare Tactics: Supernatural Fiction by American Women as a Form of Social Protest* (New York: Fordam University Press, 2008).

_____, (ed.), *Spectral America: Phantoms and the National Imagination* (Madison: The University of Wisconsin Press, 2004).

Wells, H. G., *The War of the Worlds* (1898) (New York: Modern Library, 2002).

Welty, Eudora, *The Collected Stories of Eudora Welty* (New York and London: Harcourt Brace Jovanovich, 1980), pp. 81–90.

Wharton, Edith, *Ethan Frome* (New York: Scribner's, 1911).

_____, *The Ghost Stories of Edith Wharton* (London: Constable, 1975).

Williams, Anne, *Art of Darkness: A Poetics of Gothic* (Chicago: University of Chicago Press, 1999).

Williams, Tennessee, *Plays 1937–1955,* ed. Mel Gussow and Kenneth Holditch (New York: Library of America, 2000).

_____. *Plays 1957-1980,* ed. Mel Gussow and Kenneth Holditch (New York: Library of America, 2000).

Wilson, Edmund, *The Shock of Recognition* (New York: Modern Library, 1955).

Wolstenholme, Susan, *Gothic (Re)Visions: Writing Women As Readers* (Albany: State University of New York Press, 1993).

Wright, Richard, *Black Boy* (New York: Harper & Brothers, 1945).

_____, *Native Son*, 1940 in *Early Works: Lawd Today!/Uncle Tom's Children/Native Son*, ed. Arnold Rampersad (New York: Library of America, 1991).

Wynne, Madeline Yale, 'The Little Room', in *American Short Stories of the Nineteenth Century* (London: J. M. Dent, 1930), pp. 310–23.

Yarbro, Chelsea Quinn, *Mansions of Darkness* (New York: Tor, 1996).

Ziff, Larzar, *The American 1890's: The Life and Times of a Lost Generation* (New York: Viking, 1966).

Index